THE QUEEN'S DIAMONDS

THE AFFAIR THAT LAUNCHED THE THREE MUSKETEERS

Cambridge
Academic

THE
KEY PLAYERS

LUCY PERCY

The Countess of Carlisle **Lucy Percy** is a direct descendant of Mary Boleyn and Henry VIII, her true father Thomas Percy, one of the principal conspirators in the Gunpowder Plot. The Duke of Buckingham's mistress, the brightest star of the English court, with beguiling looks and a vicious tongue, she is Anne Boleyn reincarnate. When Buckingham seduces the Queen of France, Lucy looks for a way to remove her rival.

THE DUKE OF BUCKINGHAM

George Villiers is the first commoner for the best part of a century to be made a duke, a reward for sleeping with King James I. No seduction is too outrageous for the bisexual, daring, handsome Duke of Buckingham, who also sleeps with three queens and plans to invade France to claim Anne of Austria for himself.

THE REJECTED QUEEN

The Spanish princess **Anne of Austria** is married to Louis XIII, an active homosexual whose relationship with his wife borders on repulsion and who cannot bring himself to sire an heir. Sensuous, lazy and indolent, the rejected queen finds Buckingham irresistible, playing into the hands of Cardinal Richelieu.

THE COLD-BLOODED CARDINAL

Armand-Jean du Plessis, **Cardinal Richelieu**, is first minister but not yet master of France with his own private troop of guards. He owes his rise to the queen mother, Marie de' Medici, who is determined to secure the succession even if this means removing Anne. Cold-blooded, calculating and far from chaste, Richelieu is prepared to destroy anyone in his path.

THE DARING MUSKETEER

Jean-Arnaud de Peyrer, known as **Tréville**, is the newest recruit in the King's Musketeers. A merchant's son, ridiculed at court, he takes almost suicidal risks to get ahead. Offered a dangerous mission to England to retrieve the fabulous necklace the Queen of France has foolishly given her lover, the Duke of Buckingham, Tréville does not hesitate, even though this means making a deadly enemy: Cardinal Richelieu.

*Edmund Curll, a notorious Fleet Street pamphleteer, uncovered
and published the proceedings of a secret ecclesiastical trial held in
1613 that made present-day scandals seem tame by comparison.
'Seven Matrons' investigated whether the Countess of Essex, Frances
Howard, was still a virgin, so that she could divorce one earl and*

THE CASE OF IMPOTENCY

As Debated in ENGLAND,

In that Remarkable TRYAL *An.* 1613. between ROBERT, Earl of ESSEX, and the Lady FRANCES HOWARD, who, after Eight Years Marriage, commenc'd a Suit againſt him for IMPOTENCY.

CONTAINING

I. The whole PROCEEDINGS, and DEBATES on both Sides.

II. The REPORT of the Seven MATRONS appointed to ſearch the *Counteſs.*

III. The Intrigue between Her and the Earl of SOMERSET, who after the Divorce married Her.

IV. A Detection of ſome Politicks in the Court of King JAMES the Firſt.

Written by GEORGE ABBOT, *D. D.* Lord Archbiſhop of *Canterbury.*

In Two VOLUMES.

London, Printed for *E. Curll,* at the *Dial* and *Bible* againſt St. *Dunſtan's* Church in *Fleetſtreet.* 1715. Price Five Shillings.

marry another. It led to the fall of King James's favourite, Robert Carr, Earl of Somerset, who unforgivably preferred Frances in his bed; soon both Carr and his new bride would be sent to the Tower of London, leaving a vacancy for royal paramour filled by the young George Villiers, the future Duke of Buckingham.

Also by Roger Macdonald

THE MAN IN THE IRON MASK
(2008)

THE QUEEN'S
DIAMONDS

ROGER MACDONALD

ISBN 1-903-499-52-6
978-1-903499-52-8

Printed and bound in the United Kingdom by
4edge Ltd, 7a Eldon Way Industrial Estate, Hockley, Essex, SS5 4AD.

Special jacket photography by Jeremy Hoare www.jeremyhoare.com

Cover image: Cartier's £1 million necklace, fit for a Queen of France, worn by Lucinda Nunn.

The original, given by Anne of Austria to the Duke of Buckingham during their doomed love affair, may still be worn by someone in secret to this very day.

For Jeannie and our own three Musketeers,
Sarah, Simon and Timothy

And for their grandfather, Sidney Drake

In his eighty-eighth year

Teenage ambulance man during the Blitz

Ship procurer for the Royal Fleet Auxiliary
during the Falklands War

ACKNOWLEDGMENTS

Every book must have its champions if it is to appear successfully in print. I am particularly grateful to my publisher, Ken Sewell, of Cambridge Academic press, for his sustained support for this project, and for reading the embryonic chapters with a rare enthusiasm that maintained its momentum. My production editor, Andrew Young, too, has shown exceptional commitment, patience and skill in turning the raw material into the finished article.

It is not often that an author has the benefit of another historian in the family, still less one who has just achieved a first class degree in History at Brasenose College, Oxford. My younger son Tim Macdonald has been immensely helpful in reading the text from start to finish, and making invaluable suggestions and pivotal improvements to every aspect of the book. His fellow graduate from Brasenose College, Jess Southward, also went through my final draft from the first page to last and cast a meticulous eye over its style and presentation; she undoubtedly can look forward to a very successful career in publishing.

With publisher, production editor and author often separated by thousands of miles and several different time zones, the electronic dimension of this book has relied heavily on computer hardware, software and communications. I owe a huge debt of gratitude to my elder son, Simon Macdonald, for his immense knowledge of these matters and his extraordinary ability to make everything work, no matter how dauntingly complex.

My daughter, Sarah Macdonald, has been a constant source of encouragement. Fortunately, as the book's characters are long dead and safely beyond the scope of the law of libel, her skills as a lawyer have not been needed on this occasion.

Dr Alex Drake gave advice and valuable assistance on interpreting genealogical tables.

The History Faculty at the University of Oxford opened many doors. The Bodleian Library provided access to many original documents, as did the British Library and the Public Record Office in Kew. Three Paris libraries, the Bibliothèque Nationale, the Bibliothèque de l'Arsenal and the Bibliothèque Sainte-Geneviève, as well as the Service Historique at Vincennes, responded diligently to many unorthodox requests. The London Library once again proved an invaluable source of obscure books and papers. I am grateful for the patience of the staff in each of these organisations who gave so unstintingly of their time.

My own tutor at Oxford, Felix Markham of Hertford College, introduced me to an expert on seventeenth-century French history, Anthony Levi. For those passengers who survived the G-forces close to the upper limits of human tolerance induced by Anthony's lifts in a Triumph Vitesse around the Oxfordshire countryside, he proved entertaining and erudite company. This book in many ways is the by-product of Anthony's celebrated biographies of Cardinal Richelieu and Louis XIV, as without his discovery of unpublished material about the original three musketeers who set out for England to save the Queen of France from the folly of her gift of a diamond necklace to the Duke of Buckingham, vital pieces in the jigsaw might have remained lost for ever. It all began with a meal at undoubtedly the best Italian restaurant in London, *Mamma Mia*, run by Leonardo, Guiseppe and Rosa Giannini (tel. 020 8878 3480); but such were my subsequent demands on Anthony's time, he once cryptically observed that he had come to realise the true origin of the old adage that there is no such thing as a free lunch.

As for Lucy Percy, who stole two of the queen's diamonds, her aunt, Penelope Devereux, had an equally chequered career. I am indebted to Penelope's distinguished biographer, Sally Varlow [*The Lady Penelope* ISBN 9780233002651], for reading my opening chapter devoted to this irrepressible family descended directly from Henry VIII and for making many helpful suggestions. I have made use of some of her painstaking original research into this period but reached my conclusions independently.

To replicate the fabulous necklace given to the Duke of Buckingham, I turned for advice to Edward and Christina Asprey, whose expertise on jewellery and jewellers proved invaluable. With Edward's help, we were given permission by Cartier for special photography of a necklace worth about £1 million. I am particularly grateful to Cartier's London Director, Arnaud Bamberger, and his former head of press, Sarah Carlsen, for their enthusiastic assistance. The photo shoot took place in Cartier's boardroom in New Bond Street, once the war-time office of General de Gaulle. The photographer was award-winning Jeremy Hoare, with able support from Chizuko, and the necklace modelled by Lucinda Nunn. Thanks are also due to Debbie and Phil Burks for the loan of a slightly less valuable necklace that allowed us to consider camera angles in advance.

As *The Queen's Diamonds* is a prequel to my previous history book, *The Man in the Iron Mask* (2008), it has benefited from the help and advice generously given on the original true story that involved d'Artagnan and Dumas's Three Musketeers. I am particularly appreciative of the comments made by Jane and Mike Phillips that led to significant improvements in the revised and extended second edition of *The Mask* and grateful to each of the following:

Laetitia Audumares, Burku Baikali, Stéphane Bibard, David Bloomfield of Hertford College Oxford, Jean-Pierre Boudet, Bernard Caire, L.P.B. Jeanne du Canard, Genna Gifford, Camille Lebossé, Peter Mills, Joseph Miqueu, Peter and Lorna Rogan, Claire Sauvrage and Claire Trocmé.

As always, of course, any shortcomings and errors are my own.

R.M.

CONTENTS

Principal Characters

Chronology

The Value of Money in the Seventeenth Century

Curtain Raiser: A Game at Chess

PRINCIPAL CHARACTERS

Anne of Austria: neglected wife of Louis XIII

Buckingham, George Villiers, Duke of: England's first minister; lover of James I, Lucy Percy and Anne of Austria

Brienne, Henri-Auguste de Loménie, comte de: French courtier and minister

Carlisle, Countess of: *see* Percy, Lucy

Carlisle, Earl of: *see* Hay, James

Chevreuse, Marie de Rohan, duchesse de: perennial plotter; Richelieu's enemy; confidant of Anne of Austria

Charles 1: King of England and Scotland

Devereux, Dorothy: Countess of Northumberland; Lucy Percy's mother

Du Plessis: *see* Richelieu, Cardinal

Gondomar, Diego Sarmiento de Acuña, Count of: Spanish ambassador in London

Hay, James: Earl of Carlisle; extravagant husband of Lucy Percy

Hay, Lucy: *see* Percy, Lucy

Henrietta Maria: sister of Louis XIII; wife of Charles I; Queen of England

Holland, Henry Rich, Earl of Holland: Lucy Percy's cousin; Buckingham's ally; lover of Marie de Chevreuse

James I: King of England and (as James VI) Scotland

La Rochefoucauld, François VI, duc de: French courtier; lover of Marie de Chevreuse

Louis XIII: King of France and Navarre

Marie de' Medici: Louis XIII's mother and former Regent of France

Olivares, Gaspar de Guzmán y Pimentel, count-duke of: first minister of Spain

Percy, Lucy: wife of James Hay; Buckingham's lover; Richelieu's spy

Percy, Thomas: real father of Lucy Percy; Gunpowder Plotter

Prince of Wales *see* Charles I

Rochefoucauld *see* La Rochefoucald

Richelieu, Armand-Jean du Plessis, Cardinal: French first minister

Stuart, Elizabeth: daughter of James I; Electress Palatine; Queen of Bohemia

Tillières, Tanneguy Leveneur, comte de: French ambassador in London

Tréville, Jean-Arnaud de Peyrer de Troisvilles: King's Musketeer, known as

Villiers, George: *see* Buckingham, Duke of

CHRONOLOGY

1566 Birth of James VI of Scotland

1567 Abdication of Mary, Queen of Scots; James becomes king

1580 Birth of James Hay

1585 Birth of Cardinal Richelieu

1587 Execution of Mary, Queen of Scots

1588 Defeat of the Spanish Armada

1592 Birth of Duke of Buckingham

1599 Birth of Lucy Percy

1600 Birth of Charles I

1601 Birth of Anne of Austria and Louis XIII of France

1603 Death of Elizabeth I; James VI succeeds her as James I of England

1604 Peace between England and Spain

1605 The Gunpowder Plot

1609 Birth of Henrietta Maria, Queen Consort of Charles I

1610 Assassination of Henri IV of France

1613 Gondomar arrives in England as Spanish ambassador

1614 Buckingham comes to attention of James I

1615 Anne of Austria marries Louis XIII

1617 Lucy Percy marries James Hay

1618 Defenestration of Prague

1619 Lucy Percy begins affair with Buckingham

1620 Buckingham marries Katherine Manners

1622 Lucy Percy becomes Countess of Carlisle

1623 Buckingham and the Prince of Wales ride unescorted to Madrid

1624 *'A Game at Chess'* opens at the Globe

1625 Death of James I; Buckingham in Paris

1626 Lucy Percy steals the queen's diamonds; Chalais conspiracy

The Value of Money in the Seventeenth Century

Lawrence H. Officer, Professor of Economics at the University of Illinois in Chicago, is Director of Research for measuringworth.com. By the use of comparative price data, measuringworth.com has devised an extremely plausible price index for analysing the value of money in England across several centuries in today's terms.

For example, when in January 1621 James Hay held a banquet in London at which vast quantities of food were ordered and every dish was made twice, once for display when the guests arrived, then again, freshly cooked, when they sat down to eat, it cost £3,000. The index translates this in today's money to £499,000, a staggering sum.

No such index exists for France, where the monetary system was based on the livre, which was neither a note nor a coin but a notional value used in transactions. The huge sums spent by the French royal family on jewellery, converted in this book to livres, can be best put into perspective by noting that Cardinal Richelieu's apothecary, an important person in the household of the sickness-prone cardinal, lived comfortably on an annual salary of 150 livres. One of the most utilised and essential items of the time, a candle, cost about one livre.

Gold coins used mainly by the English and French nobility, such as the sovereign or louis, were invariably interchangeable in this period when travelling between the two countries and each was the equivalent of about six livres.

How Dates Differed

Pope Gregory XIII encouraged the introduction of the more accurate Gregorian Calendar, which was initially implemented in October 1582 by a handful of Catholic countries, including Spain, Portugal and most of the Italian city states; and by France in December.

During the main period of this book England continued to use the Julian Calendar, which was ten days behind the Gregorian Calendar at the time of its inception.

The dates used in this book are those applicable in the country where the activity referred to took place.

For example, when Tréville arrived at Windsor Castle with a message from Anne of Austria for the Duke of Buckingham, on 8 February 1626 in the British calendar, it was 18 February in France. The ball where Queen Anne was expected to wear the diamonds she had given the duke had been set for 24 February, just six days away.

Great Britain and the British Empire, including its colonies on the eastern seaboard of what became part of the United States, adopted the Gregorian Calendar in September 1752.

CURTAIN RAISER:
A GAME AT CHESS

On Thursday, 5 August 1624, a satirical play full of political spin was performed for the first time at Shakespeare's Globe on the south bank of the Thames in Southwark, London's red light district.[1] Over the next ten days nearly 30,000 spectators, perhaps one eighth of the entire adult population of the capital, attended the production: it had a sensational reception. The theatre's pit bulged and its three-tiered gallery was packed to the rafters every afternoon except Sunday to see a troop of actors known as the King's Men perform *A Game at Chess*, a bawdy comedy whose nine consecutive performances established a record for the Jacobean stage.[2] It would surely have run and run had not the Privy Council, acting on instructions from the ailing James I, banned the play, closed the Globe, arrested the playwright and threatened the actors with imprisonment. Their censorship followed a vehement letter of protest from the Spanish ambassador, Don Carlos Caloma, describing the comedy as 'scandalous, irreligious, barbaric and deeply offensive to my King'.[3]

The play ridiculed Caloma's predecessor, Count Gondomar, exposing his most intimate medical afflictions amidst howls of laughter.[4] The living white and black chess pieces on stage represented England and Spain respectively, with Gondomar as the Black Knight and the Prince of Wales – the future Charles I – as the White Knight. With a little poetic licence, the playwright, Thomas Middleton, in his thirtieth work, also introduced a special piece called the White Duke, which the audience knew was code for the royal favourite, George Villiers, a commoner who had risen to the prodigious rank of Duke of Buckingham.

Middleton almost certainly had been well paid to produce a play that encouraged popular support for a radical change in foreign policy which, despite James I's misgivings, with Buckingham and the Prince of Wales behind it, was gathering a momentum of its own.[5] He did so by representing England as a realm riddled with Jesuit priests and Spanish agents and a king under the wicked spell of the Spanish ambassador, Gondomar; in his play the duke and the prince outwit the Spaniards at their own devious, diplomatic game by confronting them in their own backyard. However, Middleton portrayed as a triumph an event that in truth had been a political fiasco. A year earlier the two young men, in an unprecedented breach of convention, had arrived unannounced in Madrid to

Thomas Middleton, prolific playwright with political connections

negotiate a marriage alliance, known as the Spanish Match, and were completely outmanoeuvred. In the end, they were fortunate to be allowed to leave at all, without a Spanish royal bride, and with their tails between their legs. Soon England and Spain would renew hostilities as Buckingham threw the diplomatic levers into reverse and made overtures to the French.

The audience were fascinated by the way that Middleton had lifted the veil on contemporary politics. Had the curtain been drawn back further so that the English court and its courtiers were fully exposed to public gaze, however, their reaction might have been a mixture of incredulity and anger. Elizabeth I's grip on government expenditure and court morality had given way under the spendthrift Stuart dynasty to wholesale corruption and licentiousness on a spectacular scale. Its impetus came from the very top. James I traded jobs and titles for homosexual favours from ambitious and parasitic Scotsmen who descended on the capital, until Buckingham, an irresistibly handsome Englishman, upstaged them all to become James's established lover. Then, claimed the pamphleteers, by jumping from one royal bed to another, he ensured that the accession of Charles I enhanced rather than ended his influence.

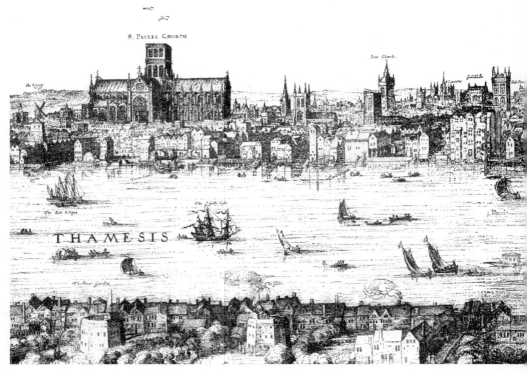

Panorama of London and the Thames circa 1600, showing St Paul's Cathedral, London Bridge and, close to the river on the south bank, the Globe Theatre.

Buckingham also liked, and perhaps preferred, women. A countess here, a duchess there, even the Spanish prime minister's wife, all served as appetisers for an unimaginably daring and dangerous main course: Anne of Austria, Queen of France. With a homosexual husband, Louis XIII, who possessed a pathological hatred of women, Anne was looking for love. She found it in Buckingham, who after the failure of the Spanish Match arrived at Paris in 1625 to collect his new sovereign's decidedly second-choice bride, Henrietta Maria, the French king's younger sister. Their affair all but paralysed the French court and turned a potential alliance into a shooting war.

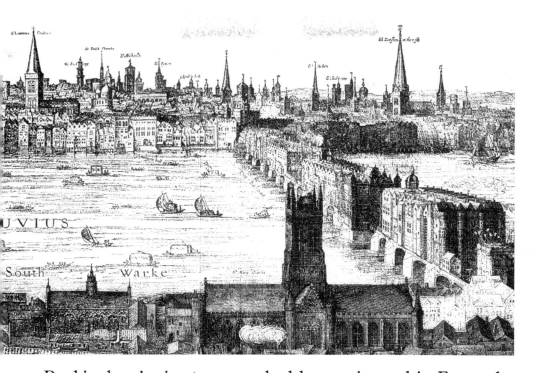

Buckingham's rise to power had been mirrored in France by Armand-Jean du Plessis, better known as Cardinal Richelieu. The childless Queen Anne made the serious miscalculation of siding with the court faction that wanted Richelieu out of the way. The cardinal needed incontrovertible evidence to prove to Louis XIII that he had an adulterous wife. Anne seemed to have provided it by foolishly giving Buckingham, as a token of her love, a necklace previously presented to her by the king. She never imagined for one moment that in February 1626 she would suddenly be asked, indeed commanded, to wear it at a Paris ball. The desperate ride against the clock to retrieve the diamonds from the duke, the central theme of Alexandre Dumas's romantic novel, *The Three Musketeers*, was fact and not fiction. Two of the diamonds were stolen at the behest of the cardinal by Buckingham's mistress, an

English countess, Lucy Percy, 'beauty, wit, harlot and traitress', a spy at the heart of Whitehall.[6] As Buckingham and Richelieu struggled for supremacy, the Queen of France was a pawn in deadly peril.

PROLOGUE:
THE UNMASKING OF LUCY PERCY

Lucy Percy, Countess of Carlisle, was a favourite subject of portrait painters in seventeenth-century England. Her picture by Anthony van Dyck graced the catalogue jacket of Tate Britain's hugely successful exhibition *Van Dyck & Britain* and the renowned artist was emulated by many others in his day. The younger daughter of the Countess of Northumberland, Lucy enjoyed a privileged lifestyle in some of London's finest houses, including, in her formative years either side of 1620, the aristocratic residence of Syon Park.

However, Lucy was no mere court lady, vacuous and transient. Behind her dazzling smile and acerbic way with words lay a burning ambition to succeed and an insatiable taste for intrigue. Her body, which many men ardently desired, was a weapon to be employed in pursuit of influence and power. In a notorious liaison that began at Syon Park, she became the mistress of the royal favourite, George Villiers, the supreme model of social mountaineering, a commoner made Duke of Buckingham. She was also Cardinal Richelieu's secret agent, the quintessence of Alexandre Dumas's fiendish Milady de Winter. Her sexual conquests included Charles d'Artagnan of the French King's Musketeers, a pleasure for which the Gascon almost paid with his life.

The trail that led to the unmasking of Lucy Percy and the extraordinary events encapsulated here as *The Queen's Diamonds* begins with the earliest biography of that famous duellist, an old and rare set of three small leather books called the *Mémoires de Monsieur d'Artagnan, Capitaine-Lieutenant de la première Compagnie des Mousquetaires du Roi*. The red and black title page of the anonymous first volume declares it to have been printed in 1700, which was true, and that the printer was Pierre Marteau of Cologne, which was not. The real printer, a Dutchman called Daniel Elvezir from The Hague, had no wish to receive a visit from the agents of Louis XIV. The king believed the best place for books that criticised his regime was in the dungeons of his feared Paris prison and depository for banned literature, the Bastille; alongside those who had dared to publish them.

The towers of the Bastille cast a huge shadow over seventeenth-century Paris. Within its walls were dozens of prisoners held indefinitely without trial, and thousands of banned books.

The mysterious author of these controversial memoirs was Gatien de Courtilz, sieur de Sandras, the writer of more than 100 provocative pamphlets, political tracts and biographies, all printed outside France to escape censorship. Courtilz dubbed Louis 'Le Grand Alcandre', a reference to Pierre Corneille's 1636 comedy entitled *L'Illusion comique*, in which an old sorcerer, Alcandre, lives in a cave with his deaf and dumb servants. The Sun King would not have liked the analogy.

He would have liked even less the fact that Courtilz, already given one long term of imprisonment for writing subversive material, had succeeded in assembling d'Artagnan's memoirs while incarcerated in the Bastille itself, from where the manuscript was smuggled out to The Hague by his wife Louise. Courtilz was released in March 1699 on condition that he left Paris and did not

return within twenty leagues; but in July 1701 he ignored this restriction, rented rooms above a Parisian upholsterers and openly hawked copies of his books around the little shops on the quai des Augustins along the Seine. He was arrested, sent back to the Bastille and thrown into its lower dungeon, where he was to remain chained in solitary confinement among the rats and the squalor for another nine years.

The only known portrait of the mysterious, elusive Gatien de Courtilz de Sandras, author of d'Artagnan's memoirs.

It proved convenient for the French *ancien régime* to dismiss Courtilz's memoirs of d'Artagnan as largely his own invention, a contention not challenged for centuries. Until, in fact, the doyen of French historians, Charles Samaran, conducted his own meticulous research into the period and in 1912 concluded of Courtilz's account, 'not only on general events, but on the deeds and actions of individuals, there are amazingly accurate details'.[1]

Few examples of Courtilz's memoirs of d'Artagnan survived destruction but a copy of volume one eventually found its way to the municipal library in Marseille, where Alexandre Dumas, just before he became famous as the author of *The Three Musketeers*, deviously acquired it in 1843 while passing through the port on his return from Italy. He seduced a lady whose brother happened to be the city librarian and illicitly took the precious antiquarian book with him to Paris; a faded index card confirms that it remains unreturned to this day.

In his preface to what in 1844 was originally entitled *Athos, Porthos and Aramis*, Dumas had the gall to declare he had found the memoirs of d'Artagnan in the Bibliothèque Nationale in Paris and that the librarian had given him permission to borrow the work. Under fierce attack at the time for shameless plagiarism in his plays, Dumas probably felt it prudent to acknowledge in passing his source for the Musketeers' names and that of their captain, Tréville: but in reality he took from Courtilz a great deal more. Dumas's account of d'Artagnan's departure from Gascony on his little yellow horse; his encounter with Cardinal Richelieu's cold-blooded assassin, Rochefort; his seduction of an elderly Paris innkeeper's attractive young wife, Constance Bonacieux; and his accidental involvement in the multiple duel that brought to a climax the heated rivalry between the Musketeers and the Cardinal's Guards, a real event that took place in May 1640, all came from Courtilz.

Above all, Dumas found in his memoirs the original of the beautiful, scheming, deadly Milady de Winter. Courtilz described her assignation with d'Artagnan and, when he frustrated her purpose, her attempts to murder him, first by her own hand and later by employing paid cut-throats in the back streets of Paris. However, Courtilz said nothing of Milady's earlier involvement in the central theme of Dumas's romance, the French Queen Anne of Austria's imprudent gift of a magnificent diamond necklace – originally a present from her husband, Louis XIII – to her lover, the Duke of Buckingham, and the desperate effort to retrieve it in time for a Paris ball. Milady's theft from Buckingham of two diamond studs, cut from the queen's necklace, at Cardinal Richelieu's behest; the race to save Anne from disgrace; the ball itself: these episodes were initially supposed to have come from Dumas's fertile imagination. Not so.

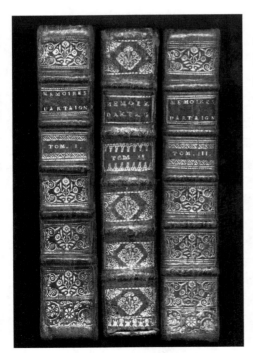

The very rare set of d'Artagnan's memoirs, published in 1700-1.

Dumas relied heavily for his research and rough drafts on a former history teacher and aspiring but anodyne playwright, Auguste Maquet, who was responsible for the central fabric of his best ideas, including *The Three Musketeers*. Dumas wrote at an astonishing pace but like his heroes, he was often barely one step ahead of his pursuers, in this case, the anxious literary editor of a Paris newspaper, Le Siècle, already in March 1844 running the unfinished story as a serial that had become an overnight sensation. 'Some copy, as fast as possible', ran one harassed note from Dumas to Maquet, 'even if it's only a dozen pages... Hammer away, hammer away... I'm completely dried up'.

Alexandre Dumas – his inspired inventions discouraged historians from pursuing the real story.

In order to satisfy Dumas's increasing demands, Maquet searched for the true identity of Milady de Winter. Courtilz had cautiously referred to her as *Miledi___*, leaving a blank space throughout the memoirs for her full name. He would only say that she was 'the daughter of a peer of England' who had been a lady-in-waiting to the French wife of Charles I, Henrietta Maria.

Auguste Maquet, Dumas's long-suffering collaborator.

Maquet found a clue in an unexpected quarter: the father of a fellow, mediocre playwright. Count Pierre-Louis Roederer, politician, lawyer, economist and historian, had died on 17 December 1835, aged eighty-one. Shortly after his death, a Nantes newspaper reported that his memoirs, which had been seized by the government in July 1834, were to be permanently suppressed. The story was picked up and repeated a few months later by the literary magazine, Moniteur.[2] Although Roederer's son, Antoine-Marie, wrote to the editor in August 1836 to deny indignantly that his family had been the victim of censorship, it was widely believed that he had been well paid not to make a fuss.[3]

Queues formed in the streets of Paris to buy Le Siècle, with the latest episode of 'The Three Musketeers'.

Pierre-Louis Roederer, forced to go into hiding during the period of the Terror in the French Revolution, had passed the time by delving into his own family history; and found that three of his antecedents had been in the service of the duc de la Rochefoucauld. He drew from their recollections to write several *comédies historiques* and reached the end of the reign of Henri IV by 1830. But then he made what seems to have been something of a Faustian bargain with the authorities. In return for the restoration of his title, originally awarded by Napoleon I, the rest of the series, including a play about Anne of Austria, was quietly dropped.

The printer, Hector Rossange, unwilling to be deprived of what had become a lucrative income,

Antoine-Marie Roederer.

induced Antoine-Marie to take over his father's project. The younger Roederer, a historian in his own right, had no reservations about including controversial material. In 1832 he assembled several new plays under the title *'Intrigues politiques et galantes de la Cour de France'*, in which *'galantes'* was undoubtedly a pseudonym for 'sexual'. It must be acknowledged, Roederer was no Molière. What distinguished his efforts was an evident determination to provide detailed reference material in the notes that accompanied each play. One was entitled *'Les Aiguillettes d'Anne d'Autriche, comédie historique en trois actes'*, or 'Anne of Austria's diamond studs, a historical comedy in three acts'. It describes *Miledi* as Richelieu's 'most dangerous spy'.

Roederer identified as his sources two obscure memoirs, those of the duc de La Rochefoucauld and the comte de Brienne, contemporaries and confidants of the Queen of France. Each confirmed that the real-life *Miledi* was Lucy Percy, Countess of Carlisle, and between them provided a full account of the diamonds affair and her role in it. Maquet's second-hand discovery was eagerly devoured by the great novelist. Indeed, a close examination of Dumas's text in *The Three Musketeers* confirms that the incorrigible plagiariser used much of Brienne's description, almost word for word, of what took place at the Paris ball in February 1626.

So why, despite this wealth of corroborative evidence, did historians hitherto tend to treat as fiction a fascinating story that is undoubted fact? In part, it may have been Dumas's unconscious influence upon them, because the great writer did add to his

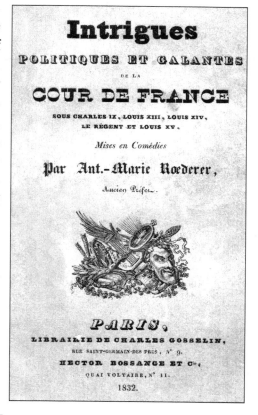

Intrigues

POLITIQUES ET GALANTES

DE LA

COUR DE FRANCE

SOUS CHARLES IX, LOUIS XIII, LOUIS XIV,
LE RÉGENT ET LOUIS XV,

Mises en Comédies

Par Ant.-Marie Roederer,

Ancien Préfet.

PARIS,

LIBRAIRIE DE CHARLES GOSSELIN,

RUE SAINT-GERMAIN-DES-PRÉS, N° 9.

HECTOR BOSSANGE ET Cᵉ,

QUAI VOLTAIRE, N° 11.

1832.

Pure Dumas: the macabre execution of Milady de Winter by the headsman of Lille on a small island in the River Lys.

novel entirely fictitious, though often inspired, events of his own: the macabre execution of Milady de Winter, for example, at the hands of the Musketeers, and their quarrels with d'Artagnan that left the impetuous Gascon with the prospect of fighting successive duels on the same day against three of the best swordsmen in France, at 12, 1 and 2 o'clock.

Dumas also took liberties with the chronology that left his historian, Maquet, in despair. The first volume of Courtilz's biography of d'Artagnan covers the period between 1640 and 1649, long after the Affair of the Queen's Diamonds. Dumas transported his borrowed characters back to 1625, the year Buckingham came to Paris and seduced the Queen of France; the episode was probably overlooked by Courtilz because at the time the real Musketeers were children and d'Artagnan still a babe in arms.

This begs the question of course, who was sent to England to retrieve the diamond necklace from the Duke of Buckingham? Anthony Levi, author of the definitive biography of Cardinal Richelieu, discovered some unpublished extracts from La Rochefoucauld's disjointed memoirs. In them the French duke named the original three Musketeers who headed north from the French capital on their dangerous mission. One was Charles d'Aramits, none other than the father of Henry d'Aramits, Dumas's 'Aramis'; and the bold young man who went all the way from Paris to Windsor and back was Jean-Arnaud de Peyrer, called Tréville; afterwards in real life, just as in Dumas's novel, he would become d'Artagnan's mentor as his Captain of the Musketeers.

Lucy Percy's role in the story began as that of Buckingham's vengeful mistress. The episode of the diamond necklace would lead to the countess becoming Richelieu's most valuable agent in England; and to a colourful career of espionage and conspiracy that eventually resulted in her imprisonment by Cromwell's Roundheads in the Tower of London.

1: ANOTHER BOLEYN GIRL

Whether heroine, harlot or arch-betrayer, Lucy Percy had the genes and the guile of another Boleyn girl.

Lucy bore the name of one of the oldest noble families in England. Led by William de Perci of Caen, the Percys arrived from Normandy with William the Conqueror in 1066 and settled in the north, running their estates as a private fiefdom. From time to time they attempted unsuccessfully to usurp the ruling monarch, suffering as the price of failure the penalties of confiscation, attainder, imprisonment and the headsman's axe.

Few died of natural causes in their own bed. The first Earl of Northumberland and his son, the heroic but impetuous Harry 'Hotspur' immortalised by Shakespeare, both ended their days during a Percy rebellion against the crown. The second earl was also killed in battle; the third was imprisoned in the Tower of London; and the fourth was murdered during an uprising. The brother of the sixth was hanged at Tyburn; the seventh was beheaded at York; and the eighth allegedly committed suicide in the Tower, shot through the left breast by no fewer than three bullets, the door of his chamber bolted from within.

Far from offering an antidote to the ill-fated impetuosity of the Percys, Lucy's family on her mother's side also played for high stakes and lost almost everything: her great-great-grandmother was Mary Boleyn and her great-great-great-aunt Anne Boleyn. Their father Thomas Boleyn came from a line of prosperous tenant farmers. He married into the nobility but reached unimagined heights because of his willingness to prostitute the females in his family to satisfy Henry VIII's insatiable sexual desires.

Whenever the king's first wife, Catherine of Aragon, was unavailable to him during pregnancy or through gynaecological problems, Henry sought satisfaction elsewhere. In 1510 he pursued Anne Stafford, the married sister of Edward Stafford, the third Duke of Buckingham, with such relentless vigour, that the duke reproached the king 'in many and very hard words' and persuaded her husband to send her to a convent to escape his attentions.[1] Although it was sixty miles away, circumstantial evidence suggests that the king nonetheless visited her several times up to 1513 for the purpose of sexual intercourse. But Henry never forgot a bad turn: in 1521 Stafford would be beheaded on Tower

The pursued: Anne Stafford.

The pursuer: Henry VIII.

Thomas Boleyn, father of Mary and Anne.

Hill, found guilty of treason on dubious evidence and the title reduced to a baronage, leaving the dukedom vacant.[2] James I would create a new dynasty by making his favourite, George Villiers, Duke of Buckingham, just over a century later.

Thomas Boleyn seized his opportunity. It was soon suspected that Henry VIII was in a sexual relationship with Thomas's wife, Lady Elizabeth Howard, the daughter of the Duke of Norfolk.[3] Possibly for turning a blind eye, Thomas received land and titles. He had high aspirations for Anne and Mary, selling the two ships he had named after them to the king. The Boleyns used their newly acquired wealth and status to send their daughters to a sixteenth-century equivalent of finishing school, the sophisticated court of France. It was, however, notoriously promiscuous. Anne seems among the few ladies to survive with her reputation more or less intact but her sister, of similar age but much the prettier of the two, with blond hair and blue eyes, may have succumbed to the attentions of the French monarch. Much later, when it became fashionable to cast aspersions on both the Boleyn sisters, Francis I called Mary 'my hack, my mule' and boasted of the number of times he had

'ridden' her, a girl barely in her teens. He told the Duke of Norfolk, Mary's uncle, with breathtaking hypocrisy, that she 'had not always lived virtuously'.

In the sixteenth century men could fornicate without attracting criticism while women were expected to be beyond reproach; the suggestion that in 1519 Mary was summoned home to avoid looming disgrace would be consistent with the dual standards of the time. The following February, Mary married William Carey, one of the sixteen gentlemen of the royal privy chamber. The ceremony was attended by the king, perhaps on a last-minute impulse, but not by her father:

Francis I, who called Mary 'my hack, my mule'.

Thomas Boleyn, who had been appointed England's ambassador in Paris, stayed abroad for another month. The date of the wedding surely could have been arranged to suit his convenience so perhaps Thomas's absence was deliberate. It may not have been the union he had intended for Mary. Although Carey had connections to the Percys through his aunt, the wife of Henry Percy, the fifth Earl of Northumberland, and for someone less ambitious than Thomas might have been seen as a good catch, he was a second son with no title and no prospect of an inheritance.

However, as one of Henry's regular hunting companions and tiltyard opponents, Carey had intimate contact with the king on a daily basis. So, too, before long, did Mary. After all, given the opportunity, who among the court ladies would not want to be adored by the handsome king's grey-blue eyes, partner the most athletic dancer in the royal palaces and be kissed by his rosebud mouth? Once Mary gave herself to Henry, he was almost certainly hers alone, with a husband who was at the beck and call of his monarch and who did not dare to assert his conjugal rights. In her psycho-analytical essay on Henry VIII, Ingeborg Flugel persuasively concludes that the king required his sexual partners to be exclusively faithful to him.[4]

Such was the naked ambition of the Howards, Mary's extended family, it seems inevitable that every intimate detail of her relationship with the king was discussed and dissected to see whether one of their line could become more than the royal concubine. If Henry made Mary pregnant, the Howards may even have hoped, however fancifully, that her marriage could be set aside on grounds of non-consummation with her husband, leaving her free to marry the king should his marriage to Catherine be annulled. As they saw it, the queen's inability to produce a healthy male heir was already a serious issue that made everything possible.

During 1522 Mary became the mistress *en titre*, displacing Elizabeth Blount, one of the queen's maids of honour. In 1519 Elizabeth had given birth to an illegitimate son, Henry Fitzroy, whom the king at first did not openly acknowledge. Anne Boleyn, newly returned from France to join the queen's household, had to bite her tongue and play second fiddle to her sister. There was often friction between them and Anne was much closer to her brother George, who also had little time for Mary.

For a brief interlude, however, it seemed Anne might confound everyone by making a splendid marriage. Henry Percy, elder son of the fifth Earl of

Northumberland, fell head over heels in love with her. In the spring of 1523 the couple became unofficially betrothed and sealed that betrothal with sexual intimacy but probably not penetrative sex. Unfortunately for Anne's hopes, Percy was already spoken for: in 1516 it had been arranged that he would marry Lady Mary Talbot, daughter of the Earl of Shrewsbury, in return for a substantial dowry. The Earl of Northumberland, seeing that Anne was hardly an heiress, was furious with his son for putting an excellent marriage settlement in jeopardy. When Percy refused to back down, the earl enlisted Cardinal Wolsey to help end the match. In an age when marriage for the nobility was a valuable political and economic commodity, Wolsey did not need any covert pressure from his monarch to act swiftly and decisively. He saw to it that the couple were separated and Anne Boleyn, in high dudgeon, was sent home to Hever. Wolsey called her 'that foolish girl yonder' and would scarcely have made such a disparaging remark in public if the king had expressed the slightest interest in Anne at the time. Henry had already demonstrated with Anne Stafford just how far he would pursue, rapidly and relentlessly, any woman who really took his fancy. Significantly, for the moment he left Anne Boleyn alone.

William Carey, the willing cuckold of Henry VIII.

The king's affair with Mary Boleyn was conducted discreetly, perhaps in an attempt to avoid further furious rows with his wife. Some of their assignations may have taken place in the royal hunting lodge in Kent, known as Penshurst Place, where later Henry would stay while courting Mary's sister Anne at nearby Hever. In about June 1524 Mary gave birth to a girl, Catherine Carey, Lucy Percy's great-grandmother, whom historian David Starkey believes was Henry VIII's child.[5] Had she produced a boy, with Anne still out of sight and out of mind, and Catherine of Aragon no longer sharing the king's bed, Henry might have been tempted to legitimise the affair and have further male children with Mary in wedlock to secure the succession; instead, he contented himself with an immediate gift of manors and estates to the obliging cuckold, William Carey. A year later Henry, perhaps despairing of both wife and mistress as a means to a male heir, formally acknowledged that he was the father of Henry Fitzroy, and positioned his illegitimate son as a possible successor by elevating him with elaborate ceremony to the peerage as Duke of Richmond and Somerset.

The timing provided a touch of pathos because, unknown to the king, Mary was once again pregnant and in February 1526 was safely delivered of a son, whom to no one's surprise was baptised Henry. A few days later the king gave the compliant William Carey the borough of Buckingham. This was to be held 'in tail male', that is to say only for the male issue of his line, which meant that in due course it would pass to little Henry and his male descendants.[6] As he grew up, the child's resemblance to the king would be noticed by those who came into contact with him.[7]

Mary Boleyn, mother of Catherine Carey and Lucy Percy's great-great-grandmother.

In May the monarch made Carey keeper of the garden, manor and tower of Pleasance in Greenwich and refurbished the tower lavishly at his own expense.[8] Soon courtiers observed that Henry VIII, accompanied by his standard bearer, Sir Andrew Flamock, sometimes took the royal barge down river from Whitehall 'to visit a fair lady... who was lodged in the tower in the park'.[9] It seems a logical conclusion that Mary, as Carey's wife, from time to time conveniently resided at this discreet rendezvous. Apparently, on one occasion the king's imminent arrival inspired him to poetry:

Within this towre,
There lieth a flowre,
That hath my hart.

Unfortunately Sir Andrew, invited to complete the verse, did so with such vulgarity that it ruined the romantic mood.[10]

But at the very moment of Mary's potential triumph, a well-connected mistress who had shown she could bear the king male children, Henry was struck, as he later put it, by the 'dart of love' launched by her own sister. Anne was back at Court as one of the queen's ladies. She had no thought at all for Mary's interests in setting her cap at the king. Anne's sex appeal, personality, intellect and wit, and bewitching black eyes that conveyed the promise of forbidden pleasure, made Henry determined to have her. But Anne, learning from her sister's experience, would not yield. Antonia Fraser concludes in her biography of Henry VIII's wives that Anne permitted her sovereign *coitus interruptus* 'with the interruption occurring at an increasingly late stage in the proceedings as the years passed'.[11] As Henry, by nature impulsive and emotional, was probably the least likely person in England to deprive himself voluntarily of full satisfaction, it seems inconceivable that Anne took any such risks. Philippa Gregory believes the lusty monarch did not 'get beyond first base'.[12] Anne's almost magical allure, Henry's willingness to wait, to play out the game of courtly love, is much more easily explained if he was surreptitiously two-timing Anne with Mary for several years.

So long as her marriage supplied a cloak of respectability, Mary remained readily available to relieve the royal frustrations prompted by her sister's resistance. But on 22 June 1528 Carey died of the sweating sickness, while Mary, in a further indication that she was his wife only in name, escaped unscathed.[13] Soon Mary was rumoured once again to be pregnant but if he was the father, nothing now could deflect the king, in a frenzy of unfulfilled lust, from his ardent pursuit of Anne. Henry disingenuously gave credence in a letter to the gossip that Mary was carrying another child, and not by him but by an unknown admirer.[14] The outcome of her pregnancy is uncertain but Mary may have miscarried. In any event, as a mistress of the king with prospects of further advancement, her time had passed.

Little Henry Carey became the ward of Anne Boleyn and was brought up in relative obscurity at Syon House. William Carey's lands and benefices were redistributed to meet his considerable debts, leaving Mary in humiliating limbo, entirely beholden to her sister and with no option but to join her expanding household. She undoubtedly made the best of it. So much so, that when in 1532 Henry VIII took Anne to France for a meeting with Francis I, far from leaving Mary behind in view of her sullied reputation among the French, they gave her almost pride of place. On Sunday 27 October Mary was one of three ladies who entered the grand reception room of the *maison des marchands* in Boulogne with Anne Boleyn, to begin a masked ball.[15]

However, just as Anne, now assured of marriage, finally began to bed Henry VIII, Mary struck up an equally intimate friendship with William Stafford, a junior member of the king's entourage. Although a distant relation of the titled Stafford family, he was a commoner and second son with almost no prospects, seen by the ever ambitious Howards as an entirely unsuitable match for the future queen's sister. In 1534 Mary became pregnant by Stafford, defiantly married him in secret, and when her pregnancy became obvious, confessed to the union. Anne Boleyn, furious, immediately dismissed Mary from court. Almost destitute, she wrote to the king's first minister, Thomas Cromwell, hoping to secure some financial support; but Mary couched her request in such provocative terms, it was doomed from the start. Of her husband, Mary said that she 'would rather beg [for] my bread with him than be the greatest Queen christened', a rebuke read by Anne that made her angrier than ever.

At first eking out a precarious existence in Chebsey, a remote village on the River Sow near Stafford, where her husband was born and had a very modest property, Mary would never return to court: when Anne fell spectacularly from royal favour, Mary's enforced absence probably saved her life.[16] In 1536, after Anne had been accused of adultery with several men and even of incest with her brother George, Mary made no attempt to intercede with the king on their behalf before their trial and execution or to visit either of them in the Tower. Aware of the close relationship between her siblings, she may even have believed them capable of incest as a desperate means to produce a healthy male heir to the throne; Mary knew only too well from her own experience that her family would stop at nothing to remain in power.[17] However, with her parents shattered by this turn of events, which hastened their deaths, ironically it was Mary who inherited the lion's share of the Boleyns' land and property. She died in July 1543.[18]

Bewitching eyes: Anne Boleyn.

*Henry Percy, 6th Earl of
Northumberland.*

Henry Percy, Anne's lost love, was forced to serve on the jury of peers that tried the queen for treason but pleaded illness, real or feigned, to excuse himself from having to decide that she was guilty. The king appointed Catherine, his daughter by Mary and still at court, an official witness of Anne's execution.[19] As he cut his psychopathic swathe through the Boleyns and their acolytes, Henry may even have thought this a merciful gesture. Catherine was made to watch her aunt's bloody decapitation at close quarters and accompany the removal of the corpse to the chapel of the Tower. No coffin had been supplied, so in return for some of the queen's clothes, her ladies begged an elmwood arrow box from the yeomen of the guard. It was too short to accommodate Anne's severed head, which had to be crammed in beside her body. Catherine was barely twelve years old and these terrifying images must have stayed with her forever.[20]

Although most of her immediate family were dead or in disgrace, in November 1539 the capricious monarch saw fit to provide for Catherine by appointing her a maid of honour to Anne of Cleves. This brought Catherine into contact with Sir Francis Knollys, one of the members of the royal household sent to welcome Henry's unprepossessing fourth wife at Dover. Within six months Catherine and Francis were married, an undoubted love match that produced at least fourteen children, all but one conceived within ten months or fewer of the last; the one exception was the result of an enforced separation when Francis, a staunch Protestant, went into exile during the reign of Mary Tudor, a fanatical catholic.[21] Elizabeth I made him treasurer of the royal household while for a decade Catherine successfully combined the role of almost continuous motherhood with that of first lady-in-waiting. When Catherine died on 15 January 1569, Elizabeth was grief-stricken and, quite out of character, paid for a lavish funeral and burial in Westminster Abbey, far more than she spent on the interment of her other close relatives. Fittingly for a half sister to the monarch, the documents setting out the arrangements for Catherine's funeral were placed with those of kings and queens.[22]

Catherine's third child, Laetitia or Lettice, Lucy Percy's grandmother, born on 8 November 1543, was also given a place at court, as a maid of the privy

Continuously pregnant: Catherine Carey.

Walter Devereux – died of a violent dysentery.

chamber. Here she met Walter Devereux, the future Earl of Essex, and their marriage in late 1560 or early 1561 allegedly produced five children. One died young and another intriguingly might not have been Lettice's offspring at all. The eldest son, Robert, said to have been born in 1566, was not entered into the Essex's genealogical register until seven years later, just after the earldom had been conferred. Attempts were made without success after Elizabeth I's death to prove that the queen had entered into a secret marriage with Robert Dudley, Earl of Leicester, with the inference, however improbable, that Robert was their legitimate son hastily fostered at birth and not a Devereux at all.

Whatever the truth of that, both Leicester and Lettice certainly behaved as though they were untouchable. Leicester encouraged Walter Devereux to accept a commission in Ireland, and in his prolonged absence, as the Sheriff of Warwickshire circumspectly put it, had 'private access to [Walter's wife] the Countess of Essex'. According to a report sent to Madrid in 1575 by Antonio de Guaras, a Spanish merchant and part-time diplomat in London, Lettice by then had borne two children by Leicester and at least one other was aborted.[23] If so, this would readily explain why in March 1576 Leicester showed himself extremely keen that Devereux, who had returned to England for three months but not to the bosom of his family, should go back to Ireland.[24] The dysfunctional relationship soon came to a head. Leicester, already suspected of murdering his first wife, who rather conveniently fell down the stairs, was accused of employing an Italian surgeon to poison Devereux, who died of a violent dysentery in Dublin on 22 September 1576, in mysterious circumstances. Two years later, exonerated by an undemanding enquiry carried out by Leicester's brother-in-law, the scandalous couple were free to marry. The ceremony took place at the discreet hour of 8 a.m. on 21 September 1578, with Lettice 'in a loose gowne' and once again obviously pregnant. No one dared tell the queen but in July 1579 the French ambassador, Jean de Simier, hoping to persuade Elizabeth to marry the Duke of Alençon, let slip the secret. Elizabeth flew into a rage, boxed Lettice's ears and banished her, shouting that just as 'but one sun lit the sky', there would be 'but one Queen of England'.[25]

Lettice left court in style, defiant to the last. Said to look uncannily like a younger version of Elizabeth, with red locks and a new wardrobe rivalling that of the monarch, she rode through the streets of London in an open carriage, followed by her ladies in two coaches and acknowledging the cheers of the populace convinced that it was the queen herself.[26]

The real Queen Elizabeth.

Lettice Knollys, often mistaken for the queen.

Already implicated in the death of one husband in the 1576 episode of the Italian surgeon, Lettice was later blamed for another. According to contemporary accounts, she had an affair with Christopher Blount, Leicester's Gentleman of the Horse. Soon after Leicester discovered this, he took Blount with him on an expedition to the Spanish Netherlands, exposing Blount to great risks in the hope that he would be killed in the thick of the fighting. When this failed, so the rumours went, Lettice – suspecting her husband's intent – disposed of Leicester by means of a poisoned cordial given to him on his return.[27] In July 1589 Lettice married Blount, far below her social station after having two earls as husbands, thereby fuelling the unsubstantiated allegation that she was a murderess. Lettice's supposed son Robert in due course became Earl of Essex and was executed for treason in 1601, followed by Blount for his complicity in this attempted coup against the crown.

Penelope, the elder of Lettice's two legitimate daughters by Walter Devereux, born in the first few days of January 1563, was implicated by Essex in the conspiracy. Examined by the Privy Council, Penelope adroitly defended herself; but many had been condemned in the past on far less persuasive evidence. Perhaps the proximity of her blood line that flowed from Elizabeth's father and Mary Boleyn made the queen merciful. Perhaps Elizabeth reckoned that her order by which Penelope would be 'sent unto my lord her husband', was punishment enough.

Penelope had been forced to marry Robert Rich, Earl of Warwick, against her wishes. Despite bearing him four surviving children, she began an openly adulterous relationship with Christopher Blount's distant cousin, Charles Blount. Together they had five children, and when Charles was made Earl of Devonshire by James I as a reward for his services in Ireland, he married Penelope even though her legal separation from Rich did not amount to a divorce. However, when Charles died, his relatives ferociously challenged the marriage and the will. After successfully rebutting charges of adultery, fraud and forgery, Penelope died on 6 July 1607.[28]

Lettice had loftier ambitions for Penelope's younger sister, Dorothy Devereux, Lucy Percy's mother, believed to have been born on 17 September 1564.[29] Early in 1583 Lettice made considerable progress towards arranging Dorothy's marriage with James VI of Scotland. Elizabeth reacted by threatening to proclaim Lettice 'all over Christendom as the whore she was', and said she

The Scandalous sisters: Dorothy (left) and Penelope Devereux.

would 'sooner the Scots King lost his crown' than be married to the daughter of a 'she-wolf'.[30]

Dorothy, described as 'less beautiful, less clever, and less amiable' than her sister, was no less wilful. To keep her out of mischief, Lettice sent Dorothy to stay at Broxbourne Manor, the Hertfordshire home of Sir Henry Cock, a senior figure in the treasury of the royal household. Dorothy, however, already had in mind a rather more secret match of her own. In July 1583 a party of gentlemen with swords and daggers concealed under their cloaks hijacked the local church, bringing with them their own vicar, who ignored all

Broxbourne Church, where the local vicar was menaced with swords and daggers while Dorothy Percy married Thomas Perrott in an illicit ceremony.

protests and proceeded to marry the eager (and possibly pregnant) Dorothy to Thomas Perrott. This member of the Welsh gentry, whose father had some pretensions to being an illegitimate son of Henry VIII, was in possession of a licence obtained, with considerable duplicity, from the Bishop of London.[31] Having to all intents and purposes eloped, the couple produced two children but quarrelled constantly and in July 1587, their initial passion extinguished, they parted company for good.[32]

Dorothy would have been seen as second-hand goods but for the queen's determination to find a suitable husband for the ninth Earl of Northumberland. In 1585 the eighth Earl had been found shot to death in the Tower of London. His lands and title went to his son, the latest Henry Percy. In eighteen months the profligate young man ran up debts from, by his own admission, 'hawks, hounds, horses, dice, cards, apparel, mistresses [and] all other riot of expense' amounting to £15,000, five times his annual income.[33] He hit upon a solution to his financial embarrassment by proposing to an heiress, Lady Arbella Stuart. As Arbella's claim to the English throne followed only that of her cousin James VI of Scotland and Henry Percy was seventh in the order of royal succession, Elizabeth viewed such a potential union with alarm, it having more royal blood than the queen herself. She put Arbella under restraint and procured

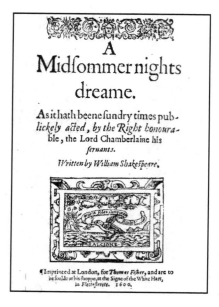

A

Midfommer nights dreame.

As it hath beene fundry times pub-
lickely acted, by the Right honoura-
ble, the Lord Chamberlaine his
feruants.

Written by William Shakespeare.

¶ Imprinted at London, for Thomas Fisher, and are to
be foulde at his fhoppe, at the Signe of the White Hart,
in Fleetefreete. 1600.

a far safer marriage, from her perspective, between Henry and Dorothy. The ceremony probably took place in Elizabeth's presence at Essex House in London on 30 April 1595, celebrated by what may have been the first performance of William Shakespeare's new play, *A Midsummer Night's Dream*. Dorothy's inconvenient marriage to (by then Sir) Thomas Perrott was ignored, perhaps because the Queen did not intend 'the mere detail of a living husband [to] thwart the course of true love'.[34] However, tongues wagged behind the scenes about Dorothy's uncertain status: 'nor maid, nor wife, nor yet widoivel', in the words of a contemporary.[35]

The 'fresh days of love' wished upon the courtly couple on stage in Shakespeare's latest comedy did not strike a chord with Henry and Dorothy as the newly weds sat in the front row of the audience. Neither had been consulted about their feelings and their marriage proved tempestuous from the start. Whereas Dorothy could always produce a caustic turn of phrase, Henry was slow of speech, a product of his deafness, and had a notoriously ungovernable temper. The 'wizard earl', as he was popularly known, spent much more time with his books and his scientific experiments than he did with his wife.

They had violent arguments and separated four times in the first five years of marriage. While Dorothy's first child as a Northumberland, christened with her mother's name on 20 August 1598, may have been Henry's, it is almost certain that her second, Lucy, born on or about Christmas Day 1599,[36] was conceived while the couple were living apart. Even though it had formed part of her dowry, in October of that year Dorothy had to leave Syon House, a grand three-storey mansion with oak-beamed hall and long gallery, crenellated roof and gable turrets, set in nearly 200 acres running down to the Thames.[37] The earl forcibly separated the heavily pregnant Dorothy from her daughter of fourteen months and made her rent for £26 a year a property in Putney.[38] This was a grand mansion, not an artisan's cottage, built by a wealthy cloth merchant, John Lacy, who had entertained Queen Elizabeth there on several occasions. Its three sides were arranged around a courtyard, with large

The Wizard Earl, Henry Percy, whom Lucy believed to be her father.

windows overlooking the river.[39] Nonetheless, given the importance of a son to inherit the title, the inability to determine the sex of an infant prior to its birth and the humiliation he was inflicting on his wife, Northumberland must have been convinced the child could not possibly be his. Dorothy pleaded her innocence in a letter to her brother, the Earl of Essex, who unsurprisingly wanted to know what had transpired. 'It was his Lordship's pleasure upon no cause given by me to have me keep house by myself,' she replied.[40] The cause she omitted to mention was her adultery with a certain Thomas Percy.

Believed by many at the time to be Henry Percy's illegitimate half-brother, Thomas Percy was in fact his second cousin once removed, being the great-grandson of the fourth earl.[41] Thomas Percy was born in Yorkshire around 1560. Educated at Cambridge, he was tall, handsome, well built, with large lively eyes.[42] 'Rather wild' in his youth, Thomas toured the country giving duelling demonstrations with other skilled swordsmen to paying customers, usually local villagers and townsfolk, a risky business as he declined to wear any protective clothing. In 1595 the earl made him a rent collector in his northern estates, a task that Thomas undertook without scruple, subsequently convicted of forgery and false imprisonment. His master, however, was only interested in results and the following year appointed Thomas Constable of Alnwick Castle. This once great symbol of power on a natural bluff above the River Aln had been rendered almost obsolete by the development of artillery. In crumbling decay, with the only serviceable lavatories at the south wall, where they emptied into the Bowburn stream, it was used as an administrative centre. Twice a year

Alnwick Castle in Northumberland, bastion of the Percys.

the earl's receivers and auditors, generously entertained by Thomas in the Auditor's Tower, checked and counted the fruits of his labours before filling the saddlebags of their packhorses with coin and returning, under armed escort, to the earl's exchequer in London.

Northumberland soon relied upon Thomas to manage most of his land and property, which stretched across eight counties of England and Wales. In doing so he came into increasing contact with Dorothy, who retained an interest in estates that had once been her own. The brooding Thomas, so often soaked in sweat that he had to change his shirts at least twice a day, was an attractive prospect for a neglected wife. Thomas was married, but bigamously: unknown to Dorothy, he had abandoned one spouse in London and saw the other only rarely in Warwickshire.[43] The earl, reconciled with his wife for a fifth time in December 1601, took credit for their second son, born on 29 September 1602. By November, after another quarrel, Dorothy found herself alone again at Syon House.[44] Northumberland was evidently unaware of the identity of her lover and sent Thomas on three confidential missions to Scotland. He was received cordially by James VI and given verbal undertakings of preferential treatment for the Catholics. Once he became king of England, however, James showed he had no intention of keeping such promises and Thomas seems to have taken this as a personal affront.[45] In 1605 he was one of the principal conspirators in the Gunpowder Plot, the prelude to a Catholic uprising, intended to blow monarch, Lords and Commons to kingdom come. But Thomas, a clever, ambitious and pragmatic man, may have been turned by the king's secretary of state, Robert Cecil. He was seen not long before the plot's denouement, according to an Anglican clergyman, Dr Godfrey Goodman, leaving Cecil's London house at the suspicious hour of 2 a.m.[46]

Thomas was always eager to preserve the conspiracy's momentum. At Easter that year he challenged his fellow conspirators, saying, 'shall we alivays be talking, and never doe anything?' His visit to Syon House on 4 November, the eve of the opening of Parliament, when he spoke to the earl in private and stayed for dinner, did more than anything else to incriminate Northumberland. Immediately afterwards Thomas went to see Dorothy, once again living separately, by then at Essex House. This prompted speculation that she was in some way privy to the plot and content for her husband to be murdered with the rest, so that her lover might become 'the best Percy in England'.[47]

The Gunpowder Plot
Thomas Percy, shown here with Guy Fawkes and their fellow conspirators, was at the heart of the Gunpowder Plot.

The following day Guy Fawkes was discovered and seized beneath the Houses of Parliament beside what subsequently proved to be thirty-six barrels of largely defective gunpowder, which might not have exploded even if lit. Thomas fled, together with several of his fellow plotters. They were intercepted and besieged at Holbeach, where Thomas and another conspirator, Robert Catesby, were brought down by the same shot. Thomas was badly wounded but little effort was made to keep him alive, suggesting that his death avoided awkward questions for the government.

Northumberland, already under arrest, sent a letter to his colleagues on the Privy Council, imploring them quickly to interrogate the traitor in case he should die from his wounds. He argued that no one apart from Thomas could establish his guilt or innocence, that is, show the earl 'clere as the day, or darke as the night'.[48] Whether his fruitless exhortation was genuine or made with the hope and expectation that Thomas was already dead, is difficult to determine. Northumberland did not help his cause by saying to his wife before James's accession that 'he had rather the King of Scots were buried than crowned'.[49] In 1605 his peer's robes had been prepared and there was every indication he intended to attend Parliament on the fateful day. But Fawkes, broken in the end by relentless, escalating torture, confessed that Thomas had undertaken to warn Northumberland to stay clear of Parliament on 5 November.[50] If Northumberland had been warned at the last moment, or had survived the blast by good fortune, as the leading Catholic lord he would surely have been the plotters' first choice to assume control of the country as its Protector.

Unable, as the earl complained, to prove a negative, in June 1606 he was fined the huge sum of £30,000 and sent to the Tower of London, where he would remain for sixteen years, cosseted by a retinue of his own servants. Northumberland was granted six rooms in the Martin Tower, which he filled with the finest furniture; a gilded cage, but a cage just the same. A plume of noxious smoke sometimes hung over the fortress, the product of the eccentric earl's unpredictable chemistry experiments. His patronage proved much more fruitful in astronomy. In July 1609 the shy, retiring Thomas Harriot justified Northumberland's generous annual pension of £80 'and board' by becoming the first astronomer to record observations of the moon through a telescope, four months before Galileo achieved immortality by doing the same.

Lucy was nearly seven when she first visited the wizard earl, believing him to be her father, and played with her sister in the prison garden tended by

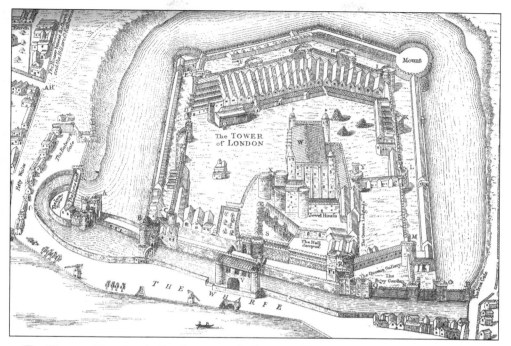

The Tower of London in the Seventeenth Century. The 9th Duke of Northumberland was imprisoned in its Martin Tower (top right, indicated by the letter 'I').

Northumberland's own horticulturists. Within a year or two she was riding tempestuous horses with the confidence of a veteran and scorning her sibling's lame efforts in the saddle.[51] She was still too young to understand the turbulent past that would formulate her future but as events would subsequently confirm, if there were genes to be found within her family for adultery, acerbity, effrontery and treachery as well as for beauty, Lucy Percy had inherited them all.

2: BEDFELLOWS

In 1566 two pregnancies ran their course in what could scarcely have been more contrasting circumstances. On 17 September Dorothy Devereux, Lucy Percy's mother, was born in the serene environment of Chartley, a half-timbered moated manor house near Stafford, sheltered beneath the battlements of a castle ruin. On 19 June Mary Queen of Scots had given birth to the future James VI (and I of England) in a tiny retiring chamber at Edinburgh Castle, whose booming guns announced his arrival. Her child had sometimes seemed unlikely to come to term.

On 19 March of that year in her apartments at Holyrood Palace, Mary's swollen belly was menaced by daggers when she tried hysterically to prevent the murder of a former wandering minstrel, her Italian secretary, confidant and probably lover, David Riccio. His assailants included Mary's own husband and debauched cousin, Henry Stuart, Lord Darnley, the father of her unborn child. The following day the queen almost miscarried with shock; and two nights later she escaped on horseback and rode, heavily pregnant and in great discomfort, twenty-five miles to Dunbar.

In June 1567 James VI's mother, on pain of death, was forced to abdicate. He was brought up by dour successive regents and often threatened or confined. Small wonder that from an early age James was nervous, restless and excitable; he had an almost pathological fear of assassination, dressing throughout his life in 'great pleits and full stuffed' that he hoped, although never really believed, made his clothing impervious to daggers, 'steletto proofe'.[1] In practice little more than a feudal chieftain at a ramshackle court, from the start James was regarded as not much of a king. Even as a boy, he seemed an unattractive specimen. He had spindly legs, probably the result of rickets, and protruding eyes he had difficulty in focusing. James's skin was lightly pitted by smallpox. He began putting on weight, the outcome of a poor diet, despite meals reckoned by foreign ambassadors to be almost inedible; his tongue was too big for his mouth and he seemed unable to eat or drink without leaving a conspicuous residue of food about his person.

James was also starved of affection, which in September 1579 made him particularly vulnerable to the attentions of Esmé Stuart, Darnley's first cousin,

Mary Queen of Scots almost miscarried from the shock of the brutal murder of her secretary, David Riccio.

James – drawn into 'carnal lust'.

newly arrived from France. Esmé, a product of the overtly homosexual court of Henry III, proceeded to 'draw the king to carnal lust'.[2] James was just thirteen, which in modern times would have characterised Esmé, aged thirty-seven, as a child molester liable for a long prison sentence. Instead, he was made First Gentleman of the Chamber, sleeping in the same room and almost certainly the same bed as the monarch, and transforming the role to one of real political power. It reflected the prevailing confusion about homosexuality, for there was no word yet to define it. Men and women to a large extent led separate lives, resulting in heightened same sex relationships. There was a prevailing belief, not altogether well founded, that sex between males was a transitional experience which would be replaced by heterosexual sex as soon as the opportunity arose. In the young king's case, however, it awakened a strong sexual disposition towards men that would remain with him for good. The besotted monarch created Esmé Earl and then Duke of Lennox and admitted him to the royal council, a pattern of advancement soon followed with other favourites. In 1582 Esmé was forced by jealous lairds to return to France, where he died unexpectedly the following May, leaving instructions that his heart should be embalmed and sent to the Scottish king.

James showed no interest in the opposite sex. A report sent to Elizabeth I said that he 'never regards the company of any woman, not so much as in any dalliance'.[3] However, at the insistence of his councillors, in 1589 he narrowed his choice of a bride to one of two princesses, both daughters of Frederick II of Denmark; the Danes forced him to accept the younger, Anne, without a dowry. Elizabeth gave the poverty-stricken monarch cash for clothes and lent him wedding plate but still James was kept waiting. Having been married to the king by

Esme Stewart – reaped a reward for sexual favours.

Anne of Denmark – inexpert shot.

proxy, aged 15, Anne was prevented three times by storms from reaching Scotland and took shelter in Oslo; whereupon, with quite untypical élan, James resolved to brave the North Sea and fetch her himself. He spent six months with his new wife in Norway and Denmark before returning home.

In sixteen years Anne would give birth to seven children, of whom three survived infancy, and had one recorded miscarriage, indicative of intermittent intercourse. There is strong evidence, however, that the king saw this as a pragmatic duty to produce heirs, not as a pleasure. He possessed a low opinion of women in general and regarded Anne, however unfairly, as a frivolous, empty-headed wife. The queen did herself no favours when, in a well-intentioned but singular attempt to involve herself in the king's main obsession, hunting, she loosed off an arrow with her eyes closed and fatally injured Jewel, James's favourite hound, causing her husband to fly into a rage.[4]

Among the king's hard drinking companions on the Scandinavian adventure had been the fair-haired, handsome Alexander Lindsay, 'sometimes his bedfellow', made Vice-Chamberlain of the royal household and subsequently Lord Spynie. James also received sexual favours from George Gordon, head of the Gordon clan and later Earl of Huntly, who often spent the night 'in the King's chamber' and would be awarded his Scottish title in 1599.[5] He was treated with extraordinary leniency by the king, despite an appalling record for sadistic violence, on one occasion seizing two cooks belonging to a rival clan and roasting them alive. As historian Maurice Lee delicately puts it, 'James overlooked Huntly's long career of conspiracy, rebellion and murder as far as he decently could'.[6]

A third contemporaneous bed partner showed that the king was far from monogamous. The writer and courtier, Francis Osborne, recorded that an

English aristocrat, Philip Herbert, also found immediate favour in 1600, when he arrived, aged sixteen, at the Scottish court and was 'caressed by King James for his hansome face'.[7] Herbert, whom the French ambassador thought 'very arrogant', received a series of increasingly important honours in the course of two years: Gentleman of the Privy Chamber, Knight of the Bath, Baron Herbert and finally Earl of Montgomery.

In April 1603, following the death of Elizabeth, James left Edinburgh to claim the English throne. The Exchequer in London was obliged to send him money, because the king, although already besieged by suitors, had only enough to get him to Berwick. After his threadbare existence in Scotland, James was stunned by the riches of his new kingdom. He took the royal barge to the Tower to feast his eyes on the crown jewels; and spent days excitedly exploring his palace at Whitehall, a hotchpotch of some fifty buildings and courtyards spread over twenty acres on the north side of the Thames between Westminster and the City, which was still surrounded by a wall and a ditch, in some places almost 200 feet wide. James's new domain consisted of grand, if faded, private apartments, with views over formal gardens, stables, bakery, cider house and coal yard. Insalubrious additions included fish stands erected by opportunist vendors against the palace walls. James was less than impressed to find that Londoners had the right to use a public thoroughfare between the King Street and Holbein gates which divided his palace in two. Tired of the constant attention of his new subjects, with a crude turn of phrase that shocked his English courtiers, he threatened, 'God's wounds, I will pull down my breeches and they shall also see my arse.'[8]

The odour derived from the king's lack of personal cleanliness was remarked upon at Whitehall in an age not conspicuous for its abundant use of soap and water. Whereas most people in society occasionally washed their extremities, James cleaned only his fingertips: not his hair, not his face, not his teeth, and never the rest of his body, even after defecating. In later life he wore his clothes until they in turn wore out. Sir Anthony Weldon, a minor government official who would accompany James on a brief return visit to Scotland, tactlessly blamed this on the habits of the Scots. Weldon declared that 'the stinking people that

Sir Anthony Weldon.

inhabited' Scotland probably did not notice their sovereign's shortcomings, what with their 'foul houses, sheets, foul linen, foul dishes and pots, foul trenchers and napkins'.[9] By no means ill-disposed towards his monarch, Weldon nonetheless reported that James had an obsessive interest in sexual perversions and sex was rarely off his mind.[10] 'His walk was ever circular, his fingers ever in that walk fiddling with that codpiece'.[11]

The young men who joined James in England included Lucy Percy's future husband, James Hay, born about 1580 into a minor branch of the family that held the earldom of Arran. He was sent to France as a teenager and taken under the wing of Charles Cauchon de Maupas, baron du Tour, with whose help he joined the Scottish regiment of Henri IV and was soon fluent in French.[12] A crack shot and renowned duellist, Maupas became Henri's royal champion and later an accomplished diplomat at the Scottish and English courts. His influence helped Hay to become a Gentleman of the Privy Chamber and shortly afterwards a knight. In March 1604 James sent Hay on a mission to Henri IV, who had pragmatically converted to Catholicism, with instructions to press the cause of the French king's erstwhile followers, the Protestant Huguenots. In identifying with their campaign for political as well as religious autonomy, he only succeeded in irritating Henri, who reduced the size of the jewel given to Hay as the traditional parting gift.[13] This left Hay considerably out of pocket because while James had given him just £300 for expenses, he had spent £6,000, an unpromising augury of the gap between his income and expenditure that would never be bridged in his lifetime.[14]

In July, eager for a new source of funds, Hay began to negotiate with Sir Edward Denny for the hand of his daughter and heir, Honoria. James paved the way by awarding Denny a barony and making Hay Keeper of the Robes, but Denny still prevaricated for more than two years, realising that his prospective son-in-law – whose family motto, appropriately enough, was 'Spend and God will send' – was already notoriously extravagant. The wedding finally took place on 6 January 1607, attended by the king. The masque that followed became equally notorious, featuring as it did a group of young men cavorting in tight fitting flesh coloured garments that made them look naked.[15]

Hay was an enthusiastic participant in the tiltyard, where an incident that occurred about two months after his first marriage lost him his position as favourite but simultaneously gained him the credit for supplying his successor.

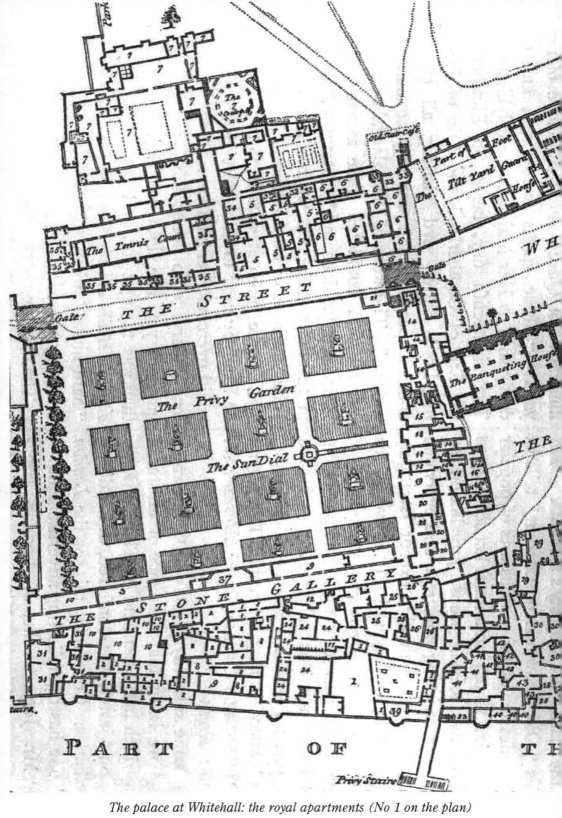

The palace at Whitehall: the royal apartments (No 1 on the plan) overlook the River Thames.

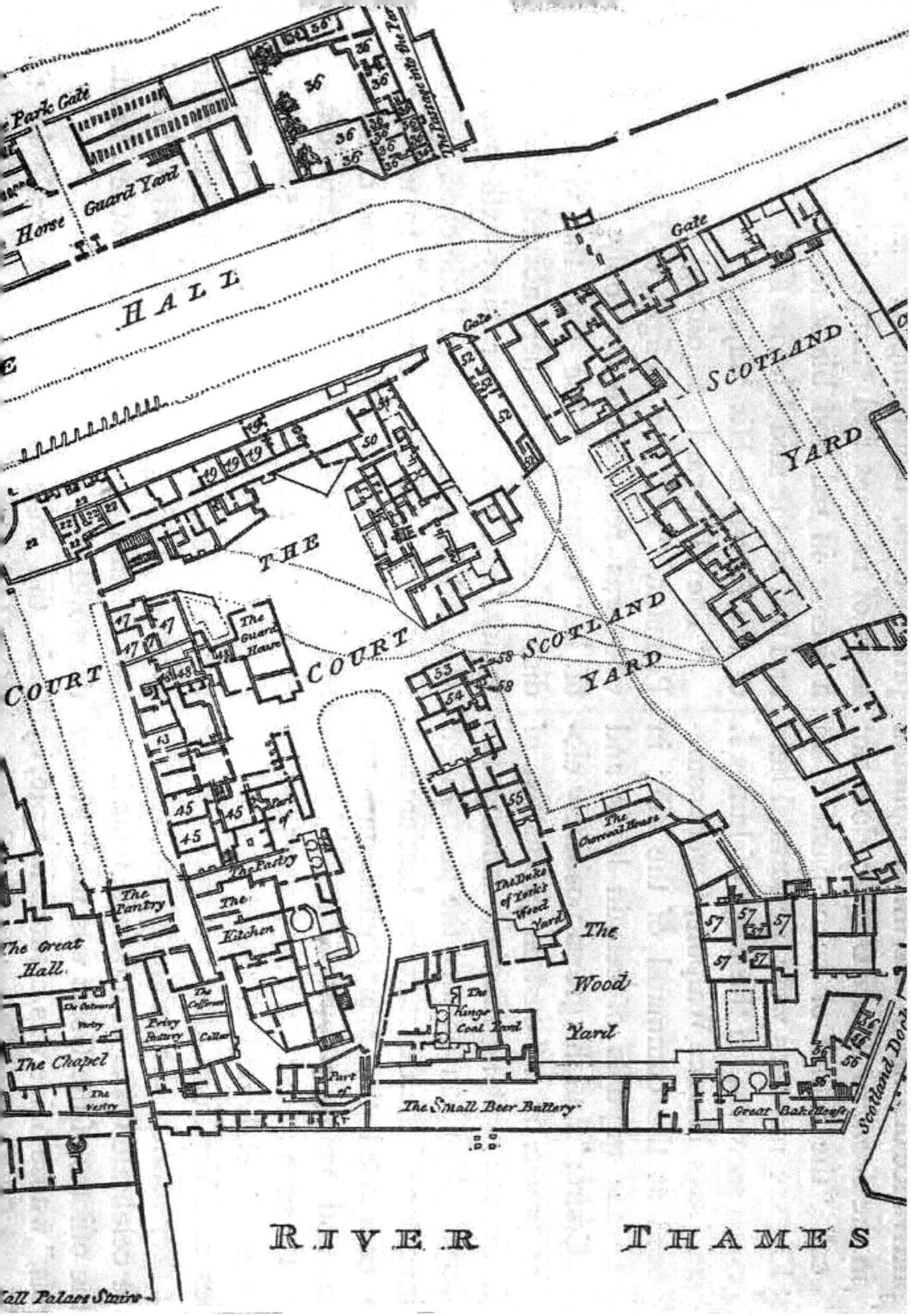

Park Gate

The Passage into the Park

36 36 36 36 36

Horse Guard Yard

HALL

Gate

Gate

SCOTLAND YARD

THE COURT

COURT

SCOTLAND YARD

The Guard House

The Great Hall

The Pantry

The Kitchen

The Pastry

The Coffee

Collar

Privy Battery

The Outward Pastry

The Chapel

The Vestry

Part of

The Cole House

The Hange Coat Yard

The Small Beer Battery

The Duke of York's Wood Yard

The Coal House

The Wood Yard

Great Bake House

Scotland Dock

RIVER THAMES

Hall Palace Stairs

James Hay: notoriously extravagant.

In presenting his master's shield to the king before he rode in the lists, Hay's squire, Robert Carr, slipped off his horse and broke his leg, rolling in agony on the ground. James, who already knew the boy as a page in Scotland, left the royal stand to see if he could help and was immediately smitten. He helped to nurse the handsome 17-year-old back to health.

The king made no attempt to conceal his feelings for the new favourite. A contemporary report observed that 'In wanton looks and wanton gestures they exceeded any part of womankind'.[16] In return for sexual favours, Carr received the manor of Sherborne, then in 1611 was made Viscount Rochester and in November 1613 Earl of Somerset. But his spectacular rise was followed by an even more spectacular fall, because before long Carr was deeply in love... with a woman. On 26 December, in the Chapel Royal, he wed Frances Howard, the daughter of the Earl of Suffolk. His bride 'was married in her haire', meaning that during the ceremony it hung down to her shoulders, a symbol of virginity.[17] The symbol was undoubtedly false on this occasion. Frances was already Carr's mistress and had obtained a controversial annulment from the Earl of Essex on the grounds of his alleged impotence, although only after James added two compliant bishops to the ecclesiastical tribunal to obtain a 7-5 majority.

For the purposes of an evidential hearing, Frances persuaded a panel of gullible matrons and midwives to certify that she was still 'a virgin untouched and uncorrupted', by inducing a young cousin, heavily veiled, to submit to an intimate examination in her place.[18] Unfortunately for her longer term prospects, her new husband Carr proved to have been 'the central figure in five erotic triangles, four of them in part homosexual'.[19] The match with Carr was vehemently opposed by Sir Thomas Overbury, who, like the king, had been one of his male lovers. 'Desire desires no triangles', as historian David Bergeron aptly puts it.[20] Overbury feared that Carr's new love – or 'that woman', as he described her, as though he were the wronged wife – would end his influence. Overbury knew too much about them both for his own good. Not content with having contrived his imprisonment in the Tower, the cold blooded couple sent Overbury poisoned tarts and jellies and a poisoned glyster, a large ivory syringe used for purging. They correctly calculated that if the former merely made him unwell, remedial use of the latter would be fatal.

When in 1615 the background to Overbury's murder began to come out, heaping sensation upon sensation, James still could have protected his favourite from trial and imprisonment. That he chose not to do so is best explained by

Robert Carr lost the king's favour by preferring a woman.

Frances Howard falsely claimed to be a virgin.

Sir Thomas Overbury

a rambling, reproachful letter in which the king complained about Carr's 'long creeping back and withdrawing yourself from lying in my chamber, notwithstanding my many hundred times earnestly soliciting you to the contrary'.[21] After finding Frances rather more to his taste, Carr had ignored all James's entreaties and withdrawn from sexual relations. If he believed his influence would survive such a snub intact and that the king would save him from criminal charges, then he was sorely mistaken. Left by the sovereign to face a tribunal of their peers, both Carr and his countess were found guilty of Overbury's murder and sentenced to death. However, Hay kept himself in James's favour by skilful negotiations that resulted in Carr agreeing to conceal his past relationship with the monarch, in return for clemency and a period of imprisonment in the Tower for himself and his wife.[22]

Hay may have felt he needed to be able to rely on the king's goodwill because of an undiscovered skeleton in his own closet. Although Honoria's marriage with Hay produced two children, she remained deeply unhappy and took a lover who was murdered by one of his Scottish compatriots.[23] Lady Mary Wroth, the daughter of the Earl of Leicester, would later claim Hay treated his first wife with such callousness that it contributed to her death.[24] In August 1614 Honoria was heavily pregnant, carrying a child that Hay surely thought might not be his own; she fell victim to a mysterious attempted robbery on Ludgate Hill in London, was delivered prematurely and died from complications within the week.[25] Honoria was buried at night in Hay's absence, at Waltham Abbey near his father-in-law's home in Essex.

Hay's public reputation remained untarnished and on 29 June 1615 he was awarded a full English peerage as Baron Hay of Sawley in Yorkshire. Hay also began to look for another wife and soon joined a series of much younger suitors for the hand of one of the Earl of Northumberland's supposed daughters, Dorothy and Lucy. Lady Mary Wroth's brother, Robert Sidney, was quickest

Lucy's sister, Dorothy Percy, eloped with Robert Sidney.

off the mark and proposed to Dorothy, only for negotiations on the size of the dowry between his father and the wizard earl, still incarcerated in the Tower, to collapse. However, in February 1616, following the tradition of a long line of rebellious Percy women, Dorothy eloped with Sidney and married him in secret.[26] The occasion was captured by a London painter, Peter Oliver, in a miniature that showed Dorothy wearing an elaborate embroidered dress with white ruff, pearl earrings and a pearl necklace, a red embroidered shawl over her right shoulder, with fresh flowers in her flowing blonde hair. Their idyllic if impecunious marriage would eventually produce fifteen children, of whom twelve survived.

Attractive though Dorothy undoubtedly was, her younger sister Lucy, the newest arrival at Whitehall, created much more of a stir. Even aged sixteen she was already held to be 'the most lovely damsel in all England'.[27] Wavy brown curls set off her oval features, swan-like neck, generous breasts and perfect complexion. Hay was soon reported 'far engaged in affection with Lady Lucy', encouraged by the Countess of Northumberland, who was seeking full rehabilitation into London society and harboured hopes that with Lucy in tow, Hay might be inclined to assist in securing her husband's release.[28]

In March the countess's two daughters had the disagreeable task of breaking news of their alliances, actual and prospective, to Northumberland in the Tower. Dorothy was already pregnant and the earl took her confession of marriage into one of the most respectable noble houses calmly, even promising a dowry of £6,000. But he considered Hay, with no lineage and no land, an entirely different prospect as a son-in-law. The proud earl 'could not endure that his daughter should dance any Scottish jigs'.[29] In an effort to persuade Lucy to let him choose another husband for her, Northumberland offered to provide a prodigious dowry, more fitting for a princess – £20,000 – if only she would agree.[30] When this largesse with strings attached did not have the desired effect, on the sisters' next visit the earl took Dorothy on one side and told her to return home at once and send for Lucy's maids, as he meant 'not to part with her but that she should keep him company'.[31] Sparks flew when Lucy discovered his intentions and Dorothy's involvement behind her back; Lucy could seem Anne Boleyn reincarnate whenever thwarted, with piercing eyes and a vicious tongue. But she could do nothing and, like Northumberland, was now a prisoner in the Tower. Under English law, until she married, Lucy was little more than a chattel that the earl could do with as he wished.

The timing could scarcely have been worse for her would-be betrothed. Hay's former patron, Maupas, had just been appointed ambassador extraordinary to the British court, and Hay had used his arrival as an excuse to plan a spectacular feast and masque. He hired the leading playwright, Ben Jonson, to produce a performance of *Lovers Made Men*.[32] Thirty cooks laboured for twelve days to prepare the banquet, at a reported cost of more than £2,200. All of this was, alas, really for Lucy, 'the most desired guest', who remained imprisoned in the Tower.[33] When Hay disconsolately went ahead with the masque two nights later without her, Lucy may even have heard the sounds of the revelry, at Hay's grace-and-favour London property, the Wardrobe in Blackfriars, echoing down river.

Northumberland did permit Lucy to visit the infamous Countess of Somerset, also held in the Tower. Branded a whore and a poisoner, with bewitching looks second only to those of Lucy herself, Frances Howard proved the worst possible influence on the rebellious teenager. She encouraged the match with Hay and enabled him to meet Lucy secretly in her apartments, so where the wizard earl 'thought he had her safest, there he lost her'.[34] Rather too late to have any effect, Northumberland sent Lucy away, forbidding her mother to take her in; and for a while she had to live with her sister in cramped accommodation at Baynard's Castle, the London residence of the Countess of Pembroke. Realising this, Hay, called upon to follow the royal progress to Scotland, invited Lucy to stay at the Wardrobe for several months in his absence, and left his delighted guest £2,000 for new clothes and entertainment.[35]

Sir Edward Hyde, Earl of Clarendon, statesman and historian, writing from almost a contemporary perspective, perceived that Hay's excesses were not some lovesick impulse but more calculating than they might at first appear. Lacking the staying power and finesse of a professional diplomat, or any military inclination or flair, Hay had to find something that distinguished him from a coterie of courtiers of similar rank. He chose to sponsor masques and banquets because they kept him in the public eye.[36] Hay could afford his extravagance because he was at the forefront of exploitation of royal finances, keeping James afloat by selling titles and pensions, collecting long forgotten debts, creating export licences where none had previously existed and creaming off revenue from commercial ventures in which the crown had a stake. He bought up narrow plots of unregistered land along the Thames waterfront, forcing developers to pay extortionate sums for the right to build. He overspent by three or four times with complete impunity the annual budget for his post as Keeper of the

Robes, becoming in addition Master of the Wardrobe from February 1613. Whilst the annual salary for running this grand office was set at £222 13s 4d, the industrious new royal treasurer, Sir Lionel Cranfield, himself no stranger to corruption, would later claim that Hay received more than £4,000 a year in bribes from aspiring suppliers to the court.[37]

It is a safe assumption that Hay, sent to the French court at the end of July 1616 as ambassador extraordinary (in diplomatic parlance, a temporary posting) did not pay the full price for his own extravagant wardrobe, ordering twenty suits, one per day of his intended stay. Each coat was actually made twice, as shortly before his departure Hay received word that the French styles had just changed and he was determined to be in the latest fashions himself. His escort, riding into Paris on horseback for greater effect, was richly attired with cloaks of white beaver edged in golden thread and embroidered gold doublets. Hay's personal mount was lightly shod in silver horseshoes so they might be easily dislodged on the cobbled streets, whereupon to the wonder of the watching citizens, a liveried attendant would produce a replacement from a tawny velvet bag and each time casually discard the original.[38]

Unfortunately for Hay's mission, the first, half-hearted attempt to betroth the Prince of Wales to a French princess, France was in no state to consider matrimonial diplomacy; the country was on the verge of civil war. Despite several extensions to his stay, Hay made no tangible progress and was recalled in October. He returned via Dieppe, complete with the parting gift from the French of a diamond worth 60,000 livres and fine wine previously laid down in the cellars of the Louvre palace; and, indicative of the modest demands of his stay, nursing a tennis injury.[39]

Although Hay had cut a fine dash in Paris, back in England another year passed for Lucy without the expected wedding. 'For so hot love, they have a great deal of patience', wrote the notorious court gossip, John Chamberlain, suggesting that the couple's ardour had cooled. Hay, however, was playing a long game that must have convinced Lucy's other frustrated suitors, gazing upon Aphrodite from afar, that he had ice in his veins. Hay rented a property near Syon House so that he could visit mother and daughter almost every day and entertained them to dinners so lavish that the countess felt intimidated and unable to reciprocate.[40] With his eye on the £20,000 dowry dangled by the earl, in late October 1617 Hay went to see him in the Tower. He suggested it might be possible to intercede with the king and accelerate Northumberland's release. The earl took the hint and reluctantly gave his blessing to the marriage;

but he declined to part with the dowry and instructed his wife not to attend the ceremony.

Although described in contemporary accounts as a radiantly beautiful bride, it seems that Lucy had fallen in love with the court rather than the courtier. Hay was far from handsome. He had an odd-shaped, triangular face, with sagging cheeks, a long thin nose and flaring nostrils. The king's daughter sometimes referred to him affectionately as 'old camel-face' and was well placed to make such an unflattering comparison following the arrival in England of five camels, a gift from King Philip III of Spain.[41] Hay, nearly thirty-eight, was twenty years older than his new wife, at a time when the average life expectancy of men in London was less than forty. He suffered from gout, the consequence of his gourmet extravagances. What he had to offer, however, was charm, grace and impeccable taste. He was also evidently well prepared for the big night, with a host of 'scents and emollients' assembled by the royal physician, including toothpaste, mouthwash, hand lotion and lozenges 'to keep the breath sweet in the bedchamber'.[42]

Lucy, sheltered from court gossip for many years because of her father's disgrace, probably knew little or nothing of Hay's earlier sexual activity with the king but she still had to contend with her sovereign's disagreeably close interest on her wedding day, 6 November, 1617. Despite his unconcealed interest in men, James had a long-established reputation for shocking prurience when he sought out newly-married couples in his circle. A courtier, Sir Dudley Carleton, recorded how after their wedding the king paid his former lover, the Earl of Montgomery, and his new bride, Lady Susan Vere, an early morning visit in his nightgown 'and spent a good time in or upon the bed, choose which you will believe'. On the morning after his daughter, the popular Princess Elizabeth, married Frederick V of the Palatinate, James made a similar unannounced visit to their wedding chamber and questioned her embarrassed husband, widely believed to be 'much too young and small timbered', as to whether he had satisfied Britain's 'queen of hearts' during the night.[43] Sometimes James's arrival for the purpose of a sexually charged bedroom tumble was even prearranged. Barely six weeks before Hay and Lucy's wedding at the Wardrobe, Sir John Villiers and Frances Coke were married at Hampton Court: 'The next morning the king visited them in bed, having first given orders they should not rise before his coming.'[44] Perhaps Hay, who spent £1,600 on his own wedding breakfast, a modest sum by his standards, should have been alerted when James insisted on giving Lucy away. A great deal of

Elizabeth Stuart: James I's fiercely ambitious daughter.

Frederick V of the Palatinate: 'too young and small timbered'.

wine was consumed by all and according to Lucy's scandalised gentlewoman, one Mistress Washington, the inebriated monarch kept wandering in and out of the bedchamber and saw as much of the bride as did the bridegroom on her wedding night.

Given the obsessive attention of her parents and despite her secret assignations in the Tower, Lucy was probably still a virgin when she wed; but if, as seems more than likely, Hay failed to make the earth move for her, the marriage was nonetheless soon consummated. By March 1618 Lucy was pregnant but at risk of having nowhere congenial to stay for her confinement. Hay, coming under the increasingly suspicious eye of treasurer Cranfield, had been forced to give up his lucrative post as Master of the Wardrobe and with it the property in Upper Thames Street. James was indifferent to corruption, endemic in seventeenth century politics; but he was trying to live more within his means rather than go cap in hand to a truculent House of Commons, and could no longer afford to have such a profligate minister in charge of a major spending department.

James I – indifferent to corruption.

In July the king showed, however, that Hay was still in favour by creating him Viscount Doncaster and his wife, of course, a viscountess. Between Ash Wednesday and Easter, Lucy wore a new dress to church on each of six successive Sundays, riding in a coach attended by four liveried footmen. Hay's biographer Roy Schreiber estimates that at this juncture the viscount owed the enormous sum of £42,000; but no one was more adept than he at keeping even his most persistent creditors at bay.[45] Quite unperturbed, Hay took a lease on part of Essex House in the Strand from Lucy's mother, spending a huge sum on renovating both the decor and its garden.[46] The work was far from complete in late November when Lucy produced a boy. He proved sickly from the start, and within two weeks had a convulsive fit and died.[47] Although only nineteen, Lucy would have no more children and there is no record of any further pregnancies. Whatever its

The Defenestration of Prague: Count Martinitz is on his way out of the far window, with Count Slavata in the foreground soon to follow.

emotional effect, from then on she was unable to conceive, an advantage in a promiscuous age when the nobility did not practise birth control.

Whether or not Hay felt inadequate to comfort Lucy, by January 1619 he was soliciting another ambassadorial task abroad. What he was given proved to be a poisoned chalice: a mission to Germany, a patchwork quilt of states divided by religion. Seven months previously in Bohemia, the modern-day Czech Republic, a Protestant assembly had decided to rid itself of two of the country's hated Catholic viceroys, both literally and politically, by throwing these symbols of Hapsburg power out of the windows in Prague's Hradčany Castle. The fall of about thirty metres should have been fatal, but the moat immediately below was clogged with refuse and excrement, which saved the pair's lives, though not their dignity.[48] This event, subsequently celebrated as the Defenestration of Prague, at first seemed more comic than catastrophic. However, when the revolt grew, the rebels offered the Bohemian crown to Frederick of the Palatinate, one of the seven German states that elected the Holy Roman Emperor. Elizabeth urged her naive young husband to accept it and take on the might of the Hapsburgs, telling him she would 'rather eat sauerkraut with a king than roast meat with an elector'.[49] It would be Hay's unenviable task to dissuade the guileless pair from almost certain disaster.

The long illness, death and funeral of Elizabeth's mother, Queen Anne, delayed Hay's departure until May, as in his usual extravagant fashion he insisted on outfitting his entire delegation in mourning clothes, about fifty in all, including soldiers, servants and his brother-in-law, Robert Sidney. Their chaplain was the formidable poet and preacher John Donne, considered ideal for the mission as a former Roman Catholic turned Lutheran.[50] Hay was kept in England still longer by a succession of storms in the North Sea. Lucy went with her husband to Gravesend and remained at his side until his ship finally set sail, an unusual display of outward devotion that surprised many at court.[51] But Hay would stay away far too long. Unbeknown to him, he already had a formidable rival for Lucy's affections, one of the guests at their wedding: the king's latest obsession, George Villiers, soon to become famous as the first Duke of Buckingham.

3: RISING STAR

Georgie Porgie pudding and pie,
Kissed the girls and made them cry,
When the boys came out to play,
Georgie Porgie ran away.

Full of cruelty, sex and death, seventeenth-century English nursery rhymes often got to the heart of the matter. As the words suggest, their subject, the future Duke of Buckingham George Villiers, was a notorious womaniser, who betrayed many of his conquests and was pursued by jealous husbands. But paradoxically he was also James I's favourite of favourites, who rose to the highest position in the land by being willing in bed to do anything and everything the king wanted him to do.

Brooksby Hall, home of the Villiers family in Leicestershire.

Like the Percys, the Villiers were part of an ancient noble family. They could trace their line back to Rodolphe le Bel, Seigneur de Villiers, who in the eleventh century fought alongside his fellow Normans but almost certainly in Sicily rather than at Hastings.[1] By the time the Villiers arrived in England, the richest pickings had already gone. They settled in Nottinghamshire until in 1235 Alexander de Villiers acquired Brooksby in Leicestershire as part of a dowry from the local heiress. Sir George Villiers, the Sheriff of Leicestershire, improved the Elizabethan manor house at Brooksby and in about 1586 employed a kitchen maid with a fine figure and good looks, Mary Beaumont, a poor relation of his neighbours and cousins. Before long Sir George with 'some importunity' had elevated Mary to be his wife Aubrey's personal maid, which meant that she worked, and slept, rather conveniently close to the master bedroom. Aubrey objected to the arrangement in vain but shortly afterwards died suddenly. Sir George, unable to keep his hands off Mary, decided despite her humble status to marry her.[2] He almost certainly did not know that ironically Mary had a rather better pedigree than his own, as she was descended, on her mother's side, directly from Henry III of England.

The couple produced three children. Their third child, George Villiers, was born at Brooksby Hall on 28 August 1592, one of eight siblings from the two marriages all brought up together. In view of her exceptional efforts to raise this large family, Lady Mary was treated rather shabbily in Sir George's will. After his death on 1 April 1606, the house and land, nearly 800 acres, went to Villiers's oldest half brother and Villiers was compelled to move with his mother to another house, much less grand but substantial nonetheless, surrounded by 360 acres bordering the nearby village of Goadby Marwood. The property apart, Mary was left in desperate financial straits, and in the following June married the former Sheriff of Nottingham, Sir William Reyner.

The Manor House at Stanton-upon-the-Woldes. (inset: the future Countess of Buckingham, Mary Beaumont.)

The marriage, it would soon be alleged by the Attorney General, was 'compassed by the enticement and persuasions of... Mary Villiers' as Sir William was almost eighty years of age, forty-three years Mary's senior, and a recluse. He spent most of his time at Stanton-upon-the-Woldes near Nottingham in the village's manor house, which was surrounded by a moat spanned by a drawbridge. Reyner was reckoned weak in both mind and body and whatever Mary may have promised, was either not permitted or unable to consummate the marriage. On 23 September, with Mary back at Goadby, the elderly knight 'did...repair unto his [Huntingdon] house at Orton Longueville, in some extremity of sickness which was not a little increased by disappointment'.

Mary, accompanied by her fourteen-year-old son, George Villiers, wasted no time in returning to Stanton. The manor was locked and shuttered but 'with false keys, picklocks and other instruments and engines, [they] broke open the doors... and did rifle and ransack closetes, chests, trunckes and cupboards and did convey away £2,000 in money and a good deal of plate'. Quite how Mary came to acquire such implements for breaking and entering is unknown. Young George's reward for his help was Sir William's feather bed, carried back to Goadby in a cart. Mary's husband died on 27 October and his will, which conspicuously failed to mention his new wife, was upheld despite her best efforts, by the Court of the Star Chamber.[3]

Having pawned the gold and silver plate from two husbands for £60 to make ends meet, Mary quickly found another rich widower. It was her third spouse, the bumbling but bountiful farmer Sir Thomas Compton, addicted to tobacco and drink, who in May 1609 arranged for a passport from the Privy Council for George and his elder full brother John 'to repair unto the parts beyond the seas, to gain experience'.[4] This description makes it sound as if the intrepid pair, accompanied by four manservants, intended to travel to somewhere like China or India whereas in fact the only salt water they crossed was the English Channel and the furthest places they reached were the chateaux towns of Angers and Blois in the Loire valley.

At Angers, Villiers was instructed in the finer points of riding in tournaments at the local Académie d'Équitation while at Blois its future bishop, Léonor d'Estampes de Valençay, taught him to read and write French.[5] But Villiers spent as much time as possible in Paris, already a city of more than 400,000 inhabitants that had spread far beyond its decaying protective wall. A perpetual haze of smoke hung over the more densely populated districts and obscured the view of the great landmarks, the steeple of Notre Dame cathedral, the crenellated ramparts of the Louvre palace, and the vast towers of the Bastille prison. After dark Paris became the dangerous realm of gangs of cut-throats, who shared the streets with roaming wolves. In summer the city had an overwhelming stench of the great unwashed, jammed into a honeycomb of tiny alleyways, trudging through a nauseating mixture of human waste and animal entrails known as *la crotte*; those with the means to leave the capital did so. Once autumn came and the court returned, even the gloomiest garret commanded an exorbitant rent. Among those competing with Villiers in 1609 for a Parisian pied-à-terre was Armand-Jean du Plessis, who would become in the course of time the de facto ruler of France and the future Duke of Buckingham's deadliest enemy, Cardinal Richelieu.

Antoine de Pluvinel.

The early lives of the two great protagonists followed a curious parallel. Du Plessis, born in Paris on 9 September 1585, the older by seven years, preceded Villiers as a pupil at Antoine de Pluvinel's military style Parisian equestrian academy in about 1602. His father, a member of the lesser nobility who rose high in government service, died from typhoid fever during a military campaign before du Plessis's fifth birthday; so the fees were paid by the wealthy Armand de la Porte, his mother's half-brother. The academy was making a loss before Villiers arrived but

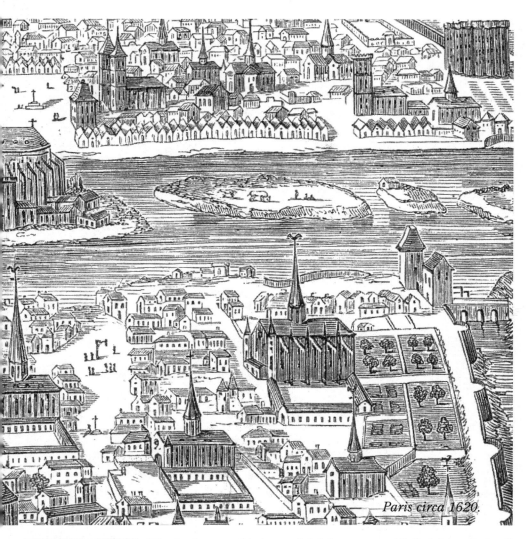

Paris circa 1620.

*François du Plessis,
Richelieu's father.*

Pluvinel turned it into a highly successful finishing school for young noblemen, adding fencing, musical appreciation, dancing, mathematics and manners to the curriculum. How du Plessis spent much of his time while at the academy may perhaps best be judged, however, by his indelicate medical problem, which had become acute in 1605. Given up as a hopeless case by other doctors, he went to see the royal physician, Jean Ribit de la Rivière. Ribit held a regular clinic with his fellow Protestant, Théodore Turquet de Mayerne, who thanks to Ribit was also on the royal payroll. Together they diagnosed *'gonorrhea inveterata'*: long-established,

Antoine de Pluvinel's military style Parisian equestrian academy.

deep-rooted venereal disease, whose unpleasant symptoms included painful erections and swollen testicles. This was particularly embarrassing for du Plessis, because he had just been nominated for the bishopric at Luçon in the gift of his family. On 31 May his name was entered in Mayerne's discreet notebook under the pseudonym of 'Monsieur du Lusson'. Du Plessis unknowingly had joined the ranks of various eminent personages with social diseases whose names appear in the book, including the future French chancellor, Pierre Séguier.[6]

Théodore Turquet de Mayerne, Richelieu's doctor.

Ribit would die unexpectedly within months, leaving Mayerne to treat their patient, based rather dangerously on the regular application of mercury. Mayerne, who subsequently became personal physician to James I, was writing the definitive work on the subject for the period. He used a crude syringe to introduce the substance directly into the penis. This understandably may have made du Plessis an unenthusiastic subject but it provided at least temporary relief for a man who showed no inclination to repent. In May 1607, when he returned to Paris from Rome, having been consecrated bishop, du Plessis is thought to have begun a passionate affair with Marie de Bragelogne, the wife of Claude Bouthillier, a family friend. On 28 March 1608 Marie gave birth to a son, Léon, comte de Chavigny, said to be the fruit of that illicit union. Du Plessis later helped the political career of Claude and Léon and each in turn would become a secretary of state.

Léon Bouthiller.

Claude Bouthiller.

However, Luçon was not a rich bishopric and in 1609 du Plessis was still seriously short of money, unable to afford accommodation in the more agreeable parts of the French capital. He wrote gloomy letters to Jeanne de Saint-Germain, the long-suffering wife of a Parisian lawyer, Jacques de Bourges, in the vain hope perhaps that his friends would take pity and invite him to stay with them. He exaggerated his financial circumstances as *'gueux'*, 'poverty stricken'. 'I am lodged very badly,' he complained. 'There is nowhere to walk, nor garden, nor avenue, nor anything else, so that my house is my prison.'[7]

Parisians became suspicious of strangers after the assassination of Henri IV in May 1610, which left his widow Marie de' Medici to act as regent on behalf of her nine-year-old son, Louis XIII. Nonetheless, Villiers did succeed soon afterwards in being presented at court, through the good offices of an English Catholic resident in Paris, Anthony Champney, a friendship that might well have been frowned upon back in London so soon after the Gunpowder Plot. Du Plessis's biographer Joseph Bergin believes that Champney, his exact contemporary at university, was also one of his 'unlikely companions'.[8] The young bishop of Luçon returned to Paris from July until late November or early December, bent on ingratiating himself with the new regime. Despite the efforts of his elder brother, Henri du Plessis, as head of the family, to rein him in, Armand-Jean succeeded in presenting a sycophantic petition to Marie de' Medici in person, which at least got the ambitious bishop noticed. Whether, through Champney, Villiers and du Plessis met socially when neither was of significance is unknown but they probably became neighbours for a time. In 1611 one of the forty-two houses in the rue de Boutier, which roughly translates as the Carpetbeater's Street, was rented by the sieurs Vilier, unlikely to be anyone but the brothers John and George. Before the end of June du Plessis took a three-year lease in the same street on a house owned by the lawyer Denis Bouthillier, brother of Claude.[9] These properties, on the unfashionable left bank and south east of the Louvre, were close to the royal garden of medicinal plants but a long walk from the palace itself, through a maze of narrow lanes lined by tiny shops whose upper stories almost touched, creating a claustrophobic passage of perpetual twilight.[10] It was a path destined to be taken many years later by the French queen to meet Villiers at an illicit rendezvous.

George Villiers as a young man.

In 1613 Villiers returned to England, aged twenty, tall and slender, having inherited his mother's good looks: he had dark chestnut hair, delicate, almost effeminate features, blue eyes, a sensual mouth with full lips, long tapering fingers and equally long and shapely legs. He could dance with brilliant athleticism and was a cold blooded fencer with razor-sharp reactions. He could control the most turbulent of horses bred for tournaments and cavalry charges with seemingly effortless pressure from thigh and knee. He had a sweet disposition, exquisite manners and subtle conversation, honed to perfection by Pluvinel in Paris. Above all, Villiers possessed compelling sexual magnetism: most men and women found him irresistible.

Like many impecunious young gentlemen, Villiers's first thought was to procure a wife who would bring a substantial dowry. In a scene reminiscent of *Pride and Prejudice*, he visited the four daughters of a neighbour in Leicestershire, the late Sir Roger Aston, Master of the Wardrobe to James I: Margaret, Mary, Elizabeth and the youngest, Anne. Villiers chose and proposed to Anne Aston, who was eager to marry him, but the elderly trustees of their estate wanted a guarantee that he possessed sufficient means. Villiers had almost no money – he was seen at Cambridge races wearing a old black suit 'broken out in divers places' – and needed help from his stepfather. Much to Villiers's initial chagrin, this was not forthcoming.[11]

Compton would never be a sophisticated member of high society – on his one recorded visit to Whitehall he got so drunk he had to be taken home for his own safety – but he had excellent political connections, influential acquaintances who persuaded him to block the local match in return for a promise to bankroll and introduce Villiers at court. Most of the expense of his wardrobe was met by Sir Arthur Ingram, a Yorkshire merchant noted for lending to the nobility on little security.[12] His second sponsor was William Herbert, Earl of Pembroke, the brother of King James's erstwhile favourite, Philip Herbert, who was on such familiar terms with the king that when James came to visit him at his country seat, Wilton House, they played practical jokes on each other. Herbert was frightened of frogs, so James put one down his neck: the earl knew that the king disliked pigs, so he pretended to make one a royal aide, indicating its special status by placing the royal chamber pot over its head. The third sponsor, Sir James Graham, was a longstanding Gentleman of the Privy Chamber, who already knew and liked Villiers. Together they schemed to place him strategically on the route of the king's next summer progress. James, ever restless, liked to switch from one residence to another and to hunt in each location with an enthusiasm that exhausted his courtiers. Many were unwilling to go to the expense of entertaining the king: it cost the Bishop of Winchester more than £2,000 for a visit that lasted just three days.[13]

Accordingly the route had to be carefully planned in advance, to take in ambitious nobles or those too rich to care. On 3 August 1614 Villiers was deliberately placed by his

Apethorpe Hall.

sponsors at Apethorpe Hall, the grand rural seat in Northamptonshire of Sir Anthony Mildmay, when the court party arrived. James was immediately entranced by the elegant young man; Villiers joined the progress and every hour that passed found him more 'in favour with His Majesty'.[14]

James, somewhat disingenuously, at first encouraged Villiers to seek preferment under the auspices of his current favourite, the Earl of Somerset, Robert Carr. Sensing a serious rival for the king's affections, Carr gave Villiers short shrift. 'I will [have] none of your service and you shall have none of my favour', was Carr's response. He added for good measure: 'I will if I can break your neck, and of that be confident.' Villiers's most distinguished biographer, Roger Lockyer, sums it up perfectly: 'It was, in effect, a declaration of war.'[15] In November Carr succeeded in blocking Villiers's appointment as a Gentleman of the Bedchamber. Instead, Villiers had to settle for the position of Cupbearer, who waited on the king at table every alternate month. But with Graham at work on behalf of Villiers behind the scenes and Carr deeply in love with Frances Howard, refusing every entreaty to come to James's bed, his resistance to Villiers only delayed the inevitable.

The catalyst for change unexpectedly proved to be James's wife, Queen Anne, equally susceptible to Villiers's dazzling looks. On 23 April 1615 at Whitehall she borrowed a rapier from the Prince of Wales, knelt before her apprehensive husband, who had a horror of naked weapons, and beseeched him there and then to grant Villiers's appointment to the Bedchamber and use the proffered sword to dub him a knight. James duly obliged. Previously existing on an income of barely £50 a year, Villiers was now the recipient of an annual pension worth £1,000. The only obstacle in his path, Carr, would soon be put on trial for murder and imprisoned in the Tower along with his new countess, thereby reinforcing the old adage that there were two types of poisoners: the infamous and the undetected.

Occasionally the subject of scandalous rumours, Queen Anne was thought by some to have had a sexual relationship with Villiers that prompted her uncharacteristic intervention on his behalf. Much later Villiers himself would tell the French Duchess of Chevreuse in a very matter-of-fact way that he had indeed slept with Anne. He was probably not her first extra-marital experience: in about April 1605, the month the durable royal adviser Robert Cecil was elevated to earl, he investigated allegations that the queen had a lover.[16] When the king and his consort engaged in sexual intercourse, the queen's chaplain

Queen Anne – seduced by George Villiers.

Godfrey Goodman had it on good authority (no doubt in the confessional) that they never spoke, so perhaps Villiers's conversational skills were a factor in his relationship with Anne.[17]

The queen and the future duke had ample opportunity for a brief affair. During Villiers's period as a royal Cupbearer, every other month was his own. Anne and James did not live together after 1607, the queen setting up her own court, first at Greenwich, where the great architect Inigo Jones was employed to design and build the Queen's House, then at Somerset House, renamed Denmark House to remind her of home. In 1615, although turned forty and putting on weight, the flaxen-haired Anne was still attractive, if in a rather masculine way, and admired for her splendid breasts. The Scottish nobles who attended her coronation at Holyrood bore witness to this particular attribute, because at James's insistence, and to the horror of the Kirk, the presiding minister had revived an ancient pagan ceremony by opening her gown and anointing her breasts with a 'bonny quantity of oil'.[18] Once James also became King of England, the queen was often inclined to do as she pleased, and hang the consequences. After attending a rather risqué masque in London, she had too much to drink, became separated from her ladies in waiting, lost her way and arrived back at her palace having hitched a lift on a cart.[19]

Despite these indications that Villiers was at least equally attracted to women, his backers surely would not have invested time, money and machinations in establishing their candidate at court unless they were confident he would give James the sexual gratification he desired. All that summer of 1615 they kept up the momentum. During his progress James stayed in Goadby Marwood at the modest 'joynture house', that is to say, the property Villiers's mother enjoyed but only during her lifetime. Villiers had already accepted a position of intimacy and subservience within the bosom of the monarch: he was 'your majesty's humble slave and dog, Steenie', so called because James thought he looked like the angelic-faced Saint Stephen.

Farnham Castle.

Then, in the last few days of August, as the wandering courtiers reached Farnham Castle in Hampshire, Lockyer concludes that Villiers gave himself to the king. He no longer had to curl up each night outside the four-poster bed, ready to hold out his sovereign's chamber pot. Much later he would recall in a letter to James, 'I shall never forget at Farnham, where the bed's head could not be found between the master and his dog.'[20] The dog, given the right encouragement, had joined his master on and in the bed. It was, on the face of it, an unedifying picture: the beautiful, physically immaculate Villiers celebrating his twenty-third birthday by engaging in sex with a forty-nine-year-old man, hair white, face red, sores on his lips, plump, clumsy, smelling abominably, sneezing constantly and sweating heavily.

In his study of homosexuality in the reign of King James, Michael Young insists 'he did have sex with his male favourites, and it is nonsense to deny it'.[21] What James actually did with his favourites in bed and in private inevitably remains conjecture. Young identifies most of them and concludes that by and large they took part in mutual stimulation with the monarch but no more than that. He believes Villiers, with his known fondness for double entendre, had this meaning in mind when later he wrote to James to thank him for making him a duke: 'There is this difference betwixt that noble hand and heart, one may surfeit by the one, but not by the other, and sooner by yours than his own'.[22] But the earlier favourites, perhaps lacking enthusiasm for their disagreeable task, did not last. Villiers was always under a great deal of pressure to do more. It was not as though other varieties of intimate sexual contact had still to be invented. The distinguished historian Lawrence Stone, in his investigation into the sexual mores of the period, referring to oral, manual and anal sex, says 'One would have supposed that these are techniques that each generation can think up for itself, without any need for transmission of information'.[23]

The circumstantial evidence suggests that each significant elevation or honour given to Villiers was prompted by his acquiescence to James's latest more demanding sexual requirement. On 4 January 1616, Villiers was made Master of the Horse, a prestigious post once held by Elizabeth I's favourites, Leicester and Essex. In April he was given the Order of the Garter. At Oxford on 27 August he was brought into the king's presence, dubbed Baron Whaddon, then taken out again, brought back a few minutes later, and made Viscount Villiers. In September he was given a package of lands suitable for his rank, with parts of Buckinghamshire at its heart, becoming Lord Lieutenant of the county. Then on 6 January 1617, James made him Earl of Buckingham. In twenty months Buckingham (as Villiers now became known) had risen from almost penniless obscurity to a seat at the king's right hand. An even higher rank swiftly followed: that of Marquis.

The imprisonment of Frances Howard, Countess of Somerset, for poisoning Thomas Overbury, damaged the faction that had most to lose from Buckingham's mercurial advance. The Howards accordingly fell back on a strategy that had served them well in the past whenever members of the family were losing their influence: they sought to gratify the monarch's sexual desires. However, this sometimes went badly wrong, as the execution of both Anne Boleyn and Catherine Howard in the reign of Henry VIII had testified. In 1618 their attempt to supplant Buckingham by introducing the handsome William Monson was a dismal failure. From the start William was an inauspicious choice: his father, Sir Thomas Monson, had been complicit in the Overbury murder.[24] The court observer, John Chamberlain, said that the Howards tried too hard in 'prancking him up, besides washing his face every day with posset-curd', a sweet drink of milk mixed with ale that may have kept acne at bay.[25] James smelled a rat. He sent a message to Monson via flunkeys saying that 'the King did not like of his forwardness and presenting himself continually about him' and the young man despondently left court. The Howards paid dearly for their deviousness. In July, Thomas Howard, the Duke of Suffolk, was removed from his position as Lord Treasurer on a charge of corruption; in October Buckingham effectively supplanted Charles Howard, the now senile, but still famous, commander of the English fleet against the Armada, as Lord High Admiral.[26]

James reinforced the Howards' discomfiture by giving Buckingham further obvious signs of his appreciation. Following the death of Queen Anne on 2 March 1619, her jewels were brought to the king at Greenwich in a procession of four carts, overflowing with boxes, cabinets and trunks. The king gave Buckingham some choice pieces of her jewellery and granted him a lease on Denmark House as his London home. James immediately became ill himself and was fortunate to have as his personal physician the services of Mayerne, who had transferred his royal practice from Paris. The doctor was unable, however, to curb James's excessive drinking, recording that he 'errs as to quality, quantity, frequency, time and order'. His discreet diagnosis was that the king had 'bilious diarrhoea' and 'voided three stones'. Buckingham stayed with him day and night for more than a week and after James was on the mend, fell ill himself in June from sheer exhaustion.

Later that summer the king, fully recovered, went with his admiral to Deptford to inspect two new warships, one of which was christened *Buckingham's Entrance*. This provoked so many ribald comments that its name was rapidly changed to *Happy Entrance*. James was sensitive to his public image and made a vigorous attempt to suppress pamphlets attacking his sexuality, including an anonymous work entitled *Coronia Regia* that pretended to praise his kingship but was in fact a scurrilous parody.[27] When stripped of its clever camouflage, it alleged that James was a pederast surrounded by young men who were 'fresh blooming and lovely', including of course Buckingham, an 'adolescent of incomparable form'.

The author was almost certainly Kaspar Schoppe, a striking figure with black bushy eyebrows, moustache and beard, described as 'a man of restless spirit and a malicious pen'.[28] A German Lutheran who had converted to Catholicism, Schoppe undertook diplomatic missions on behalf of Austrian Archduke Ferdinand and suffered a severe beating in Madrid by Englishmen who objected to his puritanical polemics. Schoppe was born in the Palatinate, which placed him at the opposite end of the religious and political spectrum to James's son-in-law Frederick, the Palatine Elector, and his daughter Elizabeth, second in line to the

Kaspar Schoppe wrote under the pseudonym 'Pascasius Gosippus'. In English 'gossip' had already come to mean someone engaged in idle, malicious talk.

British throne. The more through Schoppe Ferdinand could embarrass and weaken James at home, the less likely he was to offer tangible support to the Protestants of the Empire in general and his relatives in particular.

When Lucy Percy's husband, Hay, sailed on his diplomatic mission from Gravesend with a message from James to Frederick urging extreme caution, the Protestant cause in Germany still seemed set fair. The Bohemian rebels had triumphed at home, crossed the frontier and were encamped outside the very gates of Vienna. But no sooner had Hay left Brussels in a procession of twenty-four coaches, than the rebels were severely mauled by an Imperial army strengthened by the arrival of Spanish troops from the Netherlands, and withdrew to a defensive position around Prague. If ever there was a moment to advise the Elector and Electress Palatine to avoid any precipitous move, this was it, but on his arrival in the capital, Heidelberg, Hay found Frederick absent at a meeting of the Protestant rulers. He tried to put off seeing Elizabeth alone but she would have none of it and forced Hay, old 'camel-face', to come to dinner at the palace, forbidding local shopkeepers to sell any extra food to the embassy.[29] The way to Hay's heart was undoubtedly via

Archduke Ferdinand.

his stomach and by the time Frederick returned, Elizabeth had persuaded the ambassador to ignore his instructions and quietly acquiesce in their territorial ambitions.

He had still to get the measure of their enemy. Travelling up hill and down dale, Hay, after several frustrating near misses, finally came face to face with Archduke Ferdinand at Salzburg in July, shortly before his election as emperor, a foregone conclusion. He found a man with a penchant for trivial pastimes such as making frogs leap, as one of Hay's fellow diplomats drolly concluded, 'A strange purchase, me thought, at a time when Kingdoms are in question'.[30]

Ferdinand showed he was deadly serious, though, about one subject: he had a large army that he intended to use to crush the revolt. Bohemia was seen as an inalienable Hapsburg possession. Hay should have gone home to warn King James but instead went with half his delegation to recuperate from their travels at the waters of Spa in the Spanish Netherlands. In September, British embassy officials in Frankfurt found out before Hay did that Frederick had decided to accept the Bohemian crown and move his family to Prague. On 7 October the couple left Heidelberg with the sarcastic and prescient words of the Elector's mother, Louise Juliane, ringing in his ears: 'Oh well, here goes the Palatinate to Bohemia'.[31] But instead of recalling Hay, James sent him to offer Britain's congratulations personally to Ferdinand on his election as emperor. It was not until early November that he accomplished this new task after an arduous journey to Graz.

The new French ambassador to London had no doubt who was behind Hay's wild-goose chase. Tanneguy Leveneur, comte de Tillières, from a distinguished noble family, presented his credentials in September. By November he was sufficiently au fait with the court gossip about Lucy Percy to report back to the foreign department in Paris that diplomacy was being used to keep her husband Hay abroad and the field clear at home for her lover. 'They say it is not the King's business that necessitates the ambassador's return visit to the

Emperor,' he wrote, 'but to consummate a love that the Marquis of Buckingham has for someone very close to him.'[32]

The passionate affair between Buckingham and Lucy to which Tillières alluded almost certainly began at Syon House, where Lucy could count on the discretion of the servants, at least above stairs, and take advantage of the convenient floor plan. Its entrance hall led into a succession of narrow reception rooms on the outer perimeter of the building, where Buckingham's presence, although significant, frequent and remarked upon, was not a scandal. But behind these lay an inner sequence of private chambers that overlooked an excavated, fully enclosed courtyard garden. One set of double doors led directly to a guest bedroom that made an ideal meeting-place and where only the housemaid who afterwards changed the sheets could say with some confidence what had taken place.

Even if Lucy needed any persuading, however, the fashions of the day greatly assisted the seducer. Gentlemen still wore codpieces, fixed with small leather straps, easily undone to answer a call of nature or for sexual foreplay and coupling. Dresses were cut low, with daring décolletage, which made it easy to release what little of the breasts remained concealed. Brassieres and knickers would not become part of female attire until the late eighteenth century. Ladies wore a succession of petticoats and a shift but nothing else: if they fell over, or were caused to fall, their most intimate parts became completely exposed. Edmond Waller, a precocious young poet who became an MP at sixteen and was quickly introduced to its fringe benefits, wrote a verse entitled 'The Fall', full of sexual innuendo about what happens when one couple trip and end up lying close together on the ground:

Edmund Waller.

Then blush not, fair! or on him frown,

Or wonder how you both came down;

But touch him, and he'll tremble straight,

How could he then support your weight?

How could the youth, alas! but bend,

When his whole heaven upon him leaned?

If aught by him amiss were done,

'Twas that he let you rise so soon.[33]

The risk of the lovers being discovered was very small because Hay showed no signs of hurrying home to catch Lucy in flagrante. He was even planning a special pilgrimage to Venice until an outbreak of plague prevented him.[34] He spent Christmas at The Hague in the United Provinces, laying on a lavish New Year reception, with excessively generous presents for everyone, including the band.[35] His return to England at last in January 1620 was to a wife who greeted him coldly, showed in every glance and gesture that she regretted the union and refused him entry into the marital bed. Their rows reverberated around Whitehall and were even included as gossip in the diplomatic bags sent to British embassies abroad. One interested recipient in the Spanish Netherlands was Tobie Matthew, the gay lover of the Lord Chancellor Sir Francis Bacon, a major beneficiary of Buckingham's patronage. He could not resist sending Hay a malicious note. 'It hath been written hither', he said, 'that there is some little disgust between the noble lady (he meant Lucy) and thyself'. Matthew then added a postscript, really twisting the knife, 'saving that no disgust can be little between such a couple of creatures as you two.'[36]

Hay had to grit his teeth and maintain cordial relations with Buckingham, now powerful enough to ruin his diplomatic career. 'This poor servant of yours doth respect you with the best wishes of his soul', he wrote on one occasion to Buckingham, adhering to the conventions of the age. Buckingham replied, 'There is none living more your faithful and humble servant'. His response might well have been composed at Syon House on the guest bedroom's dainty writing desk, with Lucy lying naked on the bed a few feet away. Buckingham, however, was no more faithful to his new mistress. His cronies aided and abetted his seduction of several high-born women who thought themselves safe in their own houses.[37]

Whenever that gullible supply temporarily dwindled, they hired the boatmen at Whitehall to take them across the Thames to Cat's Dock Landing, a short stroll from a fashionable bordello known as 'The Manor'. A Flemish madam known as Donna Britannica Hollandia, unlikely to have been her real name, had bought out the English owner, six-foot 'Long Meg' of Westminster. Donna refurbished the house, brought over some allegedly 'clean' Dutch girls from the United Provinces, introduced a strict code of behaviour and put up the prices to keep out the riff-raff from the nearby Falcon Tavern. The rectangular property was protected by the Thames on one side and a moat on the remainder, filled by the tide as it ebbed and flowed from a nearby sluice gate. Its distinguished

Buckingham's brothel on "Nobs' Island".

clientele from court such as Buckingham had to cross the moat by means of a drawbridge, to reach what the irreverent population of Southwark inevitably dubbed "Nobs' Island".[38]

Such goings-on no doubt reached the ears of Buckingham's mother, Mary Beaumont, whom in 1618 the king had made a countess in her own right. She decided it was high time her son settled down and the king agreed. Marriage made his favourites more respectable but no less accessible. Her choice was Katherine Manners, the tall, aquiline, decidedly plain daughter of the wealthy Earl of Rutland. Once Buckingham had acquiesced, two obstacles still remained to the marriage: the size of the dowry and, in view of his important offices of state,

Katherine Manners.

Katherine's religion: she was a Catholic. Rutland had already refused Buckingham's demand for £20,000 and land worth a further £4,000. But early in March 1620 the countess deliberately compromised Katherine by inviting her to supper and subsequently to stay the night, without telling her that Buckingham would staying under the same roof. The earl decided this was sufficient evidence that he had slept with his daughter and compromised the family honour. He refused to take Katherine back, hoping to blackmail Buckingham into marriage; but had to beat a strategic retreat when Buckingham played him at his own game, claimed that Katherine's loss of reputation made her less attractive as a wife, and refused to marry her until he was promised his dowry.[39] Whether or not Katherine had lost her virginity on the night in question, her 'lechery', as Buckingham ignobly described her intense feelings for him, quickly won over her religious scruples. When Buckingham told Katherine it was politically untenable for him to marry a Catholic, given the widespread anti-Catholic feeling around the country, she renounced her faith. On 16 May they married in a private Anglican ceremony near London's Tower Hill.

The Earl of Rutland's humiliation was given an unexpected extra twist, courtesy of the painter, Anthony Van Dyck, who arrived in England the following October. His sabbatical, aged twenty-one, from the talented Antwerp studio of Peter Paul Rubens, was his first serious attempt to strike out on his own and Van Dyck needed commissions to cover the overheads of his five-month stay. He set out to cultivate connoisseurs and collectors of art, Buckingham amongst them. The marquis paid Van Dyck handsomely to produce a work called *The Continence of Scipio*, which depicts the Roman general's return, unviolated, of

Anthony Van Dyck.

'The Continence of Scipio.'

a young female captive when he found she had been about to be married to Allucius, an enemy chieftain, together with her ransom as a wedding present. This classical story of honour, chaste betrothal and marriage was the ironic opposite of what Rutland claimed had taken place between Buckingham and his daughter. Buckingham made sure that people got the point by asking Van Dyck to paint himself as Allucius and Katherine as his wife. Katherine's view of the picture is unrecorded but she cannot have been happy with Van Dyck's unflattering profile in which she is shown wearing a dress that fails to cover much of her less than voluptuous bosom.[40] Given Katherine's physical shortcomings, courtiers took it for granted that Buckingham had no intention of giving up his mistress; relations with his new wife, who had a fierce temper and hated Lucy Percy with an unbridled intensity, were soon, as he cheerfully put it, 'somewhat stormy'.[41]

Lucy's husband, Hay, would dearly have liked another diplomatic mission to escape from his equally stormy domestic relationship. James, however, was not impressed by his failure to dissuade Frederick and Elizabeth of the folly

Frederick, the Winter King.

of their territorial ambitions in Bohemia. Instead, in October the king sent Sir Henry Wotton to Vienna on a special mission to plead with Emperor Ferdinand II. In many ways, Wotton was a surprising choice. Almost a decade earlier James's bête noire, Schoppe, once Wotton's fellow student at Altdorf, had done his friend no favours by quoting one of his witticisms in a scurrilous attack on the king. It was the famous definition of an ambassador as an 'honest man sent to lie abroad for the good of his country'.[42] James took this as a personal slight on his integrity and for many years Wotton was left in the political wilderness. In Vienna Wotton made friends but no tangible progress. On his departure the emperor presented him with a valuable jewel, which the ambassador received with due humility; but before leaving the city he gave it to the emperor's wife, Maria Anna of Bavaria, because, said Wotton, he could not accept a gift from the enemy of the Bohemian queen.

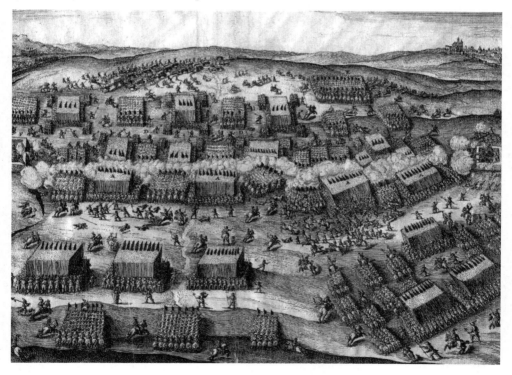

Wotton had already heard well-founded rumours of the disaster that had befallen Frederick and Elizabeth. They enjoyed just one Christmas in their palace at Prague. Frederick, a far from bellicose prince – the Spanish ambassador in London tartly observed that he knew 'more about gardening than fighting' – found himself on the battlefield, frightened out of his wits, a victim of his wife's burning ambition.[43] On 8 November their rag-bag army of rebels and paid mercenaries, despite reinforcements from England in the form of gentlemen volunteers, was decisively beaten in the Battle of the White Mountain (pictured, page 85) outside Prague; it lasted barely an hour and Bohemia was lost for good. The unforgiving Ferdinand made sure that they were unable to return to their legitimate lands in the Palatinate, as most of these were soon occupied by Spanish troops from the Netherlands, fighting on the side of the Emperor. In September 1622 even Heidelberg was captured and sacked, its English garrison overwhelmed and their English commander killed. Frederick, forever scorned thereafter as the 'Winter King', and his wife had to take refuge at The Hague.[44] Their humiliation, and James's efforts to restore the *status quo ante bellum* by anything short of military action, helped to bring about one of the most bizarre events in royal history: the journey to secure the Spanish Match.

4: AMBASSADORS

In 1588 the destruction of the Spanish Armada, more by Scottish tempest than English naval superiority, seemed to have ended the threat of invasion but it did not end the war. Once Spain had rebuilt its fleet by means of a vast levy on its people, neither side had any real prospect of landing a knockout blow. In June 1596 an Anglo-Dutch fleet of 120 ships chose as its target Cadiz, where the ill-fated and ailing Duke of Medina-Sidonia, the Armada's commander, was in charge of the garrison. Spain's largest port was devastated, stripped of its wealth and leading citizens; but four months later this did not prevent the dispatch against England of a fresh armada, which fell victim to a savage autumn gale.[1] The death of both Philip II and Elizabeth I eventually paved the way for an uneasy peace, sealed by the Treaty of London in August 1604.

James proved more than an intellectual match for the Hapsburg peace commissioners, who lacked the cunning, panache and physical presence of the Imperial ambassador Eustache Chapuys in the time of the Tudors. The Hapsburgs, ruling over Spain, the Spanish Netherlands, Austria and most of Germany, could not agree on a single spokesman. Upon learning that the Count of Aremberg, representing Austrian Archduke Ferdinand II, had gout and virtually no English – 'The Archduke hath sent me an ambassador who can neither walk nor talk', remarked the king scornfully – James deliberately arranged meetings on the top floor of his palace in Whitehall. This similarly disadvantaged the lead negotiator, Juan Fernando de Velasquez, Constable of Castile, who suffered from acute lumbago, and the Hapsburgs had to be content with imprecise assurances from James that some restrictions on Catholics practising their faith would be lifted.[2] Equally vague, with much more style than substance, was the reference in the treaty to a future marriage between James's elder son, Prince Henry, and Philip III's eldest daughter, the Infanta Anna Maria Mauricia.

However, a more agile, ambitious ambassador, a minor noble called don Diego Sarmiento de Acuña, lord of Gondomar, would soon be making his presence felt in London. In 1589, as an energetic twenty-two-year-old commander of the local militia, he had ensured a warm welcome for the expeditionary force

*Peace talks in 1604 with Hapsburg representatives Aremberg
(third on left) and Velasquez (sixth on left).*

The English delegates include Penelope Devereux's lover Charles Blount (centre right) and Robert Cecil (front right).

commanded by Sir Francis Drake that unsuccessfully attacked the coast of Galicia.[3] From the moment of his arrival at Portsmouth harbour in August 1613, Gondomar signalled the start of a fresh, more swaggering era in Spanish diplomacy. On his orders, the Spanish warships that brought him to England refused to dip their colours in salute to those of King James, whereupon the much larger English escort threatened to blow them out of the water. Gondomar sent a note to the monarch, who fortuitously was hunting nearby, explaining that his family motto was *aventurar la vida y osara morir*, 'risk your life and dare to die'. He added that he could not strike his sovereign's colours with honour and must perforce go down fighting with his ships. The new ambassador calculated correctly that James had no intention of re-starting the war over a symbolic gesture. The Spaniards were allowed to fly their flags defiantly at the top of the masthead until a favourable wind enabled their ships to depart.[4]

One of Gondomar's first tasks was to assess the political implications of the unexpected death of James's heir, Prince Henry, from typhoid fever in November 1612. Spain had already rejected the overtures of the British ambassador - since 1603 representing both England and Scotland - on Prince Henry's behalf for the hand of Anna Maria, offering instead the consolation prize of her younger sister, the Infanta Maria Anna Margarita. Seeing this as a mild insult, James I had turned instead towards France and Gondomar's first impression was that the marriage of a French princess to Henry's younger brother Charles could not be prevented.[5] But he still asserted at court in his astute, insinuating way that James could secure better terms in Madrid than he would in Paris. This prompted the king to keep his options open and had unfortunate consequences for the last of the Elizabethan privateers, Sir Walter Raleigh, as it was relentless pressure from Gondomar that brought his execution for daring to attack a Spanish settlement in South America.[6]

The ambassador's ruthless streak must have come as a surprise to many who took his avuncular appearance at face value. Prematurely bald, with a carefully cultivated beard, high forehead, bulbous nose and bags under the eyes, Gondomar was a man who enjoyed life, but paid the penalty for a rich diet with recurring piles and an untreatable fistula.[7] Equally beyond apparent remedy was the *Alice in Wonderland* scenario he inherited in which almost everyone in England in a position of authority had long been a Spanish pensioner. Spain had felt it necessary to bribe some of the prospective British peace commissioners to hasten a settlement. In an age of endemic

The arrival of Ambassador Gondomar heralded a
more swaggering era in Spanish diplomacy.

corruption, the practice rapidly spread, as successive Spanish ambassadors tried to make themselves more popular. The British establishment did nothing in return, probably because few received any money directly. Most were paid by means of a warrant from the near-bankrupt treasury in Madrid, which they invariably sold on at a heavily discounted rate, four or five to one, to leading London moneylenders such as Burlamaqui. A Spanish pension was considered an 'indefeasible prerequisite' of their post or status in society, to be accepted without stain of corruption. Perhaps this was just as well, because the recipients included the Admiral of the Channel Fleet, Sir William Monson, and the leading government minister of the day, William Cecil, followed by Carr and, in due course, Buckingham.[8] In 1615 Sir John Digby, the British ambassador in Madrid, obtained through bribery the key to the code names of Spain's list of pensioners at Whitehall. He was hugely embarrassed to discover that one of them, disguised as 'Leandro', was no less a personage than the 'King of England' himself.[9]

Only Katherine Howard, Countess of Suffolk, received her annual payment of £1,000 more or less on time, intimidating the ambassador with her haughty manners and sharp tongue if he had the temerity to plead a lack of funds.[10] The countess, though, proved invaluable in helping Gondomar to understand the resentment at Whitehall caused by what the English nobility saw as the preferential treatment given to those born north of the border. It enabled Gondomar to strike a chord with the king by representing them both as foreigners in a country where England remained the common enemy. The

British ambassador John Digby.

relationship was portrayed on the stage by the playwright Thomas Middleton as *'A Game at Chess'*, by which the Machiavellian Gondomar advanced the cause of Popery.[11] In truth, chess was an apt analogy only because it required a good deal of patience. As historian Garrett Mattingly says of the ambassador's influence, 'It was the work of years. In part it was because Gondomar was able to make James like him'.[12] The king found the Spaniard amusing, intelligent and erudite. They became intimate – although never sexually intimate – friends, 'they joked and laughed and hunted together, called themselves "the two Diegos", and drank from the same bottle'.[13]

In June 1617 Gondomar, elevated to Count by the Spanish government in recognition of his success in courting James, also showed his skill at verbal cut and thrust. His discomfited victim was Hay, whom he met, literally, on a lower staircase at Whitehall that both men were descending in pursuit of some more wine. Neither would give way until Gondomar forced the issue, saying, 'My Lord I will goe downe [to] the cellar but I will have it [precedence].' Hay responded angrily, 'Then my Lord, goe down to Hell!' Gondomar replied pithily, 'Nay, there my Lord, I leave you'.[14]

Gondomar clearly had the measure of Hay; he also had his finger on the pulse of the most intriguing relationship at court, Buckingham and Prince Charles. For a long time Charles lived in the shadow of his older, emphatically heterosexual brother. Born at Dunfermline in November 1600, Charles behaved much younger than his age, was rather short, below 5ft in height, lacking in self-esteem, shy and taciturn. A contemporary clergyman struggling to find something positive to offer in his favour said he had 'such very sweetness of manners'.[15] When Buckingham rose so fast in the king's regard that he came to be looked upon as part of the royal family, his quarrels with Charles closely resembled those between real siblings. A ring given to Buckingham by the king was the source of one squabble. Charles borrowed the ring on

the pretence of admiring it and the following day, after Buckingham had asked for the ring back, petulantly said he could not find it. When Buckingham complained, James sent for his son and used 'such bitter language' that it reduced the prince to tears. He also took Buckingham's part after Charles had deliberately misdirected the jet of a fountain flowing in Greenwich Park so that it drenched the marquis, boxing his son's ears for his impudence.[16] Buckingham, though, could be equally provocative when it suited him. At a masque to mark Twelfth

Charles, a petulant young Prince of Wales.

Night organised by Charles in 1618, James became bored by the performance of the players, including the prince himself. 'Devil take you all!' he exclaimed, then, to no-one in particular, 'Why don't they dance?' Buckingham entered the fray uninvited and to the king's delight, gave an athletic display of cutting capers, upstaging the furious Charles completely.[17]

William Laud – sexual fantasies.

The slow rapprochement between them was accelerated by the king's serious illness in April 1619, which brought home to Buckingham the risks of offending the first in line for the throne. His marriage the following year helped, too, because his wife Katherine always treated the prince with charm and respect. However, perhaps the most influential factor on Charles's attitude to Buckingham and on his own sexuality was his personal chaplain, William Laud. Historian Diarmaid MacCulloch describes him as 'a lonely little man... [with] homosexual leanings'. The cleric, later Archbishop of Canterbury, was among those who found Buckingham irresistible and had sexual fantasies about him, some of which he rashly recorded in his secret diary. Indeed, these fantasies went a good deal further, because on at least one occasion Laud dreamed vividly that he had been in bed not only with Buckingham but also with the marquis's wife, in an erotic ménage-à-trois.[18]

Perhaps the first tangible sign that Buckingham and Prince Charles had ceased their quasi-sibling rivalry and begun a more positive, intimate relationship came early in March 1620 when together they arranged a grand ball and invited 'a number of ladies, mistresses and Valentines'.[19] 'Valentines' were the recipients of bouquets containing coded messages from their lovers, which suggests this was not an event that particularly catered for the prudish. It also marked the return of Gondomar to London from Spain after an absence of twenty-one months.[20] The familiar style of the correspondence between prince and favourite on the one hand, and the ambassador on the other, is highlighted by the prince's use of a sexually charged, somewhat vulgar, Spanish word to describe Gondomar: *alcahuete*, meaning 'pimp'. It starts to occur in correspondence between them significantly before the idea of the Spanish Match had gathered momentum.[21] In what seems to be a private joke, Charles even addresses such messages 'To the Count of Gondomar, my principall Alcahuete'.[22] Did this recognise that Gondomar's efforts had been initially directed not towards a marriage between the prince and the Spanish Infanta but to bringing together, in the sexual sense, Buckingham and Charles? A letter from the marquis to the ambassador dated Wednesday 30 January 1621, or rather its postscript from the prince, implies that this could be the case. Combining a bizarre mixture of English, French and Spanish, Charles signs off with the words 'I thank you a la mode dengletere for useing my wife well'.[23] This seems to mark appreciation of Gondomar's support for Buckingham, and a reference to an already cemented sexual relationship between the marquis and the prince, rather than to his barely intended wife-to-be residing in Madrid, whom he has never seen. Historian Glyn Redworth, describing the postscript as 'one further insight into the intimate nature of the young prince's relations with the ambassador and the marquis', adds a cryptic footnote: 'Whether Charles was still of Twelfth Night cheer is not known'.[24]

Prince's lodgings, Newmarket, by Inigo Jones.

As the letter was written from Newmarket, where hunting, gambling and other more dubious entertainment often took precedence over serious government business, and not just during the Christmas festivities, it is equally plausible to suppose that he was in bed with Buckingham at the time. The prince led a highly sheltered life with few, if any, opportunities to meet eligible women, his conscience was guarded by a cleric who wanted nothing better than a sexual encounter of his own with Buckingham, and in all probability Charles had remained a virgin ripe

James I castigated the House of Commons for challenging his prerogative.

for seduction by the most attractive man in England, a man looking to secure his long-term political future.

How James viewed this relationship is uncertain. He undoubtedly welcomed the cessation of hostilities between Charles and Buckingham but surely cannot have been blind to what lay behind it. He never demanded sexual exclusivity from his favourites and actively encouraged them to marry. In the strange, intimate world unravelled by Gondomar for the benefit of his masters in Madrid, James may have actually preferred his son to enter a relationship of his own with Buckingham, rather than with an outsider who might threaten the equilibrium of the country's innermost triangle.

Like Gondomar, the new French ambassador, Tanneguy Leveneur, comte de Tillières, sent regular reports to his superiors. Tillières belonged to an ancient Norman family, one of whose ancestors had fought with William the Conqueror at Hastings. In 1609 he married Catherine, the wealthy sister of the influential maréchal François de Bassompiere. Catherine's dark brown sultry eyes, high cheek bones and generous figure attracted attention at court when Tillières presented his credentials in September 1619. She was accompanied by her niece, Renée d'Espinay Saint Luc, whom the court's self-appointed commentator, Chamberlain, an incorrigible old bachelor, described as 'a dainty young demoiselle'. Buckingham made a pass at her, but it is not known with what success.[25]

Tillières accordingly had good reason to pay close attention from the start to Buckingham's activities, and did not like what he saw. Some of his dispatches were decrypted by the distinguished German historian, Frederick von Raumer. The ambassador soon reported that Buckingham had 'advised the King to remain at Newmarket, where he leads a life to which past nor present times provide no parallel'. Pressed by the French foreign office, ever eager for more licentious detail, Tillières protested that he had 'too much modesty' to comply; but added that the king had indeed 'made a journey to Newmarket, as a certain other sovereign did to Capri'.[26] The ambassador's classical allusion can only have been to the Roman emperor Tiberius, whom historian Gaius Suetonius alleges to have engaged in all kinds of sexual perversions on the island with young boys and girls. Tillières described the king as 'plunging himself into vice of every kind' at his country estate near Newmarket and to his 'filthy and scandalous life'. He laid the blame for 'a thousand other particulars which one cannot venture to speak out' on James's friendship with Buckingham.[27]

Frederick von Raumer, who decripted Tillières's dispatches.

Leveneur de Tillières, French ambassador at Whitehall.

Whatever went on behind closed doors at Newmarket, so long as Buckingham did not make Carr's mistake of withdrawing his favours from the king, his position was secure. But as a man who apparently enjoyed sex with both men and women, he was in danger of spreading himself much too thinly among his different relationships. The price his wife Katherine exacted for accepting his longstanding affair with Lucy Percy, absolving him, as she adroitly put it, his 'sin [of] loving women so well', was to keep him at home on their new estate in Rutland more than proved prudent. Buckingham's letters to the king citing various reasons for his absence, including 'yellow janders' [jaundice], suggest he knew that the excuses were wearing thin.[28]

James relied on his ministers to manage the English Parliament, never really understanding how different it was to the Parliament of Scotland, a primitive, ineffectual, almost feudal body. Unlike the French kings through the *taille*, the British crown had no permanent tax on land, the principal source of wealth; it had to rely on Parliament to vote for 'subsidies', the main form of taxation. The king chose his ministers and they sat in the House of Lords, but the real power was already tilting towards the Commons, full of wealthy country gentlemen, who had steadily increased their land and possessions at the expense of both crown and nobility. By the end of James's reign it was popularly said that the Commons could buy out the Lords thrice over.[29] Accustomed to local authority and respect, the MPs sitting in the Commons were in no mood to be scolded and out-manoeuvred by their king.

In March 1621, when disagreements came to a head, James seized the moment to show the Marquis of Buckingham that his spectacular rise could be followed by an equally spectacular fall. Parliament, recalled after an interval of seven years because the king needed money to finance a possible war to recover the Palatinate for Frederick and Elizabeth, flexed its muscles by seeking the redress of various grievances. In particular it launched a campaign against patents and monopolies, of which Buckingham and his family had a goodly share. James privately blamed Buckingham for what he saw as this dangerous turn of events. He made an unannounced visit to the Lords, where the peers had no chance to put on their robes. Having castigated Parliament for its attack on the royal prerogative, the king invited the Lords to have no thought for Buckingham's various titles and to judge him 'as he was when he came to me, as poor George Villiers'.[30] The embryonic reports of proceedings, long before the days of Hansard, suggest that although Buckingham survived serious censure, he was taken aback by the king's remarks: 'a reminder', as Lockyer observes, 'that the King who had made Buckingham could as easily unmake him'.[31]

The response of the marquis was to move his principal residence in London as close as possible to Parliament, king and court. Wallingford House, next to the royal palace in Whitehall and overlooking St James's Park, proved the

*William Knollys, Viscount
Wallingford.*

perfect choice, with plenty of room for a large family; his wife, Kate, was already expecting their first child. Buckingham obtained the property for £3,000, perhaps a third of what it was worth on the open market. The owner, Lucy Percy's ageing great uncle William Knollys, Viscount Wallingford, agreed to the price because of a private bargain struck with Buckingham. Realising that they no longer represented a serious political threat, Buckingham arranged for Wallingford's sister-in-law, the Countess of Somerset and her husband, Carr, to be released from the Tower and allowed to live at the manor of Rotherfield Greys, Wallingford's country estate in Oxfordshire. After Buckingham had refurbished Wallingford House at a cost of almost £10,000, on 28 March 1622 Kate gave birth to a small, frail daughter following a long and difficult labour. The duchess was struck down with smallpox shortly afterwards and there were fears for both mother and child. James visited them every day and could not have been more solicitous if they had been his own kith and kin. Which, to his way of thinking, they were, and growing in number as Buckingham's closest relations steadily gained preferment. One contemporary observer soon commented upon the irony of how 'the King, who never much cared for women, had his Court swarming with the Marquis's kindred, so that little ones would dance up and down the privy lodgings like fairies'.[32]

This delightful image had its dark side. In blessing his union with Katherine, James expressed the hope that Buckingham would have offspring soon 'so I may have sweet bedchamber boys to play with me'. When his wish came to be fulfilled, in one of his letters James praised the whole Villiers family for 'breeding... pretty little ones'. Tillières said that in particular James was entranced by Buckingham's daughter, christened Mary but known as Mall, whom he 'passionately loves, tenderly embraces'.[33] This attention might have seemed innocent but for a separate dispatch from Tillières referring to Buckingham's niece, Elizabeth Villiers, the daughter of his half brother, Sir Edward Villiers. According to the ambassador, on at least one occasion Elizabeth, 'aged nine or ten years', was seen naked at Whitehall in the presence

Buckingham and family.

of the king and his favourite. James 'felt her all she would bear, then touched Buckingham's nose, and in the same place kissed him several times'.[34] The only credible explanation for Tillières's description, as Young concludes, is that 'James touched this little girl in a very personal area of her body, then transmitted the smell from his hands to Buckingham's nose, then kissed the favourite's nose.'[35] If true, at the very least Buckingham had acquiesced in a serious sexual offence involving a minor, committed by the king.

Such was the extent to which mothers among the nobility delegated the upbringing of their children to household servants, it is entirely plausible more than one of these gave Tillières reliable information that they dared not impart to their mistress, especially if their master or the king was involved. 'Had I not received this account from trustworthy persons', wrote the ambassador, 'I should have considered it impossible'.[36] However, even if the Villiers sisters-in-law, Barbara and Kate, remained unaware that their children probably were being molested in the palace, this does not explain how Kate ostensibly could remain oblivious to the persistent and growing rumours that her husband's relationship with the king had advanced to one of full-blown

Elizabeth Villiers, sexually abused as a child.

sodomy.[37] Perhaps, even in their most intimate moments, she shrank from raising it. Perhaps she believed in the strictures of the Lord Chief Justice, Sir Edward Coke, that a sin (if not a crime) could be committed by the very mention of sodomy, that 'detestable, and abominable sin, amongst Christians not to be named'.[38] Even the law lacked an authoritative definition. It would not be until 1631, in the reign of Charles I, that the House of Lords, Hay amongst those peers sitting in judgement at the trial for rape and sodomy of the debauched Earl of Castlehaven, would decide in finding him guilty that ejaculation between the thighs of another man constituted sodomy and anal penetration was not necessary.[39]

Gondomar, much bolder and coarser than Tillières, had no compunction in making a joke about James's sexual proclivities in the presence of the king. The ambassador resided on the west side of Petticoat Lane, as London's seamstress sector had begun to be called, where he could afford a grand house in the unfashionable parish of Whitechapel. He lived next door to Lady Elizabeth Hatton, Coke's estranged wife and the daughter of Robert Cecil, but for a while was unable to persuade her to give him a key to her back gate, so that he could pass through her garden to the open fields beyond. Gondomar, 'observing how King James was addicted, told him that the Lady Hatton would not suffer the Lord Cook [sic] her husband to come into her fore-door, nor he himself to come into her back-door'.[40] The king was highly amused and the ambassador subsequently penetrated all Lady Hatton's defences, in an affair that begun at a ball held at the adjacent Hatton House, when the couple had one dance before disappearing upstairs.[41]

James I, forever playing both ends against the middle, encouraged the Hays to cultivate the entourage of ambassador Tillières.[42] James Hay, now married to Lucy only in name, took the task seriously and entered into a long-term affair with the ambassador's wife, Catherine. They were of a similar age, shared a taste for rich and plentiful meals, and were soon 'very intimate'.[43] In September 1620 Tillières came to one of London's social events of the year, held by the Hays in honour of the Buckingham family. Chamberlain reported that they gave 'a great feast at Syon to the Lord Marquis, his Lady and the Countess his mother'. In entertaining his wife's lover and family, Hay was nothing if not pragmatic. Not long afterwards, of Buckingham he declared publicly, 'I am so much this noble lord's servant that I will perform whatsoever he commands me'.[44] All the patronage, each foreign diplomatic mission he so esteemed, rested upon Buckingham's goodwill. Only the previous May, the marquis had acquired for him the lifetime benefit of Keeper of the Gardens and Palace of Nonsuch, Henry VIII's Renaissance chateau rising out of the rolling countryside that formed a backdrop to the road from London into deepest Surrey. For Lucy, it was the perfect escape. If the coveted fairy-tale marriage to Buckingham lay beyond her reach, at least she could spend most summers in a fairy-tale castle.

Her winters, in residence at Syon or Essex House, were noted for lavish masques and sumptuous banquets that were Hay's answer to the wiles of

Lucy Percy's perfect escape: Nonsuch Palace in Surrey.

Gondomar. Even by his exalted standards, the dinner Hay gave in the first few days of January 1621 for a special French envoy, Honoré, maréchal de Cadenet, attended by the king and the Prince of Wales, was a truly spectacular affair. Chamberlain, as usual hot on the trail of court excesses, recorded in his newsletter that 100 cooks, including forty master chefs, were hired to prepare 1,600 dishes. So much food was ordered, that other great houses complained of a shortage and rising prices. Dozens of partridges and other birds, 240 pheasants, two huge suckling pigs, and salmon from Muscovy, together with barrels of the finest French wine, were all landed from the Thames at Essex Stairs. On the night itself the guests were ushered first into the lower gallery to marvel at the vast display of dishes. Some may have wondered whether they had misread their invitations and arrived too late, as before long a line of liveried footmen seized the myriad of trays and vanished from sight. But within a few minutes they were back with an identical second feast, steaming hot, and ready to be eaten. In an age long before kitchen inspections, this spectacular switch of one complete banquet for another have been just as well for the health of the guests. One servant sneaked several luke-warm dishes from the ante-supper home to his family, and they went down with food poisoning for the best part of a week. Maréchal Cadenet, about to return to Paris to be married, received a pair of splendid white horses, a gift from Hay, while Lucy presented him with two richly embroidered waistcoats and a set of silk petticoats for his bride-to-be, the heiress Claire Charlotte Eugénie d'Aillye. In all the occasion, which Chamberlain attacked for its 'sumptuous superfluity', set Hay back the best part of a staggering £3,000.[45]

Soon afterwards, Lucy fell ill. Like many inhabitants of large towns and cities, she sometimes suffered from stomach complaints characterised by diarrhoea and vomiting. The widespread ignorance of the need for personal and public hygiene resulted in frequent outbreaks of bacterial infections, mainly caused by contaminated food and water. The water closet was not yet in regular use and the upper classes were as bad as the rest in depositing excrement in dark corners.[46] Every basement had an unsavoury reservoir of putrid matter and latrine pits were dug close to wells, infecting the water supply. The offal of carcasses was regularly thrown into the streets, which stank unforgettably in summer. A rich, unbalanced diet accentuated stomach problems. Lucy was treated by the royal physician Mayerne, probably with pills of mercury or tin, and the symptoms subsided enough for her to take the waters at Spa in the Spanish Netherlands.

Having probably suggested the trip, Hay did not accompany Lucy: the king wanted him to return to France and had already advanced £10,000 for his expenses. Whether through guilt or generosity, or a touch of both, Hay gave Lucy half, £5,000, to spend on her convalescence.[47] It enabled her to travel in style, leaving England on 1 June with a retinue of servants, family chaplain William Woodford and her niece, Dorothy's daughter Isabella Smythe. As her husband John Smythe had just deserted Isabella and scandalously eloped to Brussels with his homosexual young cousin Tom, she understandably proved poor company: 'as dank as the weather', Lucy insensitively complained to Woodford.[48]

Hay almost died from purple fever contracted during his shuttle diplomacy.

The timing of her departure for the Continent for several months may have been accelerated by the news that Northumberland had finally permitted Hay to arrange his release from the Tower, as Lucy had no wish to see him: relations with the earl were as strained as ever. James consented to his petition and in late July Hay went to collect his father-in-law in a magnificent coach and six.[49] Soon ensconced at Essex House, Northumberland received leading lords and their ladies as though the intervening years had been but a bad dream; he reorganised the staff despite no longer paying their wages; then reclaimed Syon House for his own use.

Hay was too busy to worry about the antics of the wizard earl. Within days he left for France on a mission to plead the cause of the Huguenots, engaged in a fierce civil war with the forces of the French king. It took him more than three weeks to reach the royal camp at Moissac near Montauban, where he contracted purple fever, marked by the eruption of purple spots on the skin and transmitted by fleas. The disease cost the lives of two members of his staff and came close to killing him.[50] Nonetheless Hay recovered within a month and returned indefatigably to his shuttle diplomacy, much to the consternation of his new secretary, John Woodford, Chaplain Woodford's brother. Replying to a letter of warning from his weary predecessor, Francis Nethersole, he said, 'I find your words true, that I should spend the better parte of the yeare in a coache upon the highway'.[51]

When Hay recrossed the Channel, in February 1622, it was because of fears for Lucy's life. She had returned from the Low Countries still unwell, and the strong purgatives prescribed by Mayerne made her worse. The Venetian ambassador reported that Lucy's death appeared imminent and Chamberlain thought her 'at the last cast'.[52] Buckingham, whom Lucy most wanted to see, callously stayed away. But by the time Hay went back to France in mid-May, Lucy was on the mend. In September she learned that Hay was to be created Earl of Carlisle in recognition of his travails on behalf of his king, making Lucy a countess, a significant step up on the society ladder. Her return to court in better health was greeted with enthusiasm by some, who found her repartee amusing, but with trepidation by others, especially the plain ladies of the Buckingham family, hapless targets for her daggers of sharp wit.

5: THE HOUSE OF THE SEVEN CHIMNEYS

The Match that never was.

The internal dissentions in France confounded even James Hay, a self-confessed Francophile, seeking to cement a tangible alliance. Despite Tillières's efforts from London to prevent it, the French sent the Earl of Carlisle home empty-handed.[1] He felt betrayed and told Tillières that he was 'looking more favourably on the Spanish [Match] than he had ever done previously'.[2] In this, however, Hay seemed to be going out on a precarious limb. Throughout 1621 Parliament had showed strong anti-Spanish sentiment and was acrimoniously dissolved. Gondomar, fearing that the Commons might grant James the money he sought only if he first declared war on the Hapsburgs, in vain wrote to the Emperor Ferdinand urging a ceasefire in the besieged Palatinate.[3] But James had had his fill of disagreeable parliaments. He wanted enough Spanish gold as a dowry to free him from their purse strings. Digby was sent back to Spain 'to perfect the Match' once and for all.[4] In May 1622 Gondomar's long-anticipated recall to Madrid, at one time looking like a symbolic gesture heralding the rupture of relations between countries on the brink of war, instead was made for the specific purpose of assisting negotiations towards the marriage between Prince Charles and the Infanta.[5]

Diplomacy, especially Spanish diplomacy, proceeded at a snail's pace. Charles saw the Match as the only means of restoring the fortunes of his sister Elizabeth, who after the heady days as Queen of Bohemia had become a penniless refugee in the United Provinces.[6] There was no time to lose. On 16 May, just before Gondamar's departure, the prince made a grand gesture, an extraordinary promise, almost certainly without the knowledge and approval of either James or Buckingham. Gondomar reported that Charles had offered

Charles, Prince of Wales in 1623.

to *'poner en les manos'*, to put himself in the hands of the Spanish king and to travel to Madrid *'yncognito con dos criados'*, in disguise with two servants, if this proved to be what was needed to secure the Match.[7]

On 22 September Gondomar wrote to Buckingham from Madrid, assuring him indelicately that 'the decision has already been made, and with very great enthusiasm, that the Prince of Wales should mount Spain', by which he meant the Infanta herself.[8] But with Hapsburg troops continuing to dislodge English garrisons from the leading towns of the Palatinate, James was not so sure.[9] He decided to send a special messenger to Madrid, choosing for this

delicate task Endymion Porter, whose wife Olive was related to Buckingham by marriage. Porter himself was a distant relative of Buckingham and a close friend but in any event he was the obvious choice. Born in Seville, Porter had a Spanish grandmother, was fluent in Spanish and had once served as a page in the household of Gaspar de Guzmán, count-duke of Olivares, who in 1622 became the first minister of the young king, Philip IV.

Endymion Porter.

Porter's mission almost came to grief at the first hurdle. He was caught in a storm in the Channel, his ship and another collided, most of his papers and the servant loyally trying to hold on to them were swept overboard, and Porter himself suffered a broken shoulder bone that kept him bedridden at Calais for a week. After a painful journey he reached Madrid early in November but had to wait several weeks before Olivares would receive him. The minister, riddled with self-importance as his dual title of count-duke might suggest, found it difficult to meet on even half-equal terms a man whom he regarded as an underling. Olivares was thirty-five but Porter thought him prematurely aged, his hair combed forward to hide a receding forehead, with a thick beard cultivated in layers that descended like a black waterfall, and long curling moustaches that accentuated his flared nostrils.

The young upstart, no diplomat, paid little heed to the fact that he had an audience with one of the most powerful men in Europe. Asked bluntly by Porter if Spain would fulfil the promise it had made to collaborate with an English force in clearing the Palatinate of the occupying Hapsburg force,

Gaspar de Guzmán, count-duke of Olivares, first minister of Spain.

Olivares gave a gasp of astonishment and the mask slipped; with untypical candour he said there could be no question of the Spanish king taking up arms against his Hapsburg cousins. As to progress towards the Match, Olivares disingenuously claimed he had not been briefed about it. Porter's report of this interview, after he returned exhausted to England on New Year's Day 1623, combined with the latest official dispatch, which was 'fraught with generalities, without any one particular or certainty at all', ought to have dissuaded Charles from going to Spain.[10] Instead, they had the opposite effect: determined to help his sister any way he could, the prince resolved upon the gambler's throw, to force Spain's hand by going overland unannounced to Madrid in person, together with Buckingham, to collect his bride.

The marquis was charged with persuading the ailing king to give permission for the journey. He did so by comparing the scheme to James's own romantic adventure in sailing to Norway to bring Anne of Denmark back to Scotland. Only when James had reluctantly agreed to part with the two people he loved best in the world, did Buckingham reveal its secretive and hazardous nature. The king's response was to shed tears and retire to his 'naked bed'.[11] The next day James tried to enlist Charles's Spanish speaking secretary, Frances Cottington, against the enterprise; but intimidated by Buckingham, all the poor man could do was to agree to accompany prince and favourite.

Historian Martin Havran puts Buckingham's participation down to his 'incomparable vanity': believing that he could not bear to be anywhere but centre stage.[12] In essence, however, if the prince was determined to make the visit, the marquis had no option but to go along with it to avoid jeopardising his position in the next reign. Wisely he also spent time securing his rear. Buckingham's young cousin, Arthur Brett, had been made a Groom of the Bedchamber in April 1622. By the autumn there were rumours that James's interest in him was far from platonic.[13] Realising his enemies would plot and

William Monson: banished from court.

plan during his absence, Buckingham sent Brett abroad to travel... for more than a year.[14] William Monson, the other would-be royal favourite already banished from court, was knighted as a consolation prize but then dispatched to further his education in Italy.[15]

At 7 a.m. on Monday, 17 February 1623, Cottington, accompanied by Porter, left Holborn for Dover. Cottington had also left his wife of barely four days asleep in bed, without telling her where he was going.[16] The courtiers' instructions were to secure a ship to cross the Channel. While James played his part by taking the rest of the court to Newmarket, Charles and Buckingham slipped away to Newhall, the marquis's recently acquired house in Essex. After an over-indulgent dinner, they were late starting for Dover the following morning. Sir Richard Graham, Buckingham's Master of Horse, a dour Scot, accompanied them. Each adventurer was in disguise, wearing a hood and a rather obviously false beard; they unimaginatively called themselves Thomas and John Smith. At Tilbury, crossing the Thames to Gravesend, they gave the ferry boatman far too big a tip 'through lack of silver'. Suspecting they were noblemen bent on an illicit duel abroad, he raised the alarm. Orders were given in Rochester for their arrest but they had already passed safely through

Newhall, the departure point for Charles and Buckingham.

the town. At that moment, joining the Dover Road, they suddenly caught sight of the Imperial ambassador's train in the distance. Ferdinand de Boischot was on his way to London, where he would prove an intransigent negotiator on the fate of Frankenthal, the last surviving town in the Palatinate protected by an English garrison. The prince and the marquis leapt over a hedge and took cover in an adjacent field until he had safely passed by. At Canterbury, they again fell under suspicion. Stopped and questioned by the mayor, Buckingham had to remove his beard and explain that he, as Lord High Admiral no less, was on his way to Dover to make a snap inspection of the fleet. A local boy who had humped baggage at court recognised the prince and was less easily duped by this ludicrous explanation; but by parting with a golden guinea, 'his mouth was easily shut'.[17]

The harbour at Boulogne.

The pair arrived at Dover at six in the evening for the rendezvous with Cottington and Porter, who were waiting with two servants, a Scotsman called Kirk and James Leviston of the prince's bedchamber. However, twelve hours passed before the wind dropped sufficiently for them to embark in a fishing boat for Boulogne, and they endured six hours in huge waves before making port shortly after 2 p.m. Both the prince and the Lord High Admiral had been violently seasick and the postmaster's wife and daughter at Boulogne took pity on the wretched pair, allowing them to clean themselves up and rest for a while at their house. When Buckingham returned to Boulogne two years later, he would make a point of seeking them out and giving them a handsome reward of £30.[18]

On the road to Paris, the 'Smiths' were recognised by two Germans who had travelled in England and seen them a few months earlier, riding in a coach at Newmarket with the king. Graham, however, 'outfaced' and persuaded the Germans that they must be mistaken because of 'the impossibility to conceive so great a Prince and Favourite so suddenly metamorphized [sic] into travellers'.[19]

In their ineffectual disguise, the journey on which they embarked through France and Spain at the height of winter, by any yardstick, was extraordinarily dangerous. Buckingham and Charles could have been robbed, held for ransom or simply murdered at almost any point on the way. Safety for prince and favourite lay in speed. In 1623 every robber in France would have salivated at the thought of intercepting the heir to the British throne but fortunately for Charles, even the most valuable snippets of information moved slowly from place to place. Graham Robb, in his tour de force on the French historical landscape, deduces that 'The usual speed for an earth-shattering piece of news travelling over one hundred miles was between 4 and 7 mph', using the Fall of the Bastille as an example.[20]

A grand coach would have attracted far too much attention and still lacked the springs and chassis that would have survived such a long trip intact, on almost entirely unmade roads that turned into a quagmire in winter. The invention of the lightweight *chaise de poste* with two seats and a postillion was still almost half a century away. The only realistic option was to travel on horseback and here, at least, the infrastructure was already in place. In France a network of staging points, each sector supervised by a *maitre de poste*, supplied a string of fresh horses for royal messengers and any other traveller prepared to pay handsomely for the privilege.[21]

Buckingham and Prince Charles attended a masque at the Louvre incognito.

A Spanish writer, Almansa y Mendoza, produced a full account of the trip, stretching his reports to seventeen newsletters, each eagerly devoured by his public. According to Mendoza, half the travellers acted as an advance party, with the prince and Buckingham in the second group. Even then, they rode ahead of Cottington as though he were their master, working on the principle that any attack would be concentrated upon him. What Cottington, convinced that the whole trip was utter folly, thought of this stratagem is unrecorded.

In the late afternoon the party completed three *posts* to Montreuil, that is to say, six leagues, a distance of about twenty-one miles. They had difficulty in becoming accustomed to their hired horses, which were roughly shod, with long manes and tails, and no trimmed or cropped ears. By the evening of the third day they reached Paris, lodging above the post-house, at the Grand Cerf, a hostelry in the rue St Jacques. After a maid working there 'that had sold Linen heretofore in London' recognised the prince and had to be persuaded to keep quiet, he and Buckingham bought periwigs, 'somewhat to overshadow their foreheads'.[22] In this superior disguise, on 22 February they visited Notre Dame and other tourist sights and twice entered the royal palace of the Louvre.

Along with other citizens, they exercised their traditional right to see the French king eating his dinner in a gallery, and the queen mother at her own table. They bumped into maréchal de Cadenet, newly returned from London, but fortunately the erstwhile ambassador failed to recognise them. In the evening they were stopped at the entrance to the salon where nineteen great ladies of court were practising their steps for the *Ballet de Junon la nopcière* but on impulse the queen's chamberlain, Hercule de Montbazon, allowed them to enter 'out of humanity to strangers' and gave them two of the best seats at what proved to be the dress rehearsal.[23] Charles, although he did not know it, saw among the dancers his future wife, Henrietta Maria, the King of France's sister, in the role of the goddess Iris; but Buckingham had eyes only for 'the handsomest', the French Queen, Anne of Austria.[24]

According to the contemporary Spanish writer, Mendoza, the royal party had a third component, riding a *post* or two behind: a secretary accompanied by a herald carrying a document in which James threatened war against France if his son were detained against his will.[25] This seemed unlikely, on the face of it, to deter the French and Mendoza regarded the clandestine visit to the Louvre as 'more audacious than it was sensible'. Indeed, scarcely had the king of England disclosed the venture to his incredulous Privy Council, who heard the rumours and rushed to Newmarket for confirmation, than he began to have grave misgivings that no bombastic ultimatum carried by a herald could easily relieve. The south coast ports had been closed to prevent the news getting out but James feared there were 'many blind creeks' from which a small boat could slip across to France. What if Louis XIII did not take kindly to the clandestine passage of the heir to the British throne through his domains? So, hard on the heels of prince and favourite, went Hay with instructions to inform Louis that Charles was 'passing unknown through his country' lest, as he later wrote to the prince, 'upon the first rumour of your passing, he should take a pretext to stop you.'[26]

On 24 February Hay left Dover, taking Lucy with him. She may have agreed to go in the hope of snatching a few hours with Buckingham in Paris and the king may privately have harboured hopes that her beauty and wit would come in useful if the French proved to be seriously put out. The Channel was still anything but calm, and Hay was severely seasick before they reached Boulogne later the same day.[27] Although Lucy was Hay's equal in horsemanship, they took a day longer than the prince to ride the twenty-eight *posts* to Paris, where they found a highly disgruntled British ambassador. Edward, Lord Herbert, receiving word from Buckingham and the prince of their arrival, had invited them to the embassy; but was told they would not come and that he should keep well away from their inn.[28] Believing it prudent nonetheless to inform the French foreign ministry, on 23 February Herbert had requested an interview

Edward, Lord Herbert.

with the principal French secretary of state, Pierre Brulart, vicomte de Puisieux. Herbert was unaware that prince and favourite had left Paris for Spain at 3 a.m. that very day. Puisieux, however, already knew, telling Herbert 'I know your Business as well as you do, your Prince is departed this morning Post to Spain'. As James had feared, Louis was 'offended at this journey and at the prince having come so freely to the Louvre'.[29] Puisieux ordered a small detachment of royal guards to catch up with him and his companions for 'their convenience and safety'. Puisieux said he wanted to reduce the risk of Charles having his throat cut but, believed Herbert, in reality intended to bring him and his little band ignominiously back to Paris to explain themselves.[30]

With a thick blanket of snow and ice covering the trees, the intrepid pair took the road out of the French capital south west through Orleans, Blois, Amboise and Poitiers, staying in common inns, 'mostly terrible places', on the way. Charles and Buckingham probably shared the only private room available, tending each other's saddle sores and using their own sheets; a wise precaution because 'innkeepers along the route put fresh sheets on the beds in November and changed them in March. The trick was to slip into the envelope of grime, fully clothed, and to wrap one's head in a cloth. Sleep came quickly, despite the fleas'.[31]

The food was scarcely any better, because of Lent, and they 'could get no flesh in their Innes'.[32] Three days out, in desperation, seeing an untended herd of goats, Graham proposed to snatch and snap the neck of the plumpest. Charles, overhearing this, said with mock reproval: 'Why, Richard, do you think you may practise here your old tricks again upon the Borders?' The prince showed them all how it should be done. As the rest ran haplessly about trying to catch the young goat, Charles killed it from horseback with a single shot to the head. It was, he modestly observed, a 'fine Scottish Pistol'.[33]

Francis Cottington.

Crossing the Gironde at Blaye, and perhaps feeling themselves out of immediate danger, the party entered Bordeaux and bought five new riding coats, each in the same colour and style. Such ostentation brought them to the notice of the governor of Guienne, the duke d'Épernon, but Cottington dissuaded him from offering hospitality by claiming that they were all of no standing 'and formed yet to little courtship'.[34]

They were still ahead of their pursuers as they entered Gascony, where they experienced the same difficulties with the incomprehensible tongue of the south as later would the playwright Jean Racine, giving as an example: 'when I asked a maid for a chamber pot, she put a warming-pan in my bed'.[35] Among the troop of guards hard on their heels was a young ensign, Tréville, 'born not far from the Pyrenees', destined to play a much bigger role in the Affair of the Queen's Diamonds. Tréville was a Béarnaise, from the autonomous pocket state of Béarn. It had been annexed by Louis only three years previously and its citizens remained a law unto themselves. He spoke their language fluently and could distinguish between hostile and hospitable territory. For example, on the left bank of the river Adour, in the Chalosse region east of Bayonne, the natives were known to be 'tall, strong, well fed and welcoming'. But on the right bank, they were 'skinny, miserable and suspicious'.[36] Here all strangers were regarded as fair game, especially a Frenchman from the north, known as a 'Franchiman' or 'Franciot'.

After six weary days in the saddle, the prince's party passed through Bayonne. At the last inn before the frontier, still suffering the strictures of Lent, Charles and Buckingham lit a fire in their room and secretly broiled the remains of the goat. The smell attracted a hungry visitor also spending the night, none other than a king's messenger, Walsingham Gresley, on his way north to Whitehall with dispatches from Digby in Madrid. Perhaps sensing pursuit, in the morning they took Gresley temporarily back over the border with them, all crossing together into Spain at Irun, where the Pyrenees slip away to the sea. Only then did they feel secure enough to write letters to James that Gresley could add to his satchel. It was a prudent decision: a day later, Louis's rather disorganised detachment of guards reached Irun but had strict orders not to cross the frontier. They returned to Paris to report that the prince was no longer in the territory of the French king.

On their way back to the capital, his guards encountered Hay, travelling south, also bound for Madrid. King James intended to leave no stone unturned to secure the Match. Lucy Percy returned to London alone but only after she had attended a little soirée at the British ambassador's residence. Herbert was determined to make what capital he could out of at least one of the illustrious personages visiting Paris. Lucy was introduced to Armand-Jean du Plessis, who had been made a cardinal and was already seen by some as the emerging power in French politics.[37] He had a devoted entourage whose ability to ferret out invaluable snippets of information enabled him to survive and prosper in a potentially hostile court environment.[38] Before long, this would expand into a huge spider's web of paid informants. If Lucy was on her usual sparkling form, du Plessis no doubt would have marked her down as someone to be reckoned with. He was probably aware that she shared Buckingham's bed. This chance but opportune meeting would lead, three years later, to Lucy becoming the cardinal's secret agent at the very centre of government.

From the Spanish frontier, Charles and Buckingham took another seven days to reach Madrid. Despite receiving a warning from Gresley of what to expect, no *bandidos* blocked their way. They missed not only the prize catch of the prince but a veritable fortune: £25,000 in negotiable bonds, payable to the bearer with no questions asked; and £1,000 in gold pieces. The only risk to Charles came unexpectedly at an inn at St Augustine, a village about ten miles north of Madrid, a rough and ready place without glass in the windows, where planks served as tables and there were no napkins. They exchanged pleasantries with a Spanish diplomat on the shortcomings of the establishment. After a few glasses of wine, the prince asked whether he knew Gondomar's young successor in London, Carlos Columna, whom he joked, was far too ugly for his beautiful wife. It turned out that the diplomat was Carlos's cousin, Marco Antonio Columna, who promptly challenged Charles to a duel to satisfy the family honour. Buckingham had to intervene and hastily explain that he was threatening to kill the Prince of Wales.[39]

The British Embassy in Madrid, known locally as the House of the Seven Chimneys, stood in the calle de las Infantas, a narrow, dark street frequented by prostitutes, on the east side of the old city. The residence itself was large but far from grand, a reflection of the long period when no Englishman, not even a diplomat, was welcome in Spain. Most of the foreign embassies were much

The British Embassy in Madrid, known locally as the House of the Seven Chimneys

*John Digby, Earl of
Bristol.*

more fashionably located, near the royal palace, the Alcazar, far to the west. On Friday, 7 March, once inside the city boundaries, prince and favourite felt confident enough to ride on ahead of Cottington and Porter, with only Leviston for company. When they reached the embassy, at about 8 p.m., Charles and Leviston waited opposite in the shadows, leaving the marquis to knock on the front door. It was opened by one of the ambassador's staff, James Howell, who knew but failed to recognise Buckingham because it simply never occurred to him that the favourite could be carrying his own portmanteau. 'Thomas Smith' spun a good story in an effort to persuade the ambassador to come to his own front door and receive the surprise of his life. Buckingham claimed that Gresley 'had fallen into the hands of thieves, who had stolen all his dispatches' and said he could not go upstairs to give a full account to the ambassador because he had fallen off his horse and hurt his leg. The commotion was such that Simon Digby, the ambassador's nephew, himself newly arrived from a diplomatic posting in Vienna, came down to the hall. He recognised Buckingham, who brought in the prince, and they both went to the nephew's room. It was here that the incredulous ambassador, 'in a kind of astonishment', eventually found them.[40] Digby could scarcely believe his eyes: Charles and Buckingham were in Madrid.

Gondomar evidently had an informant at the embassy, because he knew within an hour or two of their arrival.[41] At an audience in the embassy hastily arranged for the following morning, he gave the ambassador's wife Beatrice short shrift when, no doubt put up to it by her husband, she acknowledged that Buckingham was in the city but said they were 'altogether ignorant for any intention that the Prince had of coming thither'.[42] Gondomar had received the best news of his diplomatic career and had no intention of being put off its publication. He went to see Olivares in a state of barely suppressed jubilation. The count sarcastically remarked that judging from Gondomar's mood, he must have come to report that the British king was in Madrid. 'By no means', responded Gondomar airily, savouring the moment: 'Only his son.'[43] At the end of the day he received his reward: with the Match to finalise, the long-coveted appointment to the Spanish council of state.

At first, before he received a realistic assessment of their progress, James was simply relieved that his two 'boys' had arrived safely and remained full of optimism about the marriage. Although the marquis was uneasy about the reaction back home, in May James carried out his promise to make Buckingham a duke, the first commoner to reach such heady heights for seventy years.[44] It enhanced his status in the negotiations, in which his monarch constantly tried to interfere from afar. Whilst keen that both favourite and prince should cut a fine figure at the Spanish court, the king constantly complained about the cost, regarding it as a short-term investment that he expected to recoup quickly. James soon warned Charles 'my coffers are already drained' and ordered him to ensure that the promised advance instalment on the Infanta's dowry of £150,000 was sent to London as quickly as possible.[45]

The prince, who had arrived with scarcely any suitable attire, made heavy demands on the royal purse. Over the course of six months, according to Cottington's meticulous accounts, Charles expended 80,382 reales on silks, linen, footwear, gloves and tailoring, especially on 'unmayd' cloth sent out from England.[46] This was the equivalent of £2,200 and in Spain amounted to more than seventy times the average annual income of a member of the professional classes.[47] James sent out Spencer Compton, the Earl of Northampton, with jewellery for prince and favourite to wear that he had chosen personally from the royal collection in the Tower and worth, according to one account, £200,000.[48]

Spanish courtiers spent a fortune trying to keep up and such was the drain of the festivities on the Madrid exchequer, Buckingham drolly told James that his son might go down in history as the first commander who had succeeded in sacking a city without an army.[49] This quip seemed to have increasing substance when the prince, who proved more adept at negotiating gifts of priceless works of art than securing the Match, in June acquired from Philip IV two works by Titian, *Portrait of Charles V with Hound* and the epitome of Renaissance eroticism, *Jupiter and Antiope* (pictured opposite). Soon afterwards the distinguished art expert, Vicente Carducho, recalled his astonishment when he saw *Danae* and a whole series of erotic mythological scenes by Titian (now known as the 'Poesie') 'packed into crates for shipping to England'. They, too, had been audaciously arrogated by Charles; only what Carducho diplomatically described as 'later developments' caused them to remain in Madrid.[50]

Titian's *Jupiter and Antiope.*

Back in March the rigours of Spanish protocol meant that before Charles had made his public entry into Madrid, a week after his actual arrival, he could only glimpse his future intended from inside a closed coach or hidden behind a shutter. Such restrictions did not come easily to him. On the prince's first day in the Spanish capital, Philip IV obligingly rode by in an open carriage with his sister, the Infanta Maria, in the Prado Park. Charles 'would have leapt out of his coach to salute the king of Spain but that Gondomar held him'.[51] It was not until Easter Day, 6 April that he was allowed to speak to the Infanta, and then only briefly, with the utmost formality. Maria, a rather plain sixteen-year-old with a prominent nose, red hair and green eyes, gave him no encouragement: a devout Catholic, she had no wish to marry a heretic, although she was at pains to emphasize that a Protestant husband was preferable to none and denied the rumour that she might retire to a nunnery.

The more elusive the Infanta, the more alluring Charles found her, but in an allegorical, romantic way that was perhaps only to be expected of someone whose sole sexual experience had probably been with Buckingham.

The Infanta Maria.

Festival staged in Madrid in honour of Charles, Prince of Wales.

The Walled Garden Incident.

*Archie Armstrong,
James's court jester.*

The prince's one serious effort to force himself upon the princess ended in complete fiasco. On the morning of Saturday, 17 May, hearing that Maria would be taking a walk near the Casa del Campo, in the enclosed grounds of one of the Spanish royal houses, Charles, helped up by Buckingham, climbed on to the top of the perimeter wall 'and sprung down a great height'. Alas, when Maria saw the prince she 'gave a shriek and ran back', to be swallowed up among her giggling ladies in waiting. The Infanta's guardian, fearing that he would be blamed, fell on his knees and begged Charles to leave. A small gate in the wall was unlocked for him and he departed, mortified by his failure.[52]

The only Englishman allowed near the Infanta and her ladies was, quite literally, a fool: James's court jester, Archibald Armstrong, part of a retinue of lords and retainers sent to bolster the prince's party at the Spanish court. Archie often annoyed those who saw themselves as his betters by wearing 'clothes of a style more appropriate to courtiers than to servants' and the King of Spain mischievously gave him a spectacular suit that outshone most of British party.[53] Maria, liking the way he 'flurts out what he lists', how Archie said what everyone else dared not say, gave him an unmistakeable indication of her implacable distaste for the Match.[54] As James had no doubt intended, Archie's unfettered access at the Spanish court made his letters home to the king a useful alternative assessment of how the marriage was truly progressing. When he openly blamed Buckingham for mishandling the negotiations, the duke was furious and threatened to have him hanged from one of the embassy's seven chimneys. Archie gave as good as he got. 'No one has ever heard of a fool being hanged for what he said', he replied, 'but many dukes in England have been beheaded for their insolence'.[55]

In truth Buckingham had an impossible task from the start, not helped by the plethora of British diplomats supposed to make it easier. Hay's arrival in late March from Paris, as his biographer Roy Schreiber aptly puts it, was 'one more cook with a spoon in an already well-stirred broth'.[56] James thought Hay could remove some of the rough edges on his 'sweet boys' and teach Buckingham how to deliver his vote of thanks to King Philip. Buckingham's fury can easily be imagined when he was advised to speak the words 'with the best compliments you can, and Carlisle [Hay] can best instruct thee in that art'.[57] However this exponent of sweet graces managed only a single audience with Maria, the ice princess, which lasted less than a minute because Hay 'could not draw so much from her as to put out her hand to him when he went to kiss it'.[58]

Thereafter Hay was as receptive to an excuse to depart as Buckingham was keen to find him one: it came in the form of a notice of dispensation for the marriage from the pope, meaningless because it gave no indication of the attached conditions. Hay was supposed to deliver this half-baked message to London but did not bother to do so, interrupting his journey home to remain in Paris for almost a month.[59] Another of Schreiber's broth stirrers, the British ambassador in Spain, Digby, proved an equal liability. He believed the presence of Charles and Buckingham in Madrid weakened, rather than strengthened, Britain's diplomatic hand. Digby said gloomily to anyone who would listen, 'I should rather have dissuaded them [from coming] than given any such counsel'.[60]

Initial progress towards the Match was due almost entirely to an assumption by the Spanish that Charles would never have made the journey unless he was willing to convert to Catholicism. On the Monday after his arrival, Olivares appeared so confident Rome would give its blessing that, choosing the most outrageous breach of Spanish protocol imaginable to make his point, he glibly told Buckingham and Charles, 'if the pope would not give a dispensation for a wife, they would give the Infanta to him "as his wench"'.[61] But by the end of March Olivares came to realise that neither Buckingham in Madrid nor James in London had any intention of allowing Charles to take so reckless a step with his religion. In a pointed reference to Henri IV of France, who had concluded that Paris was well worth a mass and changed his faith to secure his throne, James wrote that he was no Frenchman 'who can shift his religion as easily as he can shift his shirt when he cometh in from tennis'.[62]

At Olivares's instigation behind the scenes, the terms of the papal dispensation for the marriage, at first moderate, were altered and backdated to look as if they had been uncompromising all along.[63] The pope required nothing less than the full parliamentary repeal of England's anti-Catholic laws, which, as Gondomar in vain warned his fellow members of the Spanish council of state on 6 May, would never happen without strenuous opposition and would serve simply to bring all James's enemies together.[64] As the temperature rose in Madrid's summer heat, the tempers of the principal protagonists began to fray. Buckingham was so opposed to some of the concessions made by Charles about the up-bringing of any children from his marriage that he left the room, flung his hat on the ground and furiously trampled on it. When the duke learned of the conditions set down by Rome, he misjudged their origin and hectored the papal nuncio for three hours late at night, threatening new sanctions against English Catholics.[65] His relationship with Olivares collapsed into mutual distrust and 'darkness' and the count-duke, reacting under intense pressure and fatigue at a meeting that went on until the early hours of the morning, blurted out to Buckingham that neither Philip IV nor his father had ever been prepared to let the marriage take place.[66] The damning evidence of the truth of this was a deathbed declaration by

Philip IV: opposed to the Match.

Philip III to his sixteen-year-old heir that because of its potential impact on the faith of any children, merely to advocate marriage to a non-Catholic was a mortal sin, irrespective of any dispensation from Rome. Philip IV had revealed the declaration and his intention to abide by it to Olivares eighteen months later, on 26 October 1622, with instructions that his minister find a way to 'divert' the marriage treaty.[67] In his reply Olivares did not demur but added the qualification, 'unless the Prince became a Catholic'.[68]

This conversion was already a lost cause in May 1623. Gondomar, eager to find a way to end the deadlock, his own long-term status dependent upon a favourable resolution, suggested to Charles that a trusted emissary be sent to London to inform his father that the repeal of anti-Catholic legislation was vital to the Match. The prince seized upon this proposal as a means of escaping Olivares's clutches, arguing that he should put the case to his father in person. 'His own presence', he asserted, 'would be very necessary'.[69] Olivares politely refused to let him go. He may have heard that Charles was in no mood to make concessions. The prince had just sent a message to his sister Elizabeth, said to be 'in a pitiful case, almost distracted', that he would not consent to the marriage unless the Palatinate was restored to Frederick.[70]

As the news from Spain went from bad to worse, James ordered the royal entourage, intended to create a much grander household in Madrid for the prince, to turn back. Some of its members obeyed and some did not, with the result that they were strung out at inns the length and breadth of France, creating a demand for prime cuts of beef that could not be met.[71] These courtiers were an irresistible target for satirists back in England, who composed this little ditty:

Prince Charles can get no victuals,
Sufficient for his train,
His horses and his trumpeters,
Are all come back again.[72]

James bluntly told his son to agree to anything that would allow him to return home, 'to come speedily away if you can get leave and give over all treaty'.[73] Charles feared the worst: he knew that to all intents and purposes he had become a political prisoner, confined to two rooms at the *Alcazar* and the

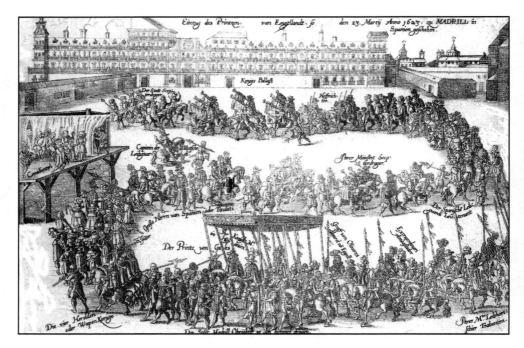

The whole of Europe was fascinated by the Prince of Wales's arrival in Madrid. This German illustration shows his arrival at the Alcazar palace in a formal procession. Within three months, Charles was desperately looking for a way out.

palace grounds. In June Charles asked his father for permission to escape at dead of night from Madrid, just 'as secretly' as he had arrived.[74] But the prince could hardly disappear without a hue and cry. In the end Charles chose a more pragmatic solution: he lied through his teeth. On 7 July, already showing an inkling of those consummate powers of deception that would cost him his head in 1649, Charles arranged a face-to-face meeting with Philip IV and said he would 'accept the proposals made to him with respect to religion, and also give the securities demanded for their due execution, and that this was the final determination of the king his father'.[75] Hay and Lucy also played their part, winning over the sceptical Spanish ambassador in London by making him the guest of honour at another monumental banquet.[76] It took until 5 August for Cottington to return to Madrid with written confirmation that James and his privy councillors had accepted all the Spanish articles, whereupon preparations could be made for Charles to depart: still without the Infanta, ostensibly held back until the promises concerning English Catholics had actually been put into effect.[77]

Countess Olivares, unable to resist Buckingham.

Buckingham, rebuked by Olivares for coming 'into the Prince's chamber with his clothes half on', practised his customary bisexuality and retaliated by seducing, or attempting to seduce, the first minister's wife, Inés de Zúñiga y Velasco, the fifth daughter of the count of Monterrey. Prima lady-in-waiting to Queen Isabella, this allegedly 'sour, elderly duenna' who 'acted the part of spy and jailer' in respect of Philip IV's politically ambitious spouse, at first had feigned outrage at reports of Buckingham's excesses.[78] Told that the duke went with prostitutes, whose beat was within easy reach of the embassy, she 'had the most diseased woman in Spain put into his bed, upon an arrangement to enjoy her'.[79]

When Buckingham subsequently exerted his charms on the countess, she was nonetheless seen by Clarendon as an unlikely conquest, 'so crooked and deformed, that she could neither tempt his appetite nor magnify his revenge'; but the historian exaggerated her physical shortcomings and underestimated the tenacity of the duke.[80] The countess, born late in 1584, was still only thirty-eight. She was Olivares's cousin and niece at one and the same time because they were related on both sides of the family. After fourteen years of a marriage that breached the medically prudent level of consanguinity, she had failed to give him the son he wanted: her two male infants were both still-born.[81] The formidable Spanish writer, Benito Pérez Galdós, was fascinated by the contradictions in her life. The countess was the inspiration for his principal character in *Doña perfecta*, 'The Perfect

Olivares: on his high horse.

Infanta Maria Anna never reached England. Eight years later she was married to Ferdinand III, King of Hungary, her first cousin. They had six children.

Lady', an attack on Catholic bigotry and hypocrisy. Its central theme, seemingly prompted by Buckingham's seduction, according to the American literary critic William Dean Howells was 'of such a brooding breathlessness, of such a deepening density, that you feel the wild passion-storm nearer and nearer at hand'.[82]

If anyone could have risen to the challenge presented by Countess Olivares, and would have taken the risk, it was surely Buckingham. When he had a fever on the eve of his and the prince's joint departure from Madrid on 29 August and could not stand, significantly it was the countess who rushed to his aid and lent him her embryonic version of a sedan chair.[83] The next day Olivares would not let his wife say goodbye to the duke. Historian Philip Gibbs sagely observes that 'Nothing could be more horrible to a Spanish grandee than to be the subject of ridicule'.[84] Their council of state met to decide what to do about the scandalous way the duke had treated Olivares 'in public and privately'.[85]

Charles saw Olivares without Buckingham at their final meeting to make a last, passionate plea for the restoration of Frederick and his sister Elisabeth to the Palatinate but it was too late for the British delegation to assuage the affront to the minister's manhood. The count's reaction, he afterwards told the Imperial ambassador, Franz Christoph Khevehülleur, was short and brutal; it amounted to *'keineswegs'*, or, 'no way'.[86] He candidly told the prince what Endymion Porter had faithfully reported and what Charles and Buckingham should have realised from the start: that Spain would never take up arms against another member of the Hapsburgs. Later Charles claimed to have responded, 'without this there is neither marriage nor friendship', but in reality he almost certainly held his tongue.[87]

The costly charade continued to the end. On the night of 14 August an extravagant fireworks display went on for hours that included hundreds of rockets and twenty-four men duelling with combustible swords. The Match, however, was already a damp squib. Buckingham's order for tilting equipment, to hold an English tourney in the Madrid bullring, was abruptly cancelled. After hunting near the royal palace of Estorial on 2 September, the prince signed the sworn authority for King Philip to act as his proxy in his marriage to the Infanta, which supposedly awaited only the arrival of a fresh dispensation from the new pope, and gave it to ambassador Digby for safekeeping.[88] The Spanish king still had no intention of going against his conscience and Olivares suspected correctly that Charles, too, had no intention of honouring his promises.

Gondomar: his ambitions gone for good.

With Buckingham in attendance, and accompanied by a gloomy Gondomar, fearing that both the marriage and his period of influence were over almost before they had begun, the prince commenced his homeward journey by way of Segovia, this time in a comfortable coach. Their destination was the port of Santander, where they were to embark in an English fleet. James, ever mindful of the cost, had already resolved that if, against all expectations, the Match went ahead and the Infanta was allowed to travel to England to marry Charles, he would not dispatch any more ships. The Spanish could 'send her by their own fleet' and, most important of all to James, the dowry, 'otherwise my baby and I are bankrupts for ever'.[89] At Segovia Charles sent a note to Digby, carried back over the mountains in a secret pouch beneath the withered arm of Buckingham's most trusted servant, Edward Clerke. The ambassador was commanded by it 'not to deliver my proxy to the king of Spain'.[90] Unsure whether Digby would comply, the prince sent another shorter letter to him 'from the seaside' to the same effect, dating it 9 October in an attempt to obfuscate its perfidious nature, before he set sail for home from Santander on 18 September.[91] An ill wind ensured a wretched passage.

As soon as he believed his son to be safely out of the clutches of the Spanish, James reinforced Charles's instructions to the luckless ambassador. So anxious was he to ensure their receipt, the king sent copies of the document by four different couriers, 'one upon the neck of the other'. It contained an unequivocal message for Olivares. The Match could only go ahead if Frederick and Elisabeth were simultaneously restored to the Palatinate. James would not allow his son to further his dynasty by marriage and at the same time 'give our only daughter her portion [her children's inheritance] in tears'.[92]

There was almost a sting in the tail – the English fleet came perilously close to sinking in a gale in the Bay of Biscay before reaching Plymouth on

5 October. Charles arrived with a heavy beard, perhaps because attempts to shave him in raging seas had prudently been abandoned. Nonetheless instantly recognised, he and Buckingham were given a hero's welcome by nation and monarch alike. The shambles of their enterprise was submerged in the euphoria at their return. Church bells rang out three days running and hundreds of bonfires were lit. Fortified by free hogsheads of wine and barrels of sherry, the jubilant London crowd shouted 'We have him, we have him' at the brideless prince.[93] James ran down the stairs to meet Charles and Buckingham, embracing them with tears of joy. On the 7 October the resident Spanish ambassador Carlos Coloma, under virtual siege from hostile Londoners at Ely House in Holborn, wrote to Philip IV to say that in his view the marriage agreement was a dead letter.[94] In fact it was much more of a volte-face than that: Charles and Buckingham now headed the anti-Spanish party clamouring for war. Only the duke knew, and empathized with, the prince's true feelings – 'what burning rage, what bitter mortification, what bleeding vanity'.[95] In the memorable words of the great historian Richard Henry Tawney, they had returned to England 'in the mood of the disappointed suitor who demonstrates the depth of his devotion by cutting the ungrateful loved one's throat'.[96]

From his shabbily furnished study in the House of the Seven Chimneys, Digby made a last-ditch stand, regarding it as a matter of honour, his and that of the Prince of Wales, to hand over his proxy and, the new papal dispensation having finally arrived, to agree a date for the wedding ceremony. James was ill, crippled by gout, which left the prince to send his harshest message yet to Digby in Madrid. 'Make what shifts or fair excuses, you will,' he wrote, but I command you as you answer it upon your peril not [to] deliver my proxy... except that the king will promise some way to restore my brother-in-law [Frederick of the Palatinate] to his honour and inheritances.'[97] In his report to Whitehall, Digby launched a pre-emptive strike in a vain attempt to avoid being made the scapegoat for the failure of the Match; but his rash criticism of the antics of both prince and favourite brought his recall on the last day of 1623 and, soon after Charles ascended to the throne, a term of imprisonment.

Spain concentrated its fire upon Buckingham by making a formal complaint, which with its strong hints of what would now be called homophobia, by implication denigrated the Prince of Wales. This served to highlight

Disaster at Blackfriars: nearly 100 were killed when the Catholics used the French ambassador's house for an illegal gathering and the floor collapsed.

what historian Hugh Ross Williamson calls 'the full meaning of Madrid, where, if Charles fell in love with anyone it was not with the Infanta but with Buckingham'.[98] A report prepared by the Spanish council of state and solemnly presented to the King of England by an ambassador extraordinary, the prickly Juan de Mendoza, accused the duke of doing 'obscene things'.[99] It did not diminish Buckingham's sexual appeal because James almost certainly was already aware of the parallel relationship between prince and favourite. However, when Mendoza, lacking Gondomar's guile, left to return to Spain, his frosty reception upon arrival was followed by an even chillier *adiós*. He was refused the traditional farewell royal audience at Whitehall and deprived of the customary complimentary coaches for his entourage to make their journey to Dover.[100]

Any thoughts that the French ambassador might have harboured of exploiting anti-Spanish sentiment were quickly dashed. On Sunday, 26 October 1623, the top floor of Tillières's diplomatic residence in Blackfriars, which contained a Catholic chapel, was given over to a sermon by a proscribed Jesuit scholar, Robert Drury. Between two and three hundred Catholics converged on the property, in flagrant breach of anti-recusant laws. The floor collapsed under their weight, as did the one below, rented out to a Catholic priest. Only the stone arch supporting the roof of Tillières's first floor drawing-room held. Even so, ninety-five people were killed and some more injured, callously refused help by a crowd of hostile Londoners. Ardent Protestant pamphleteers were quick to point out that in the Gregorian calendar used by most Roman Catholic countries, the date was 5 November, the eighteenth anniversary of the Gunpowder Plot. The demise of so many Catholics was seen, in the literal sense, as a Godsend. Tillières, first incorrectly reported killed and then depicted just above three large pieces of fallen masonry (left) still wearing his hat, had not even been present. He was summoned to Whitehall to explain why his house was being used for illegal gatherings. His dispatch to the French foreign office described his residence as a 'doleful heap of ruins'.[101] For the time being, with feelings running high, he might just as easily have been referring to the notion of a French marriage in place of the Spanish Match.

6: ESCAPE FROM BLOIS

The elder of the Spanish Infantas, Ana María Mauricia, would become known to the citizens of France as Anne of Austria, a derogatory epithet not altogether consistent with the facts. Although Anne's titles included that of Archduchess of Austria, she never went there; she was born at Valladolid in Spain on 22 September 1601. Despite having an Austrian mother and a preponderance of Austrian Hapsburg blood – and, more importantly, despite marrying into the French royal family and becoming the wife of King Louis XIII – she would show herself to be Spanish in sentiment, through and through.

Marie de' Medici, Anne of Austria's future mother-in-law from hell, was bigoted, dim-witted and conspicuously coarse in an age noted for its vulgarity; she had poor eyesight and even poorer French. The daughter of the Grand Duke of Tuscany, brought up in Florence amidst conspicuous consumption and wealth, she belonged to the Medici money-lending family that bankrolled much of Europe. In October 1600 Henri IV of France married Marie by proxy in return for a payment of 3,600,000 livres, the first instalment of her dowry. Although her initial good looks did not last, she proved reassuringly fertile, for Marie gave Henri six children, of whom the oldest would become Louis XIII. Successive pregnancies would leave her hugely overweight and she came to be known, although not of course to her face, as *'la grosse banquière'*, 'the fat banker'.

Compelled to live at the royal palaces of the Louvre and Saint-Germain-en-Laye in what might best be described as bellicose proximity to Henry's institutionalised mistress, Henriette d'Entragues, Marie abused her rival in foul language that shocked her courtiers. The king had sexual intercourse with them turn and turn about; when the two women first fell pregnant, it was within a few weeks of one another and their offspring, heirs and bastards, were brought up together. The Tuscan ambassador asked rhetorically: 'Has there ever been a brothel like this court of France?'[1]

As the legitimate first-born, Louis should have been granted a special status but found that his half-siblings often enjoyed much greater parental support and approval. Historian-psychologist Elizabeth Marvick says that his mother,

*This allegory describes France as the 'Land where truth is born' and depicts
Henri IV and Marie de' Medici with their infant son, the future Louis XIII. But
the Tuscan ambassador compared the French court to a brothel, where queen
and royal mistress lived in bellicose proximity.*

Henriette d'Entragues, Henri's mistress.

Marie de' Medici, the young queen.

Saint-Germain-en-Laye palace.

instead of showing a natural affection for her son, abdicated her position to substitutes; and that he was sexually abused by his father.[2] An insatiable womaniser, Henri revelled in his sexual performance and was obsessed by the need to confirm his son's virility. When Louis was still short of his fourth birthday, the king showed him his large, erect penis and told him this was how the Bourbons ruled the kingdom and ensured the succession. At eight years of age, Louis was taken into bed by his father, who attempted to masturbate and arouse him, apparently without success, and consequently beat his son in anger.[3]

The prince's personal physician, Jean Héroard (medallion left), disapproved of the king's violent behaviour but was powerless to intervene and by his own actions contributed to Louis's discomfiture. Already aged almost fifty when Louis was born, Héroard showed little sensitivity for the young prince's feelings and, like the king, encouraged sexual interest and play, which the

Henri IV of France.

prince's servants took as a licence to torment and humiliate the boy. They fondled his genitals to see if they could stimulate a response, threatened him with castration and mutilation, and encouraged him to simulate intercourse. As historian Geoffrey Regan comments: 'What passed for child rearing in seventeenth-century France could have provided material for a whole psychiatric conference on infant trauma and personality disorders.'[4]

A few months before his assassination in 1610, Henri asked Louis whether he would prefer to marry a Spanish or English princess. Marie de' Medici, a devout Catholic who took over as Regent on behalf of her eight-year-old son, had no such doubts. To her self-centred, uncomplicated mind, French Catholic interests and her own were best served by a marriage alliance with Spain.

After Anne of Austria had renounced any claim to the throne of Spain in front of the Spanish court at Burgos, on 25 November 1615 her marriage to Louis XIII was celebrated at Bordeaux's Saint-André cathedral. The packed audience included, at the expense of invited guests, an unusually large proportion of ordinary citizens: they discovered an unlocked door at 4 a.m. and refused to leave until the ceremony was concluded at 7 p.m., 'preferring a fast of the mouth to one of the eyes'.[5] This was not the only setback for royal protocol, which required consummation to be conclusively established to seal the union. What

Anne of Austria.

141

could happen if it remained in doubt was demonstrated in England a century earlier by Catherine of Aragon, who asserted her marriage to Prince Arthur had never been consummated and that she was still a virgin when she became the wife of his younger brother, Henry VIII; thereby famously (and perhaps falsely) challenging the grounds put forward by Henry and Cardinal Wolsey to Rome in support of an annulment.[6] In England and Spain ecclesiastical law required both penetration and ejaculation in order for consummation to be considered complete.

Having been born five days apart, Louis and Anne were both just fourteen, not considered particularly young for wedlock at the time. Nonetheless their first night together, pruriently and optimistically recorded by Héroard in his medical notebook, was a cringe-making fiasco.[7]

An account appears in the *Historiettes*, irreverent pen pictures of the prominent members of Louis XIII's court. They were compiled by Gidéon Tallemant des Réaux (pictured), a bourgeois lawyer whose wife, Elisabeth de Rambouillet, was related to the marquise de Rambouillet, Catherine de Vivonne. This was enough to secure him a regular invitation to her hôtel de Rambouillet, the Paris mansion in the rue St. Thomas-du-Louvre where from 1610 she held social and literary salons for more than thirty years. Its holy of holies was the *salon bleu*, a grand reception room with views across to the Tuileries, with blue and gold upholstery and blue silk curtains.[8] Here Madame de Rambouillet and her flock gave Tallemant a fund of stories that he cross-checked meticulously but, perhaps wisely, in the end drew back from publishing; their more salacious detail did not appear in print for more than 300 years. Anthony Levi, author of a widely acclaimed biography of Richelieu, concludes that Tallemant was 'studiously well informed'.[9] Francis J. Barnett, the most erudite editor of Tallemant's works, alludes to his 'impressive degree of accuracy' and the factual value of his conclusions because 'he did not hesitate to

Madame de Rambouillet.

doubt or dismiss as unreliable much that he was told'.[10] Philippe Erlanger, a prolific expert on seventeenth-century France, gives a great deal of weight to

Tallemant, 'who draws his facts from eyewitness informants that he never fails to name.' 'His realistic accounts', concludes Erlanger, ought to be 'preferred to other ornate descriptions'.[11]

Louis had entered Bordeaux in full military uniform but after the ceremony was sent for a brief nap by his mother in anticipation of the rigours ahead. While he was sleeping, Marie de' Medici ambushed a passing cleric and made him bless the four-poster curtained bed that was to accommodate the newly wedded couple. At 8 p.m. she roused her son, removed most of his clothes, leaving him with fur slippers and a fur dressing gown, and assembled the group of witnesses charged with taking him to the chamber where Anne was waiting with apprehensive, rather than eager, anticipation. She probably had no more understanding than Louis of what sex entailed. Her mother, Marguerite of Austria, who otherwise might have given her some idea of what to expect, had died in Madrid at the age of twenty-six just over four years earlier, in giving birth to her eighth child at the Escorial Palace.

Louis, for his part, was by no means an eager bridegroom. He refused to walk and had to be carried in a bizarre, almost farcical procession that included his own mother, Héroard, two nurses, his tutor and sundry members of the wardrobe, with Louis's premier valet de chambre, Henri de Béringhem, solemnly leading the way with a lighted candle.[12] Marie de' Medici said to Anne, 'Here is your husband, give yourself to him and love him well'.[13] Anne replied in Spanish that she was ready and everyone withdrew except the two nurses. They confirmed that the king 'did his duty' twice but as the curtains around the bed were tightly drawn throughout, in reality they could not tell.[14] After an hour Louis fell asleep and at 10.15 p.m. he was taken back to his own bed by the same procession. Héroard recorded the alleged double consummation in his journal but admitted it was only 'according to what he [the king] told us'.[15] Not that it was easy to understand anything that Louis said: he had a severe congenital speech defect and was 'so extream [sic] a stutterer that he would sometimes hold his tongue out of his mouth a good while before he could speak so much as one word'.[16]

The following morning, the queen mother crudely displayed the stained sheets to the court and falsely claimed that her son had penetrated his wife with his 'gland rouge', his erect penis, which she said had been seen when he got into bed.[17] As to the state of the sheets, Tallemant asserted that Louis merely urinated into Anne's vagina, in the extraordinary belief this was what

Louis XIII, holding the bridle of his horse.

had been expected of him.[18] Professor Lloyd Moote refers in his distinguished biography of Louis to 'the king's subsequent shrinking from any physical contact with the queen' and he refused even to take his meals with her for seven months.[19]

It must have been a miserable existence for Anne, whose substantial apartment in the Louvre did not disguise the fact that Marie de' Medici was queen of France in everything but name and treated her as little more than a tiresome child. Anne also had to put up with the morose temperament of the future Cardinal Richelieu, who had accepted the key post in her household, that of grand almoner, with anything but good grace. Armand-Jean du Plessis, bishop of the poor, remote and rural diocese of Luçon, near La Rochelle – 'the wretchedest bishopric in all France' was how he described it – had already shown by his extravagant protestations of loyalty and service after the death of Henri IV that he had developed a fantasy of himself as the means by which both family and royal prospects would be immediately enhanced.[20] He was acutely sensitive to slights and ridicule and wanted the much more important and vacant position of grand almoner in Marie de' Medici's own household. Du Plessis failed to appreciate that his eloquent address on behalf of the French clergy at the winding up of the meeting of the French Estates in 1614, the closest France came to a representative parliament, did not amount to much in terms of influence.[21] He owed his appointment as Anne's grand almoner to the fact that he was the cheapest solution for the crown. As this was deemed to be a new position, the usual rules relating to the sale of an office did not apply. No incumbent needed to be recompensed for its loss and the salary for the job could be set at a token annual payment of just 300 livres, which no other credible candidate was prepared to accept.[22]

Du Plessis also made the mistake of backing the wrong horse, ingratiating himself with Léonora Galigaï (right), the queen mother's companion, who had supported his appointment, and her Florentine husband Concino Concini. The Italian couple lacked a genuine power base even though Concini was widely believed to be Marie de' Medici's lover. On 24 April 1617, the king, despite being in a state of complete paralysis whenever he drew near the nuptial bedchamber, asserted his royal authority with unexpected political

cunning and resourcefulness in encouraging their overthrow. Concini was shot three times in the head by a captain of the guard, on the pretext that he had resisted arrest. Louis wanted his corpse hung on a gibbet. When his advisers persuaded him that this would be unwise, the king proved so indiscreet about where Concini's body had been buried, that the remains were dug up again by a mob, castrated, pulled to pieces and thrown to dogs (pictured above).

Marie de' Medici was confined to her apartments and Léonora was arrested and sent to the Bastille, the prelude to her trial for embezzlement of funds belonging to the royal exchequer and her eventual execution. In the near-hysterical atmosphere prevailing when du Plessis entered the Louvre, Louis, directing operations from the green beige top of a billiard table, caught sight of him and shouted, 'Now, at last, Luçon, I am free of your tyranny... be off and get yourself out of here!'[23] It took the prompt intervention of Louis's falconer, Charles d'Albert, the

Concini, shot while 'resisting arrest'.

mastermind behind the coup, to prevent the bishop losing much more than his post in the queen's household. At thirty-eight d'Albert, once Henri IV's page but soon to become duc de Luynes, and to all intents first minister, was much older than his sovereign. Tallemant would accuse Luynes of being Louis's lover and the king undoubtedly formed a strong emotional attachment to him.

Luynes outdid even Buckingham's family by achieving a near-monopoly of royal patronage despite being the son of a modest seigneur, on the bottom rung of the nobility. He engineered forty-two individual placements at court, including his two brothers, a brother-in-law and his father-in-law. To the leading noble families, Luynes and his brothers were the 'three pumpkins sprouting in the night and ruining everything', the crude vegetables that displace the choice plants in a garden.[24] The brothers had their uses. Anyone picking a fight with Luynes would find that one of his brothers, both expert duellists, would turn up in his place.[25] From different perspectives but with equal vehemence, Luynes was secretly loathed by both Anne of Austria and Marie de' Medici.

Charles Albert: delegated duels to his brothers.

Luynes, like Buckingham bisexual, made an advantageous marriage to Marie-Aimée de Rohan, the daughter of Hercule, duc de Montbazon. One of the oldest noble families in France, its lineage covered twelve centuries. Born in December 1600, Marie-Aimée was brought up by one of her father's mistresses, after her mother had died when she was two. Her life of capricious pleasure and infinite liberty produced first a tomboy then a young lady in every way the equal of Lucy Percy. As British courtiers would be able to see for themselves in 1625 when she nonchalantly discarded her clothes on the bank and swam naked to and fro across the Thames during a royal picnic, Marie possessed an hour-glass figure, high breasts, fine legs, entrancing aristocratic looks, reddish-brown hair she often dyed blonde, blue eyes, long lashes and tempting scarlet lips. She had a roguish wit, an enviable repartee, and an unquenchable taste for intrigue for intrigue's sake. A pamphleteer

Marie-Aimée de Rohan.

would later put his finger on Marie's weakness, observing that she was 'very clever at finding her way out of a labyrinth, but never does it without first of all getting herself into another'.[26]

At seventeen, Marie must have seemed the catch of a lifetime, which the rather dull Luynes achieved by good fortune and good timing. He found the duke beset with suitors and eager to get his wayward daughter off his hands to the king's favourite as soon as decently possible. Their betrothal took place on 11 September 1617 in the queen's apartments and in the presence of the king, who took little persuading to appoint the amusing young lady superintendent of Anne's household, on her eighteenth birthday, two months later. Marie charmed Louis into improved, though still chaste, relations with his wife, and the four all went riding and hunting together. On 25 February 1618, Luynes and Marie received the ultimate social accolade when Anne and Louis accepted an invitation to dine in their Louvre apartment. It was an extraordinary accomplishment for Marie because there was intense competition among noblewomen for the few available places in great households.[27]

As an intimacy sprung up between the queen and her superintendent, of similar age and with a similar sense of fun, Marie often led her charge astray. The king, disliking their haughty manners, had sent packing Anne's titled and severe Spanish ladies-in-waiting, so the queen's household consisted largely of vivacious young French women, who made her rooms ring with licentious laughter. The scandalised papal nuncio, Corsini, made representations to the queen about her entourage's behaviour but his initial plea fell on deaf ears. Louise Roger, a courtesan of noble blood in Tours frequented by her father and of whom it was said that she 'supplied the whole province with entertainment', had given Marie an inexhaustible range of tips on sexual techniques, highly salacious stories and pornographic literature that she shared with the household.[28] This included *Le Cabinet satyrique*, a banned volume of sexually explicit poetry. Even the worldly-wise duc de Montbazon thought it prudent to let the king know that encouraged by his daughter, the queen was perusing the illustrated edition of such a notorious volume.[29]

Hercule de Rohan, duc de Montbazon.

For the moment, this was as close as Anne could get to the real thing. Louis had an insurmountable psychological barrier when faced with the prospect of sex with women in general and with his wife in particular. Historian Auguste Bailly made a detailed study of the royal relationship and concludes that the king had for Anne of Austria a 'prodigious physical coldness bordering on repulsion'.[30] Louis told his Jesuit confessor, Père Jean Arnoux, a man recommended by

Luynes, the constant exhortations from his mother to perform sexually with Anne at Bordeaux had left him with *'répugnances insurmontables'*.[31]

But only for women. Tallemant reported that the king, when stimulated by men, was capable of sex. Not long before Louis began to rule nominally at least in his own right, aged sixteen, he displayed a full erection to the master of the wardrobe, who was helping him out of his bath. Tallemant suggested that the king's arousal was due to flagellation.[32] He compiled a list of those servants and courtiers with whom Louis had engaged in sexual relations, 'starting with his coachman, Saint Armour. Afterwards he showed indulgence for Haran, keeper

César de Vendôme.

of the kennels. The Grand Prior of Vendôme, the commander de Souvray, and Montpouillan-la-Force, a young man of wit and warmth... were removed by the queen mother one by one. Finally came M. De Luynes.' An anonymous pamphlet whose author was well informed as to the detail, especially of Louis's behaviour with Haran, makes it equally clear that sexual love was involved.[33] As Grand Prior César de Vendôme was the king's half brother – Henri IV's illegitimate son by his earlier mistress, Gabrielle d'Estrées – Louis was also involved in an incestuous relationship.

On 17 January 1619, the Spanish ambassador in Paris, Fernando Girón, reported to Madrid that 'The king and queen are still living as brother and sister'.[34] Renewed efforts were made to encourage in Louis an interest in heterosexual sex. On 20 January Gabrielle's daughter, Catherine-Henriette, Mademoiselle de Vendôme, married the duc d'Elbeuf, Charles II de Guise-Lorraine. Louis spent the evening with the twenty-two-year-old couple in their honeymoon chamber; he listened to their bawdy jokes and to the noise of their love-making behind the bed curtains while they had intercourse three times. However at 11 p.m. he left, not to visit the queen but to return to his own bedroom for a glass of tisane before retiring.[35]

Five days later the increasingly exasperated royal courtiers took matters into their own hands. When Louis, after a visit to Anne for the sake of appearances, left his wife's bedroom at 10 p.m. and returned to his chamber as usual to sleep alone, he was woken up an hour later by Luynes. After his efforts to persuade Louis to return voluntarily to his queen had failed amidst floods of tears, Luynes forcibly took the weeping, struggling king to her chamber. Héroard, on hand as ever, unpromisingly recorded that Louis 'compelled himself' to have sex with his wife but added a revealing footnote in Latin, *haec omnia nec inscio*, 'these are things I know nothing about'.[36] By 2 a.m. the king, his wife probably still a virgin, was safely back in his own bed.

Victor-Amadeus I of Savoy.

On 10 February an even more promising opportunity presented itself to show Louis what he was missing: his favourite sister, Christine, married Victor-Amadeus I of Savoy. The king escorted Christine to the bridal chamber and was invited inside, allowed even to poke his head through the bed curtains while the newly-weds made love, naked, on top of the sheets. At thirty-one, Duke Victor had a reputation for satisfying women. According to the Venetian ambassador, 'the act was repeated more than once, to the great applause and general pleasure of the king'. Christine, a generously proportioned thirteen-year-old who clearly did not suffer from inhibitions, then said, 'Sire, if you do the same with the Queen, then you will feel the better for it.'[37]

Christine of Savoy.

Alas, it was all to no avail. Héroard continued assiduously to record the king's irregular nocturnal visits to his wife's bedchamber even, on one occasion, volunteering from the wrong side of the door that Louis had made love *cum voluptate*, 'with conscious pleasure'.[38] Given that the doctor was well aware the evidence in his journal would be used in an attempt to persuade the Spanish that consummation had occurred, the figures he entered to indicate the frequency of sexual intercourse look highly implausible.

The court enlisted François Leclerc du Tremblay, Père Joseph, the original *éminence grise*, in an increasingly desperate attempt to convince the King of Spain that his daughter's marriage had been consummated. It proved a poor choice. In time, wearing the shabby grey cloak of a Capuchin monk, Joseph would become a menacing influence in the shadows behind the magnificent scarlet robes of Richelieu, the red eminence. For the moment, he was much less comfortable and adept in the spotlight, surreptitiously inspecting the royal marital sheets. On 14 February he enigmatically reported to Madrid that the king and queen had spent the whole night together and that 'several things show clearly the work of God'. His tentative report did not impress the King of Spain. Eight days later Philip III initialled the letter 'seen', as in 'seen but not believed'.[39]

Louis could no longer blame his failures upon his mother for putting pressure on him to consummate the marriage. On 3 May 1617, Luynes had successfully persuaded the king to send Marie de' Medici into a form of exile at Blois. As her party left Paris, du Plessis scrambled into the last seat in

François Leclerc du Tremblay, Père Joseph.

the last carriage, an indication of his lowly status. Greatly overestimating his influence with the queen mother, in June Louis tried unsuccessfully to have him removed.[40] Du Plessis jumped before he was pushed, making an abrupt departure to his priory at Coussay. Even this did not save him from an order made on 7 April 1618 'to leave the kingdom', although he softened the impact of his exile by spending it in the papal enclave of Avignon.

When du Plessis was at his most despondent, his fortunes were changed dramatically by a plan of which he knew nothing: to bring about Marie de' Medici's escape. Just before midnight on 22 February 1619, she scrambled out of an unguarded window 100 feet above the ground in the château of Blois. For her rescuers this presented a challenge akin to moving a grand piano from the attic, not helped by the stout lady's refusal to be parted, even for a second, from a heavy wooden box. Thus encumbered, Marie de' Medici descended a ladder almost sixty feet to the terrace below but faced by a second, even steeper ladder, could go no further; four men had to push, pull and slide her on a cloak down a grass embankment to the street below. At that moment some passing soldiers took the horizontal lady for a prostitute and began negotiating a price, which caused the queen mother wry amusement.[41] The little party crossed the bridge over the Loire to where a carriage supplied by the duc d'Épernon should have been waiting; but it was nowhere to be seen. After a moment's panic, they discovered it in a nearby lane and bundled the lady

Escape from Blois by Peter Paul Rubens.

inside. The carriage set off but had travelled only a few hundred yards when a loud cry caused it to come to a sudden halt. The wooden box was missing. It was discovered on the ground at the very spot where the coach had waited. Marie de' Medici had nearly lost the fortune in royal jewels she intended to use to support a rebellion by those persistent malcontents, the princes of the blood, and her younger son, the indecisive Gaston d'Orléans.

With the queen mother in open revolt, Luynes knew that he needed du Plessis to control her and recalled him from Avignon. Du Plessis opened peace talks on her behalf. But just when his life had taken a political turn for the better, it took an emotional turn for the worse. His patient negotiations led to the rehabilitation of what might be termed the du Plessis party, with his elder brother Henri, seigneur de Richelieu, appointed governor of the Medici stronghold

Marie de Medici, a mother-in-law from hell.

of Angers. This angered Antoine, marquis de Thémines, part of the queen mother's entourage at Blois, who coveted the governorship. Having failed to call out Armand-Jean du Plessis, who as a man of the cloth declined to fight, Thémines arranged for his younger brother, Charles de Lauzières, to provoke Henri du Plessis into a duel. Lauzières was a captain of the royal guard and an expert swordsman, so what took place at Angers on 8 July was little short of murder. During a seemingly casual street encounter, words then blows were exchanged. Both men drew their swords. Lauzières had the shorter blade but easily found a way past Henri's guard and left him dying in the dirt from a single thrust.[42]

Richelieu, as du Plessis now became by inheriting the family title upon his brother's death, was shattered by the news and for a while contemplated giving up politics altogether. He embraced his episcopal and religious duties with fervour, acquired several new benefices, and became a serious candidate for a cardinalate. Luynes, however, had the king's ear and blocked his advancement. The military campaign to reduce the Huguenot strongholds kept Luynes and Louis close together in the field.

While her husband Luynes was away, Marie-Aimée de Rohan gave birth to a son, Louis-Charles d'Albert, on the morning of Christmas Day, 1620, after Anne had sat all night with Marie at the Louvre and held her hand during a difficult

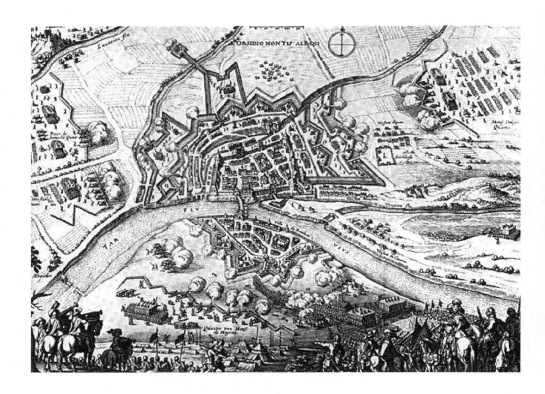

labour. Marie had begun to take lovers and Luynes was probably not the father. To discourage such goings-on, Louis, prompted by Luynes, ordered the queen's household, including of course Marie herself, to join them at the siege (above) of the Protestant fortress of Montauban that began in August 1621. Even then, they were kept apart, as king and minister took up residence in the small and draughty château of Piquecos, sending the queen and her suite to stay in the

nearby town of Moissac. From here they were expected to make regular visits to Piquecos, arriving in the morning and leaving before dark. One day they stayed much later than planned but the king sent word that they could not spend the night, as there were no beds available. Marie-Aimée shouted out, 'Surely the king has a bed', provoking a spontaneous outpouring of laughter from those who knew that her husband usually occupied it.[43]

The small and draughty Piquecos château.

Louis was not amused by Marie's frivolous reference to his sexuality and soon had an opportunity to retaliate. His army was decimated by purple fever, forcing him to lift the siege in November, but not before Luynes himself contracted the disease that had proved almost fatal to Hay on his diplomatic mission a few months previously. On 15 December, after a fever of only three days, Luynes died at the château of Longuetille near Monheurt, beside the Garonne. His last act was to plead, he believed successfully, with the king to look after his family. But Louis had always viewed his favourite's self-aggrandisement with concern – 'Here goes King Luynes!' he was sometimes heard to mutter when his interminable train of followers passed beneath his windows at the Louvre – and did not keep his promise. He removed Luynes's two brothers from office almost immediately and began to look for an excuse to dismiss Marie from the queen's service. The Papal Nuncio, seeing the way the wind was blowing, went so far as to include Marie in a message to the queen's confessor naming those members of Anne's household whom he considered to have exceeded 'all the limits of decency and respect'.[44]

It had certainly become a hot-bed of affairs. Marie's sister-in-law, the princesse de Guémenée, was living with Bassompierre, then colonel-général of Louis's Swiss Guard, while her step-mother, Madame de Montbazon, who was de Guémenée's mother-in-law, had a succession of young lovers. Another member of the household, the princesse di Conti, the sister of the duc de Chevreuse, Claude de Lorraine (right), was seen as equally promiscuous. She acted as the go-between, encouraging a relationship between Claude and Marie

and allowing them to meet secretly in her rooms. After Luynes's death, says Marie's biographer Louis Battifol, 'the two lovers exhibited their passion shamelessly. They were constantly seen together in public. The whole Court rang with it'.[45]

At forty-four, Claude de Lorraine had a string of mistresses behind him, a countess here, a marquise there. He was a deadly swordsman, so few husbands dared to call him out; one who did, Antoine de Saint-Lary, duc de Bellegarde, received a near-fatal sword thrust in a duel that took place in the lengthening shadows of the evening, in the rue de la Cerisaie, a secluded street in the Marais district of Paris. During an era when the latest duel became the principal topic of conversation at every breakfast and dinner table, it was the measure of a man. The British ambassador in Paris, Lord Herbert, overheard one young fellow asking for a girl's hand only to be told by the father he must first fight at least a couple of duels. Herbert added that there was 'scarce a Frenchman worth looking on who had not killed his man in a duel'.[46] The ambassador practised what he preached. In 1621 he even challenged Luynes on some pretext and was recalled to London in disgrace for nearly a year. Claude de Lorraine's skill with a blade got Marie into bed and then, almost inevitably, pregnant. France had advanced slightly further than England in the production of contraceptive sheaths made of sheep's gut; but they lacked sensitivity and were scorned by the upper classes. As the century's great letter writer, Marie de Rabutin-Chantal, Madame de Sévigné, later observed to her daughter, they were both 'gossamer against infection and armour against satisfaction'.[47]

With her husband dead, and a child by another man in her womb, Marie already faced disgrace. Louis at first refused to allow her to have her latest child in the Louvre, a privilege reserved for the princesses of the blood. When he relented, Marie was banished to the dingiest of rooms in the attic, where she gave birth to a girl.[48] That was problem enough, but soon events took a turn for the worst. The queen was also pregnant, and perhaps not for the first time. Encouraged by Marie to have affairs of her own, she had been seen in the company of handsome male servants from French Guiana, Saint Kitts and Senegal, still a novelty at court. One story of questionable substance had her giving birth to a baby 'with the colour and visage of a blackamoor', who allegedly died within a month.[49]

By contrast her conception in the winter of 1621/2 was an undeniable fact. It is far from certain, however, that Louis knew of her condition, even less likely that he had performed the act that brought it about. On 29 January 1622 Héroard recorded the pregnancy in his notebook. But none of the court envoys, not even that great harbinger of rumour that so often turned into fact, the Venetian ambassador, seems to have reported the event 'awaited by all Christendom'.[50] To complicate matters further, one of the princes of the blood, Henri II de Bourbon, Prince de Condé, was among the most plausible candidates to be the father. He was identified by historian Anthony Levi, whose renewed enquiries were prompted by research for his biography of Louis XIV and his growing conviction that 'someone other than Louis XIII must be responsible'.[51]

On 14 March Henri's wife, the princesse de Condé, held a glittering musical soirée in her rooms at the Louvre. Those present included the queen, Marie de Chevreuse and another of those named and shamed by the papal nuncio, Henriette de Verneuil, the mother of one of the late King Henri IV's bastard sons. Shortly after midnight the merry trio made their way back to Anne's apartments through the great hall on the first floor, used for banquets and royal audiences.[52] With Anne between them, Marie held one arm, Henriette the other, and the three women ran the full length of the hall until they reached the steps to the throne, where the queen stumbled and fell. She felt a sharp pain, was put to bed, and on 16 March had a miscarriage. Héroard noted without embellishment in his journal that at 3 p.m. the queen gave birth to an embryo of forty to forty-two days gestation. Levi observes that Anne had been, at best, 'preposterously negligent', encouraging speculation that it might not have been an accident and that she was happy to get rid of the child if she could.[53]

Louis was not told, his courtiers perhaps unable to resolve the dilemma of informing him about a failed pregnancy when he had been previously unaware that the queen was pregnant. On 20 March, Palm Sunday, the king departed for Orléans, leaving Anne behind in Paris, her indisposition attributed to some minor ailment. News quickly spread of what had really happened and several ambassadors arrived at the Louvre to express their condolences to the queen. Still the king was not informed. Finally, on 25 March, a courtier plucked up the courage to tell him. Louis flew into a violent rage and dispatched a messenger to Paris carrying letters for Anne, Marie and Madame de Verneuil. The note to his wife included not a word of affection, grief or sympathy, just the information that he had decided on a change 'to keep good order in your household'. For Marie came the blunt news that she would not only lose the post of superintendent but also must leave the Louvre altogether.

Although trumping a king was a risky gambit, Marie held a very powerful card. The duc de Chevreuse, Claude de Lorraine, besotted by his mistress, was quickly persuaded while in the throes of sexual congress to marry her. Fearing Claude might be put under pressure afterwards to change his mind, Marie persuaded him to allow her to write to Louis immediately to seek his approval of the marriage, which was expected of a duke; and when the king dithered and failed to object, went ahead regardless. In a quiet ceremony at the Louvre on 20 April 1622, Marie became a duchess and a member of one of the most powerful families in the land. Louis had gambled that the duke's relations would refuse to sign the marriage contract but he was mistaken. Sixteen of them did sign, the most important, the duc de Guise, Claude's uncle, giving a clear lead to the remainder: two dukes, two princesses and five duchesses among them. For three months Marie went on a memorable tour of her new domains, greeted like royalty by the inhabitants, before returning to Paris and the queen's household.

Louis, by now reunited with his mother, was furious. Although he never withdrew the order for Marie to leave court, he could never enforce it. Claude was too powerful – his apartment at the Louvre was immediately above that of the king himself – and Louis could not afford to offend the House of Guise.

On 17 May Michel de Marillac, keeper of the seals and a creature of the queen mother, Marie de' Medici, wrote to a trusted confidant to say that the king 'had conceived a great hatred' against the duc and duchesse de Chevreuse. And of the queen, he added ominously, *'Le roi n'est pas content de la reine'.*[54]

Michel de Marillac.

Marillac's confidant was Richelieu, who soon realised that his prospects of a cardinalate would be greatly strengthened in Rome if he could present himself as the successful peace broker between the king and the queen mother, rather than as a member of Marie de' Medici's party, where he was superintendent of finances and her chaplain. The death of Luynes removed the last obstacle. On 5 September 1622 Pope Gregory XV announced Richelieu's appointment as cardinal. In December he received the coveted red hat at Lyon from the king, in the presence of the queen and the queen mother; and with the touch of a consummate politician, immediately laid it at the feet of Marie de' Medici.

His elevation to cardinal encouraged gossip-writers and pamphleteers to try to undermine Richelieu's growing influence in government. In particular, they accused him of sleeping with the queen mother but his only proven intimacy with Marie de' Medici was to join her in taking lessons from the distinguished music teacher, Ennemond Gaultier, in playing the lute.[55]

Richelieu could be both charming and circumspect, making the evidence of his sexual conquests purely circumstantial. One rumour that persisted

Rubens's picture of the reconciliation of Louis XIII with his mother hints at an incestuous relationship.

throughout the rest of his life, started by his brother-in-law Urbain de Maillé, marquis de Brézé, was that Richelieu himself had sired the four children of his niece and superintendent of his household, Marie-Madeleine de Vignerod, Madame de Combalet.[56] The queen, asked for her opinion, produced an exquisitely malicious response: 'We can never believe more than half of what Brézé says.'

However, the enigmatic relationship between Anne of Austria and the cardinal always promised to be more than that of queen and minister. Erlanger, in writing the most extensive biography of Richelieu, suggests that the cardinal secretly desired Anne.[57] There were several plausible witnesses to the notable occasion when Richelieu risked ridicule by dancing for her in private the Saraband, described by the German musicologist Kurt Sachs as 'a sexual pantomime of unparalleled suggestiveness'.[58] Told by the mischievous Marie, who would prove a thorn in the cardinal's side as the duchesse de Chevreuse, that this would show him willing to do anything to win her affections, Richelieu dressed comprehensively for the part. He arrived wearing green pantaloons, silver bells on his garters, and castanets on his hands, and performed the Saraband to music on the mandore, a forerunner of the mandolin, played by the distinguished court musician, Boccan. The cardinal was unaware that hidden behind a screen sat several of Anne's confidants, including Marie, Béringhem and Henry-Auguste de Loménie, comte de Brienne, each shaking in silent hysterics. Years afterwards, Brienne could not prevent himself from bursting into laughter at the very thought of it.[59]

If Richelieu made any tangible progress in his suit, it would come much later, when Anne was in fear of her life. For the moment, encouraged by Marie, Anne showed only contempt for the cardinal and could always be relied upon to produce an injudicious *bon mot*. Richelieu already suffered from haemorrhoids, and often had to travel in a horizontal position. A bungled operation to remove them, no light undertaking in this medically ignorant age, had resulted in a near fatal abscess. Yet Anne persisted in calling him *'cul pourri'*, 'rotten arse', in her private, but often read and intercepted, correspondence at court. Hostilities had been declared and Anne was about to give Richelieu a golden opportunity to retaliate. It was nearly time for the arrival in Paris, all amorous guns blazing, of the Duke of Buckingham.

7: DANGEROUS LIAISONS

Buckingham had plenty of time on his hands in Spain to reflect on the yawning gap between himself and Olivares in the acquisition and exercise of power. Whereas the duke had enjoyed the rewards of favour, treated by James I the way a man in this bygone age ordinarily might treat a beautiful wife, in political terms he was still subordinate to the prejudices of the king, who determined policy and expected his ministers to abide by it.

James kept Buckingham on as tight a rein as a flow of messengers between London and Madrid would permit: 'they go up and down like a well with two buckets' was Chamberlain's sardonic observation.[1] In contrast Olivares, although also a *privado* or favourite, was given real *privanza*, political supremacy. King Philip IV delegated all the powers relating to decision-making to him and he became the country's real ruler. Recognising this, Buckingham returned to England determined to wrest control of the machinery of government from James and become in the modern sense his first minister.

His rekindled ambition was assisted by James's physical decline. In November 1623 the king fell ill and became almost crippled with gout. He was in constant

James I in decline.

pain and Buckingham spent long hours by his side; but as nurse, rather than lover. A month or so later, when James was evidently feeling better, he wrote to the duke 'praying God... that we may make at this Christmas a new marriage ever to be kept hereafter', in other words suggesting a resumption of sexual relations. The letter ends 'God bless you.... and grant that ye may ever be a comfort to your dear dad and husband'. James had originally ended with 'master' but then evidently had second thoughts: the pendulum was swinging in favour of the prince and the favourite.[2] They had forged a bond of friendship, which his biographer Lockyer describes as 'not only unbreakable but even unshakeable'.[3] This was reinforced by sexual intimacy, not flouted, as James

Duke of Buckingham, 1624.

Queen of France, Anne of Austria.

did with Buckingham by caressing him in public, but more than enough to satisfy 'Charles's libidinal drives'.[4] Under the protection of anonymity, commentators put it bluntly, stating that Charles 'was known to have committed all manner of lewdness with his confidant the duke'.[5] It assured Buckingham of continued favour into the next reign. As the rehabilitated diplomat, Sir Henry Wotton, observed, 'by so long and so private... consociation with a prince... he had now gotten two lives in his own fortune and greatness'.[6]

The duke's transformation from playboy to statesman was at its most obvious on 29 February 1624, when Buckingham gave a compelling analysis

from his perspective of British foreign policy and the perfidy of the Spanish to a joint session of Lords and Commons, crammed on to wooden scaffolding erected specially for the occasion inside the Banqueting House at Whitehall.[7] Only a handful among the audience were aware, however, that a few days earlier the duke had opened negotiations for a marriage treaty with France, by sending his close friend and subordinate, Sir Robert Rich (pictured left), to Paris.

Within a few hours of his arrival, on Sunday 25 February, Rich was granted an audience with Louis XIII and invited that very night to attend a ballet at the Louvre arranged by the Queen of France, in which both she and the king's unmarried sister, Henrietta Maria, took part. Although Henrietta for Rich was a 'lovely, sweet, young Creature', the queen was charming to him and made a much greater impact. He wrote to Buckingham, 'She is so very *French*', with scant regard for her Spanish upbringing but wetting the duke's appetite.[8]

Rich, created first Baron Kensington at Buckingham's instigation a year earlier, would shortly be elevated to the new earldom of Holland, although the 'Holland' in question was in Lincolnshire, not the Dutch United Provinces. Holland, as he would become known, had extremely good connections. He was the second son by the Earl of Warwick of Lucy Percy's aunt, the infamous Penelope Devereux, and accordingly was Lucy's first cousin. Anne of Austria's confidential manservant, Pierre La Porte, described him as 'one of the most handsome men in the world' but nonetheless thought him 'effeminate'. Holland, however, was resolutely heterosexual and had delayed his opportunity for preferment under James for many years 'by turning aside and spitting after the king had slabbered his mouth'.[9] Aged thirty-four, he had 'a lovely and a winning presence and gentle conversation'.[10] Holland was at his most attractive to women and, it would prove, to one woman in particular.

Marie de Chevreuse.

The hôtel de Chevreuse, set in a quiet quarter between the Louvre and the Tuileries, close to rue Saint Honoré, had been renovated almost regardless of expense by the royal architect Clément Métézeau. Its grand entrance, embellished by pillars, pilasters and statues, opened into a series of imposing drawing rooms; a sweeping staircase led to the principal bedrooms. Unbeknown to the duc de Chevreuse, often away on business, his wife Marie de Chevreuse

was soon regularly entertaining Holland upstairs under the covers. It was during some post-coital conversation, despite Holland's extremely poor command of French, that these ardent lovers became inspired to bring together their master and mistress.[11] As one of Anne's loyal supporters disingenuously later put it: 'To do honour to their own passion, they planned an adventure of interest and gallantry between the Queen and the Duke of Buckingham'.[12]

Anne, made aware of Marie's liaison with Holland, invited the couple privately to her apartments in the Louvre, where they cleverly turned the conversation to the considerable attributes of the duke: 'brilliant, supple, with a fascinating glance, smiling sensual lips, gentle, coaxing, haughty, passionate, violent, all at once, Buckingham's personality might well have disturbed the most placid imagination'.[13] Anne was drawn surreptitiously upon a dangerous path of what remained, for the time being, suppressed emotions: Buckingham, although present only in the form of a miniature portrait (page 165) that Holland brought with him, had stirred the heart of the Queen of France.

Back in England the great man himself was under enormous strain, managing Parliament and the king, reorganising the navy, and planning a military expedition to recover the Palatinate. In April he fell ill. His physicians reported that he had a yellow skin and was discharging yellow urine and yellow bile; he complained of weakness, so they bled him, making him weaker than ever. Buckingham did not fully recover until the end of July. Much to his wife's satisfaction, Lucy saw very little of him, for she, too, looked thin and ill and was under the solicitous care of Hay's friend, the wealthy Earl of Norwich and ambassador to France, Sir George Goring.[14]

The duke's distractions multiplied in a way that, given his reputation, Lucy would have seen as ironic. The estranged wife of his full brother John, Viscount Purbeck, who had accompanied him to France in 1609, was Frances Coke, daughter of the jurist Sir Edward Coke. Frances, forced into marriage at seventeen, now lived apart from her mentally unstable husband at Denmark House; her lover, Robert Howard, a younger son of the Earl of Suffolk, was often seen climbing over the rooftops to her rooms.[15] When Frances gave birth to a boy in secret Buckingham still had no son of his own, so despite his dubious parentage, her child automatically became heir to the duke's fortune and titles.[16] Frances and Robert admitted intimacy but denied intercourse. Buckingham pursued Frances through the Court of High Commission, which merely sentenced her to do penance in a white sheet at the Savoy church in London. She escaped this penalty by flight, but it hung over her for many years.[17]

Meanwhile in France, Holland, who clearly had a flair for romance, succeeded in exciting princess Henrietta Maria at the prospect of a marriage to Charles.[18] But the nuances of a complex political treaty were beyond Holland, so Hay, the fluent French speaker, was once again dispatched to Paris to join him. Apparently still oblivious to what was going on in his own household, the duc de Chevreuse organised a lavish reception for Hay and Holland, attended by 200 of the nobility and by Henrietta, who was flattered when both honoured guests bowed low enough to kiss the hem of her skirt.[19] It would be Hay's first and last flamboyant gesture. Faced with demands that were almost identical to those sought by Spain a year earlier, and remembering that he had been given the run around once before by the French, Hay was determined 'not be humiliated by these people' again.[20]

In June he engineered the recall from England of Tillières, who no longer supported the marriage alliance, the first of several diplomatic manoeuvres designed to throw the opposing negotiators off balance. Summoned to a meeting, Hay and Holland sent a message that they were still sleeping. As soon as they got up, they asked for an immediate audience with Louis. When this was refused, they said they must take further instructions. Then they declared that the terms of the treaty were impossible and they were going back to the Spanish.[21] As Hay patiently explained to King James, well enough again to take a close interest, the only way to negotiate successfully was to defend the critical points tenaciously but reliquish the rest to allow France to save face.[22] It seemed he had got his way when Charles, marquis de La Vieuville, the French first minister, agreed that a private assurance from James to improve the lot of his

The shop-soiled Prince of Wales.

Catholic subjects would suffice. But on 7 August, after Hay and Holland asked Louis to endorse the terms that Vieuville claimed already had his approval, the king said ominously that his minister had lied, on this and other matters besides.[23] Six days later Vieuville was arrested and from then on the council of state was dominated by Richelieu, although it would be five years before Louis began to address him as the *'principal ministre'* he had effectively become.

The cardinal understood that the security of France depended upon pushing back its boundaries, largely at the expense of the Hapsburgs, in Artois, Flanders, Alsace, Lorraine, Franche-Comte, Savoy, Nice and Roussillon; on every point of the compass from north-north-west to south-south-east. For this France needed allies and England, as Spain's traditional enemy, was the obvious choice. That Richelieu succeeded in securing the marriage treaty, his first diplomatic success, without significant concessions, owed much to his negotiating skills; but even more to the anxieties of the shop-soiled Prince of Wales, fast running out of eligible princesses. He wrote to Hay in October and gloomily predicted that if the treaty

The army of thieves and vagabonds sent to recover the Palatinate was
unwanted at home.

fell through, 'then Spain will laugh at us both'.[24] The final terms – toleration for
recusant Catholics, the children of the marriage educated in the faith until they
were thirteen, a huge, evangelizing French household in London for Henrietta
– amounted to almost a complete surrender on the critical points.

France also refused to allow safe passage for a British mercenary army
to recover the Palatinate, and in the spring this poorly led and provisioned
force melted away in Germany with the snow. Only its composition, largely of

thieves and vagabonds, whose home towns were delighted when they failed to return, avoided this debacle becoming a serious political embarrassment. Of 12,000 who set out, by 17 June only 600 were left, and they were keeping starvation at bay by eating stray horses and cats.[25]

Buckingham remained optimistic that France might still be induced to participate fully in an anti-Hapsburg League and, perhaps deliberately, remained ignorant of the minutiae of the marriage treaty. Accordingly when Hay and Holland proposed that the duke should travel to Paris to collect Charles's bride, Tillières, for ever briefing against Buckingham, pointed out to the *conseil d'état* that this 'hot and haughty' character 'would fly into a passion' over some of the clauses in the contract.[26] Richelieu agreed but thought 'disobliging' Britain's most powerful minister would be a diplomatic blunder. Louis, perhaps with some sixth sense that nothing good would come of the visit, objected weakly. Marie de' Medici, her heart set on a good marriage for her daughter, was strongly in favour and got her way.

In mid-March 1625 Buckingham sent coaches laden with his baggage towards Dover and was on the point of following them when he received news that the king had fallen gravely ill. Already crippled with arthritis throughout Christmas, with Buckingham at his bedside, James suffered a severe, intermittent fever, which turned into convulsions, terrible dysentery and finally a fatal stroke on 27 March. Charles took the grief-stricken duke with him to London in his own carriage and ordered lodgings prepared for him at St James's, next to his own apartment. The following day he gave Buckingham the golden keys which supposedly unlocked every door in every palace, an indication that the duke's influence was as strong as ever.[27]

On 1 May, with James still unburied, in the French capital Hay and Holland went by coach to collect the duc de

The proxy marriage of Charles and Henrietta Maria.

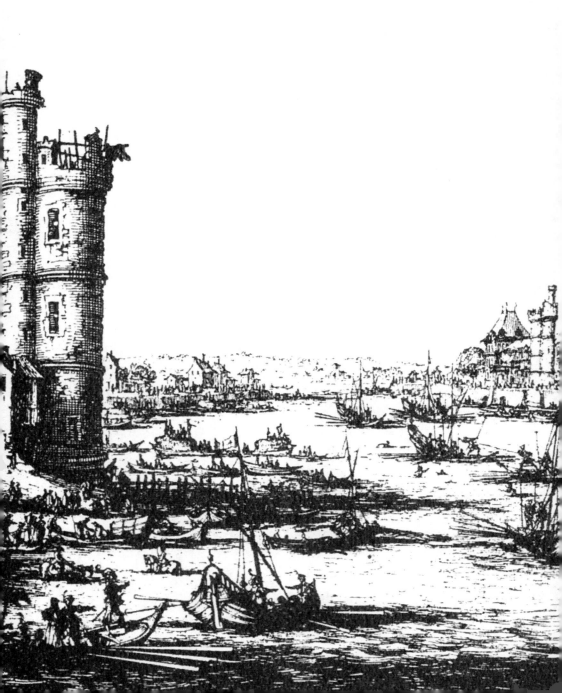

Boats of all shapes and sizes cluster on the Seine between the ruined tour de Nesle and the Louvre for a glimpse of the Duke of Buckingham.

Chevreuse, who was to stand in proxy at Notre Dame for Henrietta Maria's marriage to the new king, Charles I. In the procession, just behind Louis, Marie de' Medici, Anne of Austria and sundry princesses, came Marie de Chevreuse, flanked by two courtiers, her long gown supported by an equerry. She had just written Anne an indiscreet note, urging the queen to accept Buckingham as a lover.[28]

The object of Anne's imminent affections set out for France on 12 May in calm seas, reached Boulogne in four hours and rode *post* to Paris. Much of his entourage had gone on ahead and the *Mercure de France* reported that Buckingham travelled 'with more pomp and glitter than if he had been king'. He was accompanied by twelve other nobles, twenty gentlemen, seven grooms of the bedchamber, thirty chief yeomen, twenty-seven cooks and twenty-four outriders, one to each horse, three teams of eight for three coaches lined with padded velvet edged in gold lace. A personal barge took him on the Seine through the city centre, rowed by twenty-two watermen decked out 'in sky-coloured taffaty'.[29] Taking into account 'eight score musicians richly suited', and copious pages and footmen, his train consisted of almost 700 persons. Buckingham arrived on the evening of 14 May, to be lodged sumptuously at – where else – the hôtel de Chevreuse, said to have the finest furnishings in all France. Here his hair was prepared by his host's personal barber, with such skill and finesse that Buckingham tipped him £100 so he could take one of his assistants back to England.[30]

The meeting that every titled lady was waiting for, between Buckingham and the queen, took place in her packed apartments on the second day of his visit. Holland had described Anne to him in such a glowing manner that it made the duke eager to see her again in the flesh.[31] What Holland wrote was undoubtedly an exaggeration, for more objective observers concluded that the queen's nose was long and thick, her green eyes were too big for her head and her complexion had touches of acne.[32] But Marie had showed Anne how to make the most of her assets: flowing chestnut hair that curled at the ends in a tantalising way, large breasts and white slender hands. The queen took hours to prepare, spurred on by a letter from

Anne's apartments, the scene of her first meeting with Buckingham.

172

her sister in Spain describing Buckingham's 'supernatural beauty'.[33] Maria, supremely indifferent towards Charles, evidently had lusted after the duke in secret from the moment she saw him.

Among Anne's ladies, talk was of what James I always referred to as the 'codpiece point', whether Buckingham's beauty extended to his most intimate parts. Apparently Marie's sister-in-law, the princesse di Conti, who shared his carriage on formal occasions and would have liked to have shared his bed, was thought to have first-hand information. In this age men often casually exposed their penises when ladies were present, not least because plumbing was non-existent, even in the royal palaces. Nobles thought nothing of relieving themselves 'on the balconies, and staircases, and behind the doors'. Status was no barrier whatsoever to such behaviour. When Anne's chevalier d'honneur, Charles, comte de Brancas, marquis de Maupec and d'Apilli, was escorting

Louvre quarter circa 1620.

his mistress to a dance at Saint-Germain, he did so hand in hand, as etiquette required.[34] Finding his bladder disagreeably full, he undid the large button that fastened the front flap of his culottes, known as *'la braye'*, and urinated over a set of drawn curtains, before taking the queen's hand again as if nothing untoward had happened. The incident was reported only because Anne later remarked to her confidants upon the generous proportions of the comte's penis and the prodigious distance he achieved. Such coarse habits died hard; more than a generation later, the author of a manual of manners, Antoine de Courtin, still felt it necessary admonish courtiers for exposing themselves in mixed company.[35]

The scene at the Louvre had a touch of the Montagues and the Capulets in Shakespeare's Verona as Buckingham arrived, surrounded by effortlessly arrogant Englishmen, and bowed to Queen Anne, surrounded by her French household, all aristocratic elegance. Juliet had finally met her Romeo. 'The duke,' said Tillières, scarcely renowned for his romantic

Louvre façade.

173

Louvre quai.

instincts, 'was seen by the queen regnant with great joy, which was not only written on her face, but went straight to her heart. From this very first day, the freedom between them was as great as if they had known each other for a long time.' For the moment it was all perfectly innocuous but, added Tillières with almost infinite understatement, 'its appearance was anything but that'.[36]

La Porte, the queen's aide, observed at first hand what he had heard previously only by repute, the magnetic effect that Buckingham had on everyone who saw him. He was 'the best built and best looking man in the world' who filled 'the ladies with delight and something more (La Porte meant lust of course), the gallants with jealousy, and the husbands with something worse'.[37] Among their number from a distance was Louis, increasingly perturbed by reports of a growing relationship that for all his royal power he must have felt helpless to prevent.

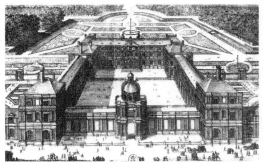

Luxembourg Palace.

It was given an unexpected impetus by the great painter, Peter Paul Rubens, who had been working feverishly in Paris since February to complete the last fifteen canvases of a ludicrously hyperbolic cycle on the life of Marie de' Medici.[38] On 11 May they went on display, with due ceremony, in a gallery in the west wing of the Luxemburg Palace, leaving Rubens to concentrate on other commissions. These included a portrait of Anne of Austria that was nearing completion but because the artist was unable to walk – a shoemaker had badly wrenched his foot while attempting to force it into a new boot – the queen had to attend the final sittings at his temporary studio.[39] Located in an inaccessible attic with excellent light, a long way from the royal quarters overlooking the rear gardens, this would

Peter Paul Rubens.

Louis had no idea how to deal with the increasingly public relationship between his wife and the Duke of Buckingham.

Anne of Austria by Rubens, with reputedly Buckingham's bust circled.

have provided a perfect opportunity for the prospective lovers to meet in private, because Buckingham wanted Rubens to paint him and was prepared to pay £500 if he began immediately. According to Louis Hourticq, a formidable art historian and member of the renowned French Académie des Beaux-Arts, the duke also persuaded Rubens to make significant changes to the queen's portrait. In the background he added an arched doorway opening on to a distant view and decorated by the bust of a man wearing the crown of Love whom,

176

says Hourticq, is none other than Buckingham himself. At the same time Rubens removed from the picture the queen's wedding ring. Hourticq adds that the duke then gave the picture to Anne, who surely must have been party to the little conspiracy, leaving Rubens and his acolytes to make several copies.[40] One, without the changes, probably went to Louis XIII, leaving him none the wiser.[41] Another, identical to the gift, went to the duke, who back in England draped it in cloth of gold embellished by two burning candles of white wax in golden candlesticks, as though worshipping at an altar.[42]

Rubens's preliminary sketch of Buckingham.

In painting Buckingham himself, relying primarily on an initial sketch of his features in black and white chalks, Rubens captured for posterity the duke's new, exquisite Parisian curls and immaculately trimmed beard. Depicted on horseback in martial glory, a trifle premature perhaps for a man yet to command any military force in the field, Buckingham exudes wealth and power. Gold appears everywhere: the shining black armour edged in gold, the saddle embroidered with golden thread, the golden spurs, and the golden sword on its golden hangers. With the exception of the billowing black cloak and blue sash, the costume existed only in Rubens's imagination but if anything, Buckingham's real wardrobe of twenty-seven outfits surpassed it. One suit of purple satin was 'embroidered all over with rich oriental pearls'; another of 'white satin uncut velvet' was 'spangled with diamonds' that broke off his shoulders as the duke strode through the corridors of the Louvre and left onlookers scrambling for valuable souvenirs on the marble floors. He also sported a hunting cap that resembled Sherlock Holmes's deerstalker. It became the height of fashion and because the visitor of the moment was known as the duc de Bouquinham, his hat became naturalised as *un boukinkan*.[43]

Buckingham had entranced the queen and dazzled Paris; but he would need more than charisma to get the better of Richelieu. After resting in his house at Limours, where he had been in poor health, the cardinal returned to the capital for a long meeting with the duke. Unexpectedly, both men kept their temper, helped, perhaps, by the delay whenever Hay had to translate. Buckingham spoke French fluently, so this was probably a device to give him time to formulate his

The finished martial portrait of Buckingham, by Rubens.

replies. The duke feared that he might be set a trap or two by the wily cardinal but need not have worried. Richelieu was new to government and surprisingly ill-at-ease. According to Erlanger, his biographer, the cardinal envied Buckingham's self-assurance and all-powerful splendour, and his ability to seduce the queen, whom Richelieu also wanted but who seemed impervious to his advances.[44]

When small talk gave way to serious negotiations the meeting proved unproductive. Richelieu wanted peace with the Hapsburgs in order to deal with the Huguenot threat, 'the state within a state', as he described the French Protestants. Militant Huguenots based at the port of La Rochelle had seized the Île de Ré, the strategically important island that dominated sea routes to the city. Buckingham already knew from Hay and Holland that the French army, bivouacked on their eastern border and ideally positioned to help British interests in the Palatinate, instead was destined for La Rochelle.[45]

*Paris celebrations in 1612 of the betrothal of Louis and Anne, recalled by
Buckingham as an excuse to show the queen hands-on English dancing.*

The duke made much more progress with the queen. An anonymous
correspondent of society's chief source of information, the *Mercure de France*,
adroitly described the purpose of his visit as to 'speed up the departure' of
Henrietta Maria when prominent Parisians already suspected that he had an
entirely different queen on his mind. Louis XIII remained by and large a sulky
absentee, so Buckingham found himself sitting beside Anne at a series of grand

dinners, 'none equalled' by that in the Luxemburg hosted by the cardinal. This could scarcely have been an accident; a case, perhaps, of Richelieu giving the couple enough rope to see if they hanged themselves. According to the *Mercure de France*, 'the air was filled with the 'noise of cannon shot and pistols' and in the morning with gossip about the banquet.[46] But this was nothing to what occurred the next afternoon when at the Louvre Buckingham told the queen how, back in April 1612, as a young man he had danced in the place Royale during a festival to celebrate Anne's betrothal to the French king.[47] Marie de Chevreuse was within earshot and asked whether he had danced in the English or the French style. Told it had been the English, with feigned innocence she arranged for the duke to give a demonstration. Before long, with the queen as his impromptu partner, and courtiers looking on in amazement, Buckingham went through his brilliant repertoire of English country dances.[48] Unlike their French equivalent, they were designed to facilitate rather than frustrate close bodily contact, breast against breast, hands entwined or around the waist, sometimes accidentally straying lower. The court had never seen anything like it.

Duke and queen sat together again at a concert in the hôtel de Rambouillet in the rue St Thomas de Louvre, next door to the hôtel de Chevreuse. The principal performer was Angélique de Paulet, the most famous singer of the time, and the mistress of the duc de Chevreuse.[49] Marie was not the least put out by her husband's infidelity; her marriage was increasingly one of mutual convenience and anyone who was anyone in Paris took a lover. The queen, sensuous, lazy and indolent, with few ideas of her own, was about to sail in Marie's licentious wake.

The duchesse de Chevreuse, the arch go-between, rose to the challenge of arranging a discreet rendezvous for the would-be intimates. She disclosed its location, and what happened there, to Paul de Gondi, the future Cardinal de Retz, the bandy-legged, short-sighted nephew of the archbishop of Paris. Some historians have challenged the reliability of Retz's memoirs as a source, pointing to the fact that later he fell out with both Marie and Anne of Austria. He was on the opposite side to the queen during the Fronde, a French civil war; and when discarded as a bedmate by Marie de Chevreuse, noted that she burned her old skirts and would have liked to eliminate her old lovers in the same way when she grew tired of them.[50]

But Retz's raison d'être was always self-deprecating humour rather than calculating malice. His vision of life was a game, an entertainment, 'one huge

Paul de Gondi, later Cardinal de Retz.

practical joke'.[51] He never saw his memoirs as such and made no attempt to publish them in his lifetime. He valued the approval of his niece, Madame de Sévigné, and much of what he wrote was an attempt to justify his notoriously bad behaviour during his youth.[52] Retz's underlying defence was the discrepancy between codes and ideals and the reckless behaviour displayed by men and women 'in excitement'. As such, the dangerous liaison between Anne of Austria and the Duke of Buckingham, reported to him with highly plausible detail by Marie de Chevreuse, must have seemed the perfect example: discovery *in flagrante* would have meant death for them both.

The French historian Louis Battifol doubts the truth of his account because according to Retz, as Battifol interprets it, Marie arranged for the pair to meet in the little walled garden of the Louvre, later known as the Jardin de l'Infante. 'Had they desired to meet unseen,' he argues, 'the very last [place] would have been a corner overlooked by more than sixty of the palace windows'.[53] However, Levi examined some of the original untidy manuscripts left by Retz, and concludes that *'petit'*, 'little', could just as easily be read as

Back streets near lovers' rendevous.

'physik', a word of German origin but in wider use, meaning the royal garden of medicinal plants close to the lodgings Buckingham took during his first period in Paris. As such it was free from prying eyes, easy for the duke to find, and not an impossible distance from the Louvre.[54]

Marie kept watch a discreet distance away. According to her account, afterwards Anne came to see her in a state of 'feverish excitement' and the following morning sent the duchess 'to ask Buckingham if he was quite certain she was not in danger of becoming pregnant'.[55] As Marie's extensive experience of such matters had not enabled her to reassure the queen herself, there is only one plausible explanation for such concern. The succession of petticoats on top of a chemise worn in both England and France offered no serious obstacle to male advances, especially if the female partner was willing, so Buckingham would not have needed long. The indication was that he had intended to practise *coitus interruptus* with the queen, and she feared the duke had got carried away in the heat of the moment, with potentially disastrous consequences. Some historians give credence to a persistent rumour that Anne became pregnant and had a miscarriage, possibly self-induced, in the winter of 1625-6.[56] Among those to point out that the duke did not practise what he preached was his sister-

in-law, the wanton Lady Purbeck, who fled to France and frustrated every effort to bring her back.

Buckingham, in every sense, had gone too far with Anne. The 'familiarities between the Duke and the Queen Regnant and her affection for him increased by the day', according to Tillières, 'which enraged both the King her husband and the Queen her mother-in-law'.[57] They dispatched a member of their inner circle, Henry-Auguste de Loménie, comte de Brienne (pictured), to confront Buckingham. Brienne, a master of 'diplomacy and intrigue', appointed a secretary of state ten years previously when he was aged 20 in 1615, was 'in constant and often intimate contact with the highest affairs and some of the deepest secrets of the realm'.[58]

Brienne tried to play the patriotic card. According to his memoirs, and acknowledging that some high-born women found it impossible to resist amorous advances, he suggested to Buckingham they ought to be *'courtisées'* by a 'cavalier' who lived at court, not seduced by a stranger passing through. Brienne may have been fortunate that despite his fluency in French, Buckingham probably did not quite grasp the full implications of the actual words used by the count, who described him as a 'passe-volant', the name for the worst dregs of soldier passed between one captain and another to keep up their numbers during inspections.[59] In any event, Buckingham took no notice of Brienne, and soon after their unproductive meeting Henrietta Maria's departure for England was brought forward in the hope that the affair would die a natural death.

Although many of the roads were flooded because of the spring thaw, at 5 p.m. on 22 May Henrietta left the Louvre for what she fully expected to be the last time, carried in a litter of red velvet with gold braid, escorted by the good burghers of Paris as far as the city gates.[60] Buckingham travelled with her. Marie de' Medici and Anne, whom Richelieu deliberately kept apart from him, had already started by another route in the company of the King of France. Louis abandoned his wife and mother on the third morning, claiming he was unwell; but then promptly went hunting at Fontainebleau. Brienne attempted to persuade the queen to return to Paris but she refused.[61] After successive nights at Stains, on the outskirts of the capital, and Compiegne, Henrietta's train was joined by that of Marie de' Medici and Anne of Austria at Montdidier,

a small town in Picardy. It quickly became obvious that Anne's equerry, Tomas de Morel, sieur de Putanges, had been given orders not to let her out of his sight and a detachment of Swiss Guards, who in normal circumstances hardly ever left the king's side, surrounded their quarters.[62]

Marie de' Medici fell ill with a bad cold, so the single night's stay at Amiens (pictured) turned into several. Brienne advised her to send Henrietta ahead, which would have obliged Buckingham to follow, and she agreed that she would do so if still unwell after two more days.[63] The queen mother and Anne were lodged separately, Anne in a large house whose garden ran along the bank of the Somme.

On the last, balmy evening in Amiens the duchesse de Chevreuse arrived there without warning, together with Buckingham and Holland, and suggested a walk along the river. Anne agreed and Buckingham took her arm, with Marie and Holland, entwined as always, following them. Putanges, La Porte and Anne's ladies scrambled to catch up with their mistress but were caught out by the impulsive spontaneity of it all. If they could see the queen, it was only at a considerable distance. As dusk came, Marie and Holland contrived to fall behind, leaving Anne and Buckingham completely alone at the corner of a wooded alley, hidden by a cluster of shrubs.

What exactly happened then is uncertain but when the princesse di Conti belatedly arrived on the scene, the gold lace on the duke's tunic had left telltale marks on the queen's breasts, and the very best that Conti could say of the episode was that she would answer to Louis for his wife's virtue but only from the waist down, *depuis la ceinture jusqu'aux pieds*.[64] In the intervening period, as much as fifteen minutes' duration but probably no longer, Buckingham may again have engaged in sexual intercourse with

princesse di Conti.

the queen. Either he was rebuffed for fear of discovery, or rapidly succeeded, because Anne uttered a loud cry and as the others scurried towards them, the duke, perhaps still in a state of *déshabillé*, disappeared into the gathering gloom.[65]

Marie de' Medici, supplied with an edited report of what had taken place, forbade her daughter-in-law to proceed any further. The following morning Anne was compelled to say farewell to Henrietta and, it seemed, to Buckingham, two leagues outside the town. The duke and Henrietta travelled by way of Abbeville and Montreux to Boulogne, where they were due to embark for Dover, together with the duc and duchesse de Chevreuse, who refused to leave Holland's side despite being several months pregnant. Each day Anne kept up an active correspondence, carried by her confidential servant La Porte, which historian Noel Williams concludes can only have been destined for Buckingham.[66] 'I came and I returned,' La Porte wrote in his memoirs, 'I carried letters to Madame de Chevreuse, and returned with her replies, which appeared to be of the utmost consequence, because the Queen gave orders to the duc de Chaulnes to take care that the gates of Amiens were never closed, so that I might not be delayed at any hour, even at night.'[67] No letters from the duchess herself would have been so important.

Twenty assorted vessels had arrived at Boulogne to collect Henrietta but a storm was raging, making departure that day impossible. The fleet brought dispatches for the queen mother, including a tentative offer from the British government to use English warships against an enemy of France, the Genoese.[68] Holland and Marie de Chevreuse suggested to Buckingham that he might carry these dispatches to Amiens himself. With love letters from the queen already in his pocket, perhaps suggesting a further rendezvous, he needed little persuading; Buckingham took post-horses and rode back to Amiens without a stop. Here he saw first Marie de' Medici and then, with her permission, Anne, who had already retired to bed; although it can be safely assumed that Marie de' Medici did not intend Buckingham to see her daughter-in-law without the presence of a chaperone.

While accounts differ, the queen's companion, Françoise Bertaut de Motteville, usually an apologist for her conduct, admitted she was 'assez seule', meaning in its context 'quite alone'.[69] Levi also found an extract from some memoirs attributable to Marie de Pagan, Anne's maid of honour, who said that the senior lady-in-waiting, the comtesse de Lannoy, was already asleep in her

Sanitised Victorian view of Buckingham's unchaperoned visit to Anne's bedroom.

own room.[70] This was entirely plausible because the comtesse, *première dame d'honneur* since 1623, was very old and she would expire from natural causes in September of the following year.[71] Anne claimed that Buckingham merely knelt at the foot of her bed but significantly no explanation was forthcoming (or, on the balance of probabilities, really needed, given previous events) about where the duke, with no accommodation arranged, had spent the rest of the night. The queen also received him again most cordially, in front of her increasingly apprehensive retainers the following morning before he returned, tearfully, to Boulogne.

With Lannoy anxious to avoid admitting she had failed dismally to keep the lovers apart, Marie de Pagan was suspected of leaking the story that everyone else was keen to suppress. She was the youngest sister of Blaise François de Pagan, comte de Merveilles, highly regarded as a fortifications engineer by both Richelieu and Louis XIII, and the obvious conduit of information through him to them both.[72] During a frosty public reunion with her fully-briefed husband at Fontainebleau, Anne remained defiant. In front of the whole court she told the king that 'she could not have prevented the Duke of Buckingham from admiring or even loving her', while giving the distinct impression that the attention had been more than welcome.[73] On 20 July the furious Louis, encouraged by the cardinal, struck at Anne's household. Putanges, La Porte (at two hours notice), her aide François de Rochechouart, the Chevalier de Jars, her principal physician Pierre Aliot Ripert, one of her ladies, Mademoiselle du Vernet and Vernet's manservant, Datel, were all dismissed from her service.[74] The queen sent her husband an icy note, asking him to confirm that no more dismissals were to follow. Of her relationship with Buckingham, La Porte observed that 'The King testified [displayed] the strongest jealousy at all these proceedings, and believed the malignant interpretation put upon them by Her Majesty's enemies'.[75] With hints of treason in the air, those with access to the inner circle spoke in cautious whispers. The Venetian ambassador in Paris, Marc Antonio Morosini, was frustrated by the failure of his usual informants. He complained, 'There is much gossip about the journey to Amiens, of the queen herself, Buckingham, the English ambassadors, the princess and the Duchess of Chevreuse, but it is all kept very secret'.[76]

What the king did not know was that Anne of Austria had made a promise to the duke between the sheets which before long would place her in mortal peril. It was probably Buckingham who pressed the queen for a tangible sign of her love at their last intimate meeting in Amiens. He was aware that the customary gift to distinguished visitors made during a state visit had not so far been forthcoming, even though, as the Venetian ambassador had noted in April, jewellery for this purpose had been ordered to the value of 900,000 livres.[77]

Louis had refused to grant the duke a final audience and Buckingham, whose income could never keep up with the expenditure that went with his image, may have feared he would not receive anything. The French ambassador in London eventually presented him with a circlet, a gold headband studded with diamonds, worth a mere 480,000 livres, but only after a delay of several months.[78]

Dover Castle.

Buckingham was probably aware that Anne possessed a variety of personal jewellery: bracelets, belts, chains, rings, earrings and pearls. The jewellery that formed part of her dowry from Spain was worth a great deal more, and included a long chain and necklace of wrought gold enamelled in green, grey, red and white set with diamonds, worn only on state occasions.[79] However, according to the memoirs of her confidant, Brienne, despite the wide choice available to her, the fabulous necklace the queen recklessly promised Buckingham, containing twelve magnificent diamond studs, had been given to Anne by the king just before Buckingham's visit – not as a token of his affection but to keep up appearances, knowing that the duke himself would be sure to be magnificently attired.[80] Anne had worn the necklace at her first, formal encounter with Buckingham at the Louvre. Her only touch of prudence was to leave a decent interval before, using an intermediary, she dispatched it to her lover.

On 12 June the sea had subsided sufficiently for Henrietta and Buckingham to embark in a three-decker, *The Prince*, but the crossing to England still took almost twenty-four hours. Henrietta occupied the cabin that had been lavishly decorated in vain two years previously to accommodate the Infanta. An 'orchestra of lutes, viols and other delicate instruments' attempted unsuccessfully to assuage her sea-sickness and Charles, all too conspicuously, was not waiting at the quayside for her arrival. Henrietta spent an uncomfortable night alone in a nine-room apartment in Dover Castle high above the harbour but her unwieldy entourage, including Tillières, back in England as her high chamberlain, suffered worse: no food was provided for them and they had to walk into the town for refreshments, then trudge back up the hill to the castle in the dark.[81] The following morning the first salvo was fired in what would become a running battle to reduce the French influence in the queen's household. Buckingham ordered Henrietta's most favoured lady-in-waiting, Madame Saint Georges, to give up her seat in the first coach to her intended replacement, his half-sister Susan Villiers, Countess of Denbigh. If the opening round went to the Buckinghams, many more would soon go to the queen. For several months she refused point blank to give anyone foisted upon her the traditional welcome kiss on both cheeks and would 'scarce speak to any Lady that speaks French to her unless they be Papists...so all the English ladies are gone from her Court'.[82]

Charles and Henrietta spent their first night together at Sir Henry Wotton's country house outside Canterbury, after the King of England had frustrated the usual coarse revelries by surreptitiously slipping away from the nuptial breakfast with his bride and bolting from the inside the seven doors and four windows that gave anticipated access to their wedding chamber. The bridegroom almost certainly had no previous experience of heterosexual intercourse and accordingly the occasion was not a conspicuous success. Henrietta's humour the next morning after possibly (but by no means certainly) losing her virginity was described as 'moribund', that is to say, in a state of terminal collapse. For all his forced jocundity, Charles was disappointed with his fifteen-year-old bride, whom he found puny, bony, poorly endowed, with big eyes and buck teeth. He would quickly discover that she also possessed an incandescent temper invariably presaged by a distinctive frown. 'None but a queen could have cast such a scowl', wrote the memorialist Joseph Mead upon seeing Henrietta in a foul mood.[83] Within six weeks to all intents and purposes king and consort had parted company.

Not long afterwards, at the palace of Nonsuch, Buckingham slept with Henrietta, which said a great deal for the sexual magnetism of a man she had been told by her household to look upon as the enemy; indeed, despairing of her spectacular ignorance of English history, on one occasion, with more than a hint of menace, he told her 'there had been queens in England who had lost their heads'.[84] The duke admitted his latest seduction to Marie de Chevreuse – referring in the same vein at one and the same time to the past and present British queens and to the Queen of France, no mean accomplishment – using to describe what he had done with each of them the French word 'gourmer', a derivative of 'la gourmette', 'the bridle', which could mean to take the bridle off a tamed filly or to give way to one's passions.[85] This casual confession came in pillow talk with the duchesse, as following her arrival in England, Holland had allowed Buckingham to share her favours. Indeed, according to Retz, the duke had already dabbled in Paris, making 'violent love' to Marie while staying under her roof.

The head of Henrietta's household in London, grand almoner Daniel de la Mothe du Plessis Houdancourt, developed an intense dislike of Buckingham. He said of him 'We have no worse enemy' and was scandalised by his latest

Daniel de la Mothe.

behaviour.[86] Recently appointed Bishop of Mende, a town at the crossroads of Languedoc and Auvergne, the evangelical ecclesiastic ran his bishopric from afar like a medieval fiefdom, collecting a *péage* at its borders on every wagonload of goods. Mende reported to his cousin, Cardinal Richelieu, that 'Madame de Chevreuse is shut up for five or six hours every day with Buckingham: Holland has made over his prize to him'.[87] The gossip writer Chamberlain, intolerant as ever, said that Marie 'though she be fair, yet paints [applies make-up] foully' when he saw her parading heavily pregnant in public. Chamberlain thought Marie's mouth much too bright and odorous. Fortunately in this age before dentistry, bad breath proved so commonplace, it was not seen as a serious impediment, even for a deity of love.[88]

Efforts to recall Marie and her acquiescent husband to France failed because Charles I, who delighted in her company, said Marie's pregnancy was too far advanced for her to make the journey. For the last few weeks leading up to her confinement Marie moved in with Holland, then on medical advice to Hampton Court Palace, where she gave birth to a daughter, probably his. Richelieu was furious at her brazen disregard for social convention and wrote to Mende about Marie, saying that 'when she does come back, we won't need to fetch any *guilledines* from England!' – an allusion to men who *couraient le guilledou*, 'run after a prostitute'.[89] The enmity between the duchesse de Chevreuse and the cardinal would soon take a more sinister turn.

8: 'THE KILLING BEAUTY'

Heaven has no rage like love to hatred turned,
Nor hell a fury like a woman scorned.

Playwright William Congreve's much-misquoted epigram from the seventeenth-century had a special resonance in Whitehall.[1] Buckingham and Anne of Austria were still exchanging billet-doux via Marie de Chevreuse, the latest brought across the Channel by the Chevalier de Jars, who had yet to learn of his dismissal in his absence from the French queen's service.[2] The duchess de Chevreuse was not noted for her discretion, and Lucy Percy, still the duke's mistress *en titre*, could scarcely have been unaware of the twin targets of Buckingham's recent affections.

Lucy Percy.

It was time to make use of all her assets. The Countess of Carlisle had become, as one besotted nobleman put it, 'the killing beauty of the world'.[3] Schreiber acknowledges that 'men of all descriptions virtually worshipped her as a goddess'.[4] In June 1625 the royal secretary, Sir Edward Conway, wrote to Hay extolling the virtues of his wife in suspiciously familiar terms but fortunately his handwriting was so illegible that the recipient read only half of it.[5] Even the worldly-wise Earl of Exeter, Thomas Cecil, at the age of sixty-one sent Lucy this eloquent eulogy from his country seat:

The night is the mother of dreams and fantoms, the winter is the mother of the night, all this mingled with my infirmities have protracted this homage so due and so vowed to your ladyship, least the fums and vapors so arisinge shuld con-taminate mie so sacred and pure an intention. But

mutch more pleasure it were to me to performe this duty in your lodginge at
Court when you see your perfections in the glasse addinge perfection to perfection
aproovinge the boune mots there spoken in your presence, moderatinge the exscesse
of compliments, passing over a dull gest, without a sweete smile, givinge a wise
answer to an extravagant question but why do I regrete these absent pleasurs, and
find defects in my condition since it pleased God so to determine but were I yonge
againe I shuld be a most humble sutor that you would be pleased to vouchsafe
that your lodginge might be my academie quittinge to the rest both Italie and
France.[6]

The Countess of Carlisle was aware that, Buckingham apart, men of intelligence and status had begun to take her seriously, to treat her almost as an equal. Lucy was now consciously setting out to cultivate and influence them, not just with her body, but with her mind as well. Not everyone had appreciated how the political world in Britain and France was subtly changing. 'Women wielded significant power through their skill in managing human relationships and in their ability to call into play affinities that sometimes extended across national frontiers'.[7] Soon Lucy would demonstrate this power and teach the duke a lesson.

In mid July 1625 the duc and duchesse de Chevreuse left London for Paris. At the French court Marie found Anne had been like a rudderless ship without her friend and mentor, although inclined to lay the blame for her depleted household at Richelieu's door. The duchess returned in time 'to transform a mere inclination into a living force'.[8] The queen needed little encouragement from Marie to fulfil her promise to send the diamond necklace to Buckingham, thereby defying the cardinal and reinvigorating the clandestine relationship that already had cost some of her supporters dearly.

Their natural choice for a discreet intermediary was Balthazar Gerbier, an accomplished Dutch Huguenot from a family of cloth merchants.[9] Fluent in several languages, Gerbier could turn his hand to mathematics, architecture and painting – he received regular commissions from James I – and later would prove a skilful diplomat. He became Buckingham's chief agent and art buyer, supervising the construction of the Great Chamber, a large paved room to display the collection, at York House, the duke's magnificent property in The Strand.[10] In 1625 he wrote to Buckingham: 'out of all the amateurs and Princes and Kings, there is not one who has collected as many pictures in forty years as your Excellency has in five'.[11] Needless to say, Gerbier omitted to mention that the collection's common theme was the depiction of naked female flesh.

The jewels may have been smuggled to London in the container holding Buckingham's new portrait by Rubens, a close friend of Gerbier; but if so, this was not without its risks, as Rubens was an agent of Spain who would not have hesitated to pass on any information potentially to the duke's disadvantage. It was probably Anne of Austria's first lady-in-waiting, the comtesse de Lannoy, however, who told Richelieu that the queen had given away such an important gift from the king. Frustrated by her

Balthazar Gerbier.

failure to keep Anne and Buckingham apart on his return to Amiens, out of sympathy with the younger coterie of women in the queen's household, the comtesse had good reason to make life difficult for Anne. With constant access to the collection of state jewellery held at the Louvre, she would soon have realised what was missing.

Before the end of 1625 the necklace sent by Anne was probably in London, fermenting the duke's conceit and Lucy's anger. The Bishop of Mende reported to the cardinal that Buckingham was 'wearing the Queen's portrait, toasting her at banquets, and conducting himself generally like an accepted lover'.[12] For his part, Richelieu bided his time until the forthcoming *bal du roi*, an annual event celebrating the Fete of Saint-Jean, held at the expense of the Paris bourgeoisie. Although only the more respectable Parisians were invited, André Félibien, the official court historian, records that from time to time things got out of hand: in 1620 many valuable faïence plates were broken that had been borrowed from the Louvre to help with the catering.[13] The royal family was expected to attend and regularly put on a ballet or masque in which its members performed. Back in February 1623 Buckingham and Charles had watched the final rehearsal for one such entertainment when they passed anonymously – or so they thought – through Paris.

On 3 February 1626 Nicolas Bailieul, sieur de Vattetot-sur-Mer and Soisy-sur-Seine, counsellor of state and prévost for the merchants, was granted an audience at the Louvre and extended the traditional invitation to the king. The date of the ball was confirmed on the following day as Tuesday 24 February, a much shorter interval than usual, leaving only just enough time for the necessary

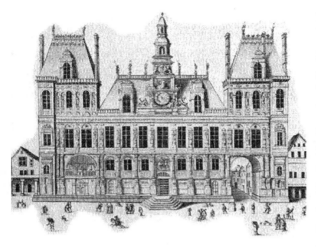

Hôtel de Ville, Paris City Hall.

preparations to enable the bourgeoisie to receive their monarch *'somptueusement et superbement'* at the Hôtel de Ville in the place de Grève.[14] With the help of every stonemason and carpenter in Paris, they turned the Grand Hall on the first floor into a magnificent theatre especially for the occasion, complete with stage, tiered seating, boxes and staircases. Hundreds of holders for burning torches were assembled for walls, booths and tables.

The scheme to snare the queen by using the missing necklace and giving as little notice as possible of the impending ball was hatched between Richelieu and Père Joseph. Although the cardinal's confidant spent much of 1625 in Rome on diplomatic initiatives with the papacy, he remained editor of the *Mercure Francois* (right), and so transformed this Parisian journal that it became the precursor of

the modern newspaper, with a thorough coverage of domestic and international events.[15] Its discernible editorial line, no doubt determined by Richelieu, was the elevation of royal authority at the expense of self interest, be that religious or secular; there was no place for the disloyal, the privileged or the irresponsible. Using his secretary, Ange de Mortagne, as a go-between, the Capuchin monk urged the cardinal to send a message that no one was untouchable if their actions undermined the interests of the state.[16] As events would show, and perhaps Joseph and Richelieu already suspected, the Queen of France was involved in much more than a clandestine love affair.

Courtiers fawn as Father Joseph, the grey eminence, descends the staircase in solitary study: behind him, a tapestry depicting the crest of his patron, Cardinal Richelieu.

Louis, prompted by Richelieu but almost certainly unaware of the significance of his request, sent a note to the queen, commanding Anne to wear at the ball the diamond necklace he had given her for the visit of Buckingham. Once the queen had recovered from the initial shock, Anne knew that she had to act quickly and decisively to preserve her reputation, perhaps even her life. The queen needed someone willing to go to London to recover her gift to the duke, a dangerous undertaking made all the more desperate by the approaching deadline. She took a huge risk by confiding in Charles de Bérard, marquis de Montalet, the inaugural captain of the Musketeers, an elite force established in 1622 to ensure the king's safety,

Louis XIII and Richelieu: uneasy partnership.

if necessary at the expense of their own. They accompanied Louis on official visits and military campaigns, guarding the perimeter night and day wherever he slept.

Montalet, a minor noble from Languedoc, one of five brothers in the household divisions, might have gone to the king, in which case the game would have been up. Instead, he surreptitiously encouraged three of his men to undertake the mission. They were not the Three Musketeers immortalised by Dumas or even Charles d'Artagnan, at the time still a babe in his mother's arms at château Castelmore near Lupiac in Gascony. Dumas's Three Musketeers were not that much older. Isaac de Portau, known as Porthos, was nine, residing in Pau with his father, principal secretary to the Béarn parliament. Armand de Sillègue, known as

Home of Charles and Henri d'Aramits.

Athos, was a ten-year-old living with his mother Nicole and his father Adrien, lord of Auteville and Athos, a little village near the town of Sauveterre-de-Béarn. Henri d'Aramits, known as Aramis, and about the same age, lived in the abbey of Aramits, a village in Béarn. His mother Catherine de Rague, a wealthy member of the local nobility, was left to bring up Henri and his two sisters, while his impecunious father, Charles d'Aramits, followed in the family tradition of serving the king – or in this instance, the queen.

Montalet successfully approached Charles d'Aramits, one of his original recruits for the Musketeers, and Jacques de Terride, seigneur de Labenne and de Floris, who came from a village in Gers and had been a Musketeer for little more than a year. His choice to lead the little expedition, however, was a man who already had a reputation for taking almost suicidal risks, Jean-Arnaud de Peyrer. Under French law the oldest male child inherited everything and Jean-Arnaud, the youngest son of a prosperous architect and trader, Jean de Peyrer, knew that he had to make his own way in life. Born near Oloron in Béarn late in 1598, he left home against his father's wishes in 1616. Jean de Peyrer wanted him to follow in the family business and made his departure as difficult as possible. Aged seventeen, Jean-Arnaud travelled to Paris *pédestrement*, on foot, with all his worldly possessions in a small battered valise and wearing an old borrowed sword that was much too long for him and kept grazing his calves. His only advantage was the privilege he enjoyed of being received at court. Almost a decade earlier Jean de Peyrer had purchased the *seigneurie* of Troisvilles, whose seemingly grandiose 'trois villes' or 'three towns' were tiny hamlets in the back of beyond; but they afforded his family a place on the very bottom rung of the aristocratic ladder. The impoverished and ill-clad youngster was the butt of many jokes at the palace of Saint-Germain and his heavy, guttural, almost incomprehensible accent altered 'Troisvilles' for ever more to 'Tréville'. Starting as an unpaid gentleman cadet in one of the Regiments des Gardes, Tréville showed such courage under fire in September

Mill at Saucéde, birthplace of Tréville.

1621, during the unsuccessful siege of Montauban, that maréchal de Bassompierre recommended him to the king for a commission. Tréville declined, preferring to wait for a more junior appointment in the Musketeers, which he achieved in 1625, with the rank of cornette.

The trio's journey from Paris was recorded by François VI, duc de La Rochefoucauld, prince de Marcillac, a member of one of the leading aristocratic families of France. A well-educated, intelligent young man, Rochefoucauld was taught Latin and mathematics alongside dancing, fencing and etiquette; at the age of fifteen he commanded his own regiment.[17] Much of his life was dominated by a series of sexual and political escapades, in which his principal source of information, Marie de Chevreuse, was a constant influence, at best mischievous, at worse malign. La Rochefoucauld's realisation that he was only one of her many lovers added to his bouts of melancholy but that very condition helped him to focus his ideas on the

La Rochefoucauld.

fundamental laws of human nature. He believed that altruism, friendship and even love were facades that shielded self-interest from discovery. He honed his ideas into maxims, captured perfectly in concise, elegant statements, which have stood the test of time. Long before *schadenfreude* was invented, La Rochefoucauld anticipated the concept by observing, 'In the misfortunes of our best friends, there is something that does not displease'.[18]

The duke first recounted the Affair of the Queen's Necklace to his aunt, Marie-Claire de Bauffremont de la Rochefoucauld, marquise de Sennecey, who would become one of Anne of Austria's maids of honour and a governess to Louis XIV.[19] Alas, he was no Dumas, and little of the danger and drama of this desperate venture emerges from his sparse recollections.

The life-size picture of Tréville (left), now lost, was the joint work of two famous artists, Mathieu and Antoine Le Nain, the only portrait Antoine ever signed. It was painted about 1636, when Tréville had become Anne of Austria's handsome lover and was at the height of his powers.

The Le Nain brothers kept the picture at their Paris studio in the rue de Vieux-Colombier for more than twenty years because Tréville could not afford to pay for it. In the early 1660s, however, he hung it above the drawing-room fireplace in his new, magnificent chateau of Troisvilles (below) near Tardets, built with money from the Queen for his silence...and from the corrupt finance minister, Nicholas Fouquet, for his secrets.

There were plenty who would have wanted
Tréville to fail but the cardinal did not yet
possess the resources for a full-scale pursuit. He
sent messages to his agents by carrier pigeons,
leaving them to recruit men locally who would
rob and kill without question. The original three
Musketeers left Paris with several
spare horses (which they used
to barter for fresh mounts at
country inns) by way of Porte
St Denis, Tillart, Beauvais
and Oudeuil. A group of
armed ruffians ambushed
them at Poix and Jacques de
Terride, who was wounded,
had to be left behind. On
the second day the surviving
Musketeers' route took them

*Desperate venture:
the ride from Paris
to Calais.*

through Ayrenes, Abbeville, Nouvion, Bernay, Nainpont and Montreuil until
they reached the village of Franc, where Aramits's last horse was killed during
another attack. This left Tréville on the third day to ride on alone through
Neufchatel, Boulogne and Marquise, before taking ship at Calais.[20]

Tréville's task was more difficult than he realised. According to La
Rochefoucauld, Richelieu sent a courier of his own to London who had a
head start. He carried a message for the Countess of Carlisle describing
Anne of Austria's diamond necklace in detail and the cardinal's suspicions
that it was now in the hands of the Duke of
Buckingham. Although presuming upon
their brief conversation of more than two
years earlier at the British ambassador's
soirée, Richelieu had a shrewd idea
that Lucy Percy would not take lightly
this tangible evidence of Buckingham's
betrayal. His letter encouraged her to find
an opportune moment to remove some
of the diamond studs from the queen's
necklace. Richelieu also offered her a large

Calais Gate.

Richelieu's armed ruffians, men who would rob and kill without question, ambush the original Musketeers at Poix.

sum of money, much greater than would be required to cover her expenses, to bring the stolen studs to him in Paris personally. The cardinal's offer was particularly welcome because the Carlisles, more than usual, were hard-pressed by creditors. Their famous banquets, cut back, had been eclipsed by Buckingham's prodigious feasts at York House.[21] Lucy's husband no longer kept up with new styles regardless of cost. 'But for the Earl of Carlisle, the wearing of ruffs and the gartering of silk stockings would be forgotten', said

Buckingham's residence on the Thames, York House, with its ornate water gate.

the dapper secretary of state Conway, cruelly suggesting that Hay's clothes were no longer *à la mode*.[22] The Earl of Northumberland, riding about in a coach pulled by eight horses to make his point, dismissed the ageing mounts attached to Lucy's carriage as 'six carrion mules'.[23]

It was not, however, the Carlisles' newfound need for economy that made Charles I's coronation, postponed for ten months because of the plague running through London, an unusually subdued occasion. On the chosen date, 2 February 1626, the sun shone but the king's mood was anything but bright because his queen, Henrietta, refused to take part, instead watching part of the procession from a private house.[24] She had imposed the impossible pre-condition that the Bishop of Mende, a Catholic, instead of the Anglican Archbishop of Canterbury, should place the crown of England on her head.[25] There was no banquet or masque and the grand ball planned for Windsor on 7 February went ahead under a considerable handicap: the king and queen were not on speaking terms. Buckingham, however, enlivened the party by arriving in a costume of breathtaking magnificence. His pourpoint, the stuffed quilted doublet that remained the height of seventeenth-century fashion, was made of 'black velvet embroidered with gold and, to hold the cross-belt, on the left shoulder a large node of blue ribbon from which hung the twelve diamond studs'.[26] Lucy, expected by some onlookers to snub the duke because of increasing rumours of his dalliance with the Queen of France, instead welcomed him with open arms. Buckingham would soon discover the reason why. For the moment, suspecting nothing, the duke monopolised his mistress, ending up in bed with Lucy in one of the castle's finest suites.

When Buckingham awoke, Lucy had already left for Essex House. At first he did not notice anything was wrong. Then one of his valets, tidying his clothes,

Windsor Castle

fearfully pointed out that two of the jewels were missing, neatly cut from his coat. There could be only one culprit. A messenger was sent at once to Essex House but he returned to report that according to the servants, the countess

had returned briefly before dawn before departing by coach for an unknown destination. Soon afterwards Buckingham's worst suspicions were confirmed by the arrival, bearing a note from the Queen of France, of the exhausted Tréville, who had spent the night at the *newe inne* (left) on Windsor's Church Street.

The duke, as Lord High Admiral, acted swiftly to close the ports, thereby, he hoped, preventing Lucy Percy from taking the stolen diamonds to France. According to the Venetian ambassador, even the king's own messengers were 'stopped at the coast... they say the duke delayed them in his own interest'. Three weeks later the same ambassador was still complaining, 'My despatches have all been stopped at Dover and there is no means of getting them across except by an extraordinary courier and with his Majesty's permission or by satisfying the duke, but this would be difficult in his present disposition.'[27]

With the whole diplomatic community in a state of fury about the blockade, for which no explanation was forthcoming, all normal government business

came to a halt. Buckingham spared no effort or expense to have replacements made for the missing jewels. The jeweller to James I, famed for his skill, a Scotsman called George Herriot, unfortunately had died almost two years earlier, leaving the business to his son, Alexander.[28] The duke promised him a king's ransom if his staff could find and fashion two extra stones in forty-eight hours that no one could tell apart from the originals, and reassemble the complete necklace in its original form. When Tréville received the finished product from Buckingham (pictured), all twelve diamonds did indeed look identical; but the work had taken longer than expected and the ball in Paris was just four days away.

In the meantime the Countess of Carlisle succeeded in crossing the Channel, the combination of a beautiful woman and a bag of sovereigns proving irresistible to some enterprising captain willing to sneak past the naval vessels guarding every harbour. From the French coast, under Richelieu's patronage, Lucy travelled by private coach to Paris, and, said La Rochefoucauld, arrived with her stolen pair of studs on the morning before the ball, 24 February. The restored necklace was not far behind. Realising that the usual *post* service would be carefully watched, Buckingham had Tréville landed at Ambleteuse south of Calais and arranged relays of fresh horses along the route.

According to the comte de Brienne, who had an intimate knowledge of state matters, the ball was a late affair, due to start shortly before midnight.[29] Two hours previously, at 10 p.m., with still no sign of Tréville, Richelieu ordered an enseign in the household guards to requisition from Clément, the Hôtel de Ville greffier, the city hall clerk, the key to every lockable door in the building, running into dozens, if not hundreds. As several guardsmen struggled with the task of labelling this heap of keys under Clément's exasperated supervision, and identifying everyone who needed access to any part of the Hôtel de

The Musketeers' skirmish is halted by the Queen.

Ville, their compatriots began to block the surrounding streets (pictured, page 203). At 11 p.m. they were reinforced by more household troops commanded by the duty captain of the guard, Duhallier, under the watchful eye of Marie de Chevreuse's father, the duc de Montbazon.

Inside city hall, at midnight one of the ball's institutions, widow Croisier, brought out her famous annual banquet, including more than 600 *bouties*, miniature sweets; but wisely she put off cooking the fish, laid out enticingly on a huge row of trestle tables. All the dignitaries of the city and the bourgeoisie were already in their places, the ladies wearing their best dresses and pearls. The orchestra, complete with twenty violins, began to play but none of the women would dance, for fear of losing their seats. It would prove to be a long wait. The queen, perhaps aware that a winged messenger in the shape of Tréville was approaching Paris, did everything in her power to delay and dragged out her preparations for another three hours, to the increasing exasperation of the king. But at 3 a.m. she was forced to enter her carriage and join the procession from the Louvre to the place du Grève, along avenues lit by hundreds of multicoloured paper lanterns, escorted by two companies of guards, one French, one Swiss, marching to the beat of a single drum. Inside city hall the royal party put on their costumes for the ballet, an exercise that the queen managed to stretch out for another hour.

Anne appeared at last. Her neck was bare. Marie de Chevreuse stood behind her, clutching tightly the wooden case in which the diamond necklace was normally kept. Richelieu and Louis stood waiting, deep in conversation. The cardinal, having concealed in his sleeve a tiny box containing the two diamond studs given to him by Lucy Percy a few hours earlier, confidently predicted that the necklace would be incomplete. He implied that the queen would be unable to explain why. Louis impatiently seized the wooden case from Marie de Chevreuse and opened it himself. To his surprise the necklace was there in all its glory, with twelve identical diamonds glittering under the torches of the Hôtel de Ville. Tréville had managed to find a way into the building and pass his precious package to Marie, although, according to La Rochefoucauld, only after a bloody skirmish in the corridors. Seeing that Tréville was about to be arrested, several of the King's Musketeers intervened on his side, and three of the household guards were wounded in the mêlée before it was halted by the dramatic appearance of the queen herself.

Anne upstages Richelieu.

The cardinal tried to recover by offering Anne as a gift the two, now superfluous, additional diamond studs, which she graciously accepted; but it did not save him from an angry reproach from the king, for the moment conveniently disregarding his own suspicions on the matter, for casting such doubt upon the queen's honour. Anne, helped by Marie, triumphantly put on the necklace. Humiliated in front of the two women who hated him most in all the world, Richelieu left the Hôtel de Ville without another word. His seat for the entertainment to come would remain empty, as no one else dared sit in it.

Louis entered the improvised theatre, surrounded by his court, to frenzied applause from the bourgeoisie, because this was a signal that at last the ball was beginning in earnest. The king, in a remarkably good mood, apologised profusely for the delay, referring, with studied ambiguity, to something being not quite ready. The exhausted members of the city orchestra, which had been playing for four hours without an interval, thankfully gave up their seats to the royal violinists to provide the music for the ballet. With twelve members of the royal family taking all the parts and the queen, wearing the diamond necklace, looking radiant, it lasted just under three hours. Louis played a Persian gentleman in Act II, and a Spanish guitar-player in Act III.

Finally it was time for the feast. The king admired the wonderful display of fish, which by now had been well and truly fried, and sampled some of the meat. The confectionery was covered by white napkins, and as these were removed, Louis pretended to fall back as though amazed at the variety. He took three pieces for himself and retired to the pavilion reserved for the nobility. As he did so, the starving bourgeoisie scrambled for the food, the trestle tables wobbled and finally collapsed into a heap on the floor, much to the king's unconcealed amusement. Later he appeared in public again, seized a glass of wine from a startled citizen, and toasted the guests. It was 9 a.m. before Louis clambered back into his carosse, to the roar of cannons and cheers from the crowd. 'Vive le roi!' they cried as he drove back to the Louvre. The king stood up and waved. The upstaging of the cardinal, whose influence he was already beginning to resent, had made it a wonderful day.

Afterwards, the original three Musketeers who had risked everything for the queen would enjoy mixed fortunes. Charles d'Aramits became maréchal des logis, the Musketeers' quartermaster, a post that offered almost unlimited opportunities for making money on the side. A decade later he would retire to Bearn and his *abbaye laïque* in Aramits, so called because it was not attached

to any religious order; women often said they felt safe with either Charles or his son Henri, one of Dumas's Three Musketeers, believing them both to be men of the cloth, until it was too late.

Jacques de Terride, nursing a leg injury, was not a lucky soldier. No sooner had he returned to action at the fourteen-month siege of La Rochelle from August 1627 until its fall in October 1628, than he was wounded again, in what appears to have been an imprudent picnic in no man's land, undertaken for a bet made by Tréville, newly promoted to sub-lieutenant. In March 1629, when the Musketeers would lead the main French attack at dawn on the Pas de Suze (pictured), the gateway to Savoy and Italy, Terride was badly injured by a bullet that struck him in the shoulder and he was forced to retire from military service. In contrast, with king and cardinal both present, in the same action Tréville, pushing ahead at a furious pace in the snow and ice, wounded and disarmed Jean Cerbelloni, captain-general of the Spanish artillery, in a fierce sword fight and almost captured the opposing commander, the Duke of Savoy himself. For this glittering feat of arms, Tréville was feted at court and promoted to lieutenant.

His commanding officer, the marquis de Montalet, was much less fortunate: he died mysteriously from poison and the position of Captain of the Musketeers went to his nephew.[30] Although Richelieu rarely bothered about the small fry, he could be ruthless when opposed by those close to the seat of power. His efforts to disgrace the queen by forcing her to admit she had given away her diamond necklace to Buckingham were not motivated entirely by malice, although this was a sentiment he could never completely suppress. From 'early in 1626 the government knew that it was menaced by a huge conspiracy', in which Richelieu strongly suspected both the duchesse de Chevreuse and Anne of Austria were intimately involved.[31] Between 1626 and at least 1628, one of his secretaries, Cheré, taking dictation from the cardinal of confidential dispatches on their activities, used as the code for the queen, 'La Chesnelle'.[32] This was a seventeenth-century term that appeared in inventories of jewellery to describe a chain, usually of gold or silver, often threaded through the clasp of a series of diamond pendants or studs and assembled as a necklace.[33] The code for Marie de Chevreuse was 'La Lapidaire', which meant an artisan in a jewellery workshop who cuts and shapes diamonds.[34] The use of two such

Gaston d'Orléans.

significant code words could scarcely be a coincidence. It was easy to see what recent event rankled with the cardinal.

There proved plenty to report. On 25 April the king's younger brother and heir, Gaston d'Orléans, celebrated his eighteenth birthday. Sly, debauched and dissolute, with an ambition to succeed to the throne that was frustrated only by his chronic indecision and cowardice, he wanted what he saw as his rightful place on the royal council. Much to Richelieu's unease, Gaston's governor and the head of his household, Jean-Baptiste d'Ornano, the son of a Corsican bandit, 'the ugliest man possible to imagine', also claimed a place on the council for himself.[35] When, predictably, this was refused, Ornano, a close friend of Hay, threw himself into the plot that became known as the *Conspiration des Dames*. The principal conspirators were Anne of Austria and Marie de Chevreuse, who set about persuading first Ornano and then Gaston himself that the prince should refuse to marry the bride that had been arranged for him almost since birth: Marie de Bourbon, the duchesse de Montpensier, the richest heiress in France.

Anne's motive was self-evident. Louis had already rejected all encouragement to make him sire a son and if Gaston were to father a male child in wedlock with the young duchess, thereby starting a new dynasty, Anne's already precarious position would take a turn for the worse. However, Gaston found Marie de Bourbon unappealing and was much more enamoured of the queen. The proposal, put forward by Marie de Chevreuse with Anne's approval, was that Gaston should wait until the queen became available to marry him instead. This might occur innocently if Anne became a widow, because Louis's

health was already causing concern; or by an annulment of the marriage on grounds of his impotence, although Marie de' Medici had already undermined any such basis by her extravagant claims of consummation on the king's wedding night. Always implied, although perhaps never spoken out loud in the presence of the queen, was that Louis might simply be deposed or put to death. As to the cardinal, the king's half brothers, Caesar (pictured, page 210) and Alexandre de Vendome, both numbered among the conspirators, had no doubt that Gaston should 'use threats and violence to Richelieu'.[36]

Louis acted precipitously before Richelieu had acquired the solid evidence he needed. On 4 May he invited Ornano to dinner at Fontainebleu, then called the sieur de Hallier, the duty captain of the guard, and had him arrested. Ornano was taken to the prison at Vincennes, whose disagreeable dungeon, 'worth its weight in arsenic' according to Madame de Rambouillet, brought on tuberculosis and an attack of dysentery.[37] After an illness of eleven days, Ornano expired on 2 September.

Marie de Chevreuse as Diana.

His arrest had caused consternation among the principle plotters. The comtesse de Lannoy, with a piercing thrust at the duchesse de Chevreuse's easy virtue, said of her, 'I thought there could not be a man left in the kingdom, so deep was the dejection written on her features!'[38] But the duchess had another shot in her locker. She turned her amorous attentions towards Henri de Talleyrand, the marquis de Chalais, a young man of eighteen who was the unwilling subject of Louis's sexual attentions at court, where as Keeper of the King's Wardrobe he had constant access to the king. Chalais fell hopelessly in love with Marie de Chevreuse and became involved in a plot to murder Richelieu, before getting cold feet and confessing everything. It was planned that Gaston and his aides would hunt in the Fontainebleau forest and seek impromptu shelter at the cardinal's house in Fleury-en-Bière. Then, over dinner, they were supposed to instigate a spurious quarrel that would come to blows, one of which would just happen to kill the cardinal. Richelieu pre-empted the assassination attempt by setting out for the palace of Fontainebleau before dawn and rousing the prince from his bed. Handing the startled Gaston his shirt, he said laconically, 'Monsieur, you have not risen early enough; your quarry is no longer at home!'[39]

The heir to the throne was summoned to Nantes to account for his actions. Once Chalais (right) had been

The marriage of Gaston d'Orléans to Marie, duchesse de Montpensier, was an ill-fated affair. Marie died the following May, shortly after the birth of her daughter, the future Grande Mademoiselle.

arrested on 8 July for high treason, Gaston took fright and informed Richelieu and Louis of the conspirators' every move, including the entreaties made by Anne and Marie on 2 August, when both went down on bended knee to beseech him not to marry the duchesse de Montpensier.[40] But on 5 August the unhappy pair became formally betrothed in front of Richelieu himself and went on gloomily to wed the following day without music, or a banquet, and dressed in their ordinary clothes.

On 18 August Chalais was found guilty and sentenced to death. The next afternoon the regular Nantes executioner, bribed by Gaston, did not turn

Chalais's execution.

up and a shoemaker due to be hanged was offered a pardon to undertake the beheading. He missed Chalais's head completely with a Swiss sword and turned to a cooper's adze, a tool used primarily for smoothing rough-cut wood. The victim remained conscious until the twentieth blow, crying out constantly, 'Jesus Maria!' and even after the thirtieth the amateur headsman had to 'turn the head round the other way before he could cut it quite off'.[41]

By then, Marie de Chevreuse, banished from court, was on her way to her husband's château at Dampierre, near Rambouillet. But for the intervention of the duc de Chevreuse, who unwisely gave an undertaking as to his wife's future good conduct, Louis would have signed the warrant for her arrest based upon Chalais's evidence. Forbidden to contact the queen, forbidden to go to England, and hearing rumours that she might be shut up in the château du Verger, in distant Poitou, Marie took flight. 'Transported with fury', wrote Richelieu in his memoirs, and vowing vengeance, she sought asylum with her husband's kinsman, Charles IV of autonomous Lorraine. Aged twenty-two, like most other young noblemen, he would prove to be putty in her hands.

The net closed around the queen. Whenever Louis went south to the war with Spain, she would no longer be regent of Picardy. Anne ceased to have precedence over the queen mother, who was determined to secure the succession, if needs be, by removing her daughter-in-law altogether. On 27 August Anne was forbidden to grant any private audience without first informing Marie de' Medici or the cardinal, and explaining whom she wished to see and why. From that date an order signed by the king and countersigned by Richelieu, prevented any nobleman or gentleman, apart from those attached to Anne's household, to enter her apartments.

On 10 September Anne was summoned in front of a special session of the council of state, attended by the queen mother, Richelieu and, most reluctantly, Gaston, still the heir to the throne despite his treachery. The queen was made to sit on a little folding seat, as though she were a common criminal, and listen while the king accused her of conspiring against his life by planning to take his brother as her husband. Afterwards Louis would tell his confessor, even on his death bed, that he did not believe her denials.[42] But Anne brazened it out and produced a memorable, spirited response that saved the day. Pointing to Gaston, making faces as he always did, with a drooping lower lip and a huge open mouth, she replied scornfully that she 'would have had too little to gain in the exchange'.[43] However, for the next decade, until the extraordinary birth of a dauphin, the queen, in the vernacular of the time, remained *deux doigts de sa perte*, a finger's breadth or two from disaster.

What had most disconcerted the conspirators was the cardinal's ability to discover the details of their plans, even those made after Chalais's arrest. Richelieu was certain that both Hay and Buckingham had direct knowledge of the plot.[44] The principal leak was in London. Schreiber concludes, 'From the evidence collected by Richelieu and his agents, it is plain that Carlisle [Hay] and his political allies in England were more than passive observers of the events across the Channel... they had done everything possible to encourage those who were personally involved'.[45] After the French ambassador, Jean de Varignies, seigneur de Blainville, left England at the end of April 1626, he continued to receive high value information that must have come from someone at the very centre of affairs. For example, on 4 July, he was able to give Richelieu word for word the contents of Gaston's letter to Hay 'full of hatred and scorn for the King' and not long afterwards to disclose that Hay had promised Gaston British aid.[46] The cardinal sent a playwright, Guillaume Bautru, to visit his secret agent and to 'ensure she is well looked after'.[47] With her husband, Hay, in direct contact with the plotters, only Lucy Percy had the necessary access to him and Buckingham.

When in the previous February Lucy had left Paris after succeeding in her mission but failing to humiliate the queen, she was forced to wait a fortnight at the coast for the English ports to reopen. The duke's blockade, which had already served its purpose, remained in place primarily to teach her a lesson. However, it probably never occurred to Buckingham that Lucy had acted at Richelieu's behest and the duke did nothing to disrupt their sexual relationship. Buckingham did not pursue vendettas.[48] The cardinal's discomfiture, however unintended by Lucy, had been for him a most agreeable outcome.

For her part, Lucy was determined that she would no longer be at the duke's beck and call. She became more promiscuous and spread her favours much more liberally. Among her lovers was a young Cambridge undergraduate called John Suckling, the inventor of cribbage, who funded his law degree by teaching the nobility card games. As the precocious Suckling preferred to play cards in bed, and spent most mornings there, it is not hard to see how during Lucy's tuition one thing led to another. Suckling's poetic talents commended him to Charles I, and if his works lacked inspiration they fully compensated with candour. In his poem, 'Upon my Lady Carlisle's walking in Hampton Court garden', Suckling describes her vulva as a fountain.[49] One verse that was too much for the Victorians, and remained excised from his works until the 1970s, defended his desire to drink from this fountain on the grounds that many others less deserving were finding the countess an easy conquest:

> *Troth in her face I could descry*
> *No danger, no divinity.*
> *But since the pillars were so good*
> *On which the lovely fountain stood,*
> *Being once come so near, I think*
> *I should have ventur'd hard to drink.*
> *What ever fool like me had been*
> *If I'd not done as well as seen?*
> *There to be lost why should I doubt,*
> *Where fools with ease go in and out?*[50]

What Lucy was able to discover from Buckingham, and others, in bed would have been invaluable information had the French been in a better position to act on it. The duke remained inviolate, so much so, that when in May the House of Commons attempted to impeach him, the king, accompanied by Hay, Holland and Buckingham himself, ordered his barge rowed from Whitehall to Westminster and arrested the leading trouble-makers, Sir John Eliot and Dudley Digges.[51] Buckingham saw Henrietta's huge household as a threat to his position and with Hay's help, played on the king's suspicions of those around the queen. They said, or at any rate strongly implied, that a man unable to control his own wife would never rule his kingdom.[52] In July one of the few nights the royal couple spent together was taken up by a spectacular row during which Henrietta handed Charles the names, both English and French, of those whom she was willing should serve her, a list based on recommendations from a woman who terrified the king even though they had never met, his mother-in-law Marie de' Medici.[53] On 1 August Henrietta refused to attend a meeting of the Privy Council, claiming she had toothache but when Charles stormed in to confront her, he found she was holding a party.[54] This was the final straw. The king told Henrietta he was sending her servants back to France, whereupon she went wild with fury, and smashed the windows of her bedchamber with the heels of her shoes. On 7 August Charles wrote to Buckingham leaving him in no doubt that he had to

'send all the French away... driving them away like so many wild beasts... and so the Devil go with them'.[55]

In a desperate effort to prevent the expulsions, Henrietta had dispatched Tillières to Paris to ask Louis XIII to intervene. The day after the high chamberlain's departure, leaving his wife Catherine behind in Hay's bed, the duke carried out King Charles's order. Hay, as well informed as ever, and Buckingham gambled correctly: across the Channel, the French, in domestic disarray, could do nothing. After a futile last-ditch stand by her maids of honour, forming a physical barrier on their final day at court, most of Henrietta's French attendants were sent packing; those that remained were already in Buckingham's pay.[56] Charles promptly descended on his wife, haranguing her even while she was relieving herself on a *chaise percée*.[57] Henrietta was forced to accept as her ladies Buckingham's wife, sister and niece.[58] However, she would not accept Lucy, to whom, she told the king, she had a 'great aversion', adding that 'it would be very difficult to accommodate herself to the humours of the Countess of Carlisle'.[59] But it was not Lucy's disposition that worried Henrietta: it was her looks. The Bishop of Mende, Henrietta's confessor, voicing the Queen of England's well-founded suspicions, told Richelieu that Buckingham's 'principal aim now was to give his master new affections'.[60] According to Schreiber, Hay, pliable as always, and vainly hoping for fresh preferment, actively supported the duke's idea of placing Lucy in the king's bed.[61]

Lucy would surely have seen this as a means to an end: she had a strong motive to bring about a thaw in the frosty relationship between Henrietta and

Henrietta Maria after Lucy's makeover, wearing rouge and powder.

Charles. On 2 August, in one of his final dispatches to Richelieu before returning to France, the Bishop of Mende warned him 'it had been settled between Madame de Chevreuse, the ladies (the Princesse di Conti and others) and the

217

gallants (Buckingham and Lord Holland) that twice a year they would cross the water under pretext of settling the difficulties between the King and Queen of England, and that [Marie de' Medici] the Queen Mother, in her fear that [otherwise] her daughter might be badly treated, would obtain this freedom for them. As they believe the Cardinal may cross their plans, they desire to bring about his ruin'.[62] Richelieu's natural instinct would have been to acquaint Lucy with Buckingham's intentions to continue his liaison with the Queen of France. Lucy removed the duke's pretext for visiting her rival and allayed Marie de' Medici's fears of reprisals against her daughter by removing the prime cause of Henrietta's unhappiness. She began by helping the Queen of England with her make-up, encouraging her, against the respectable fashions of the time, to wear rouge and powder. One scandalised courtier said of Lucy's efforts to make the queen look more attractive, 'She has already brought her [Henrietta] to paint [her face] and in time will lead her into more debaucheries'.[63] This meant, in effect, as the Bishop of Mende tacitly acknowledged, showing her the means to more and better sex.[64] As for Henrietta's hapless royal husband, in the utmost secrecy, Lucy also set about educating the king between the sheets. With her help, Charles acquired sophisticated sexual manners and techniques that enabled him to satisfy Henrietta, so successfully that before long they actually fell in love. The new French ambassador in London, Tillière's brother-in-law Bassompierre, saw Charles, quite uncharacteristically, caressing his wife over and over again in public and not long afterwards the king presented her with an exquisite diamond bracelet.[65]

It was only then that Charles, placing Lucy on the same level in his own court as her husband, much to Hay's chagrin, ratified the Countess of Carlisle's appointment as a Lady of the Queen's Bedchamber. If Henrietta still had reservations, they were quickly dispelled at private, exclusive little dinner parties where Lucy entertained the queen with her biting sarcasm, usually at the expense of Buckingham's relations. The gossip writer John Hope observed that 'the Duke's mother his lady and sister do hate her even to death, not only for my Lord Duke's lying with her but also for that she has the queen's heart above them all, so in comparison she values them as nothing.'[66]

The irony of it was that Henrietta would almost certainly have continued to keep Lucy at arm's length but for the avalanche of criticism of her conduct communicated on Buckingham's orders to Paris to justify the expulsion of her household. Henrietta wept for two days when she heard from Tillières what

Katherine Villiers hated Lucy Percy 'even to death'.

had been falsely alleged, then hit back effectively, The private dinner parties arranged with Lucy were a stroke of genius, a conspicuous social slight that the Buckinghams found almost insufferable. 'The duke and his sister are jealous

Richelieu en route, he hoped, to becoming master of Europe.

beyond measure', Henrietta reported to Tillières. But then, in a part of the secret dispatch that no longer survives – 'Show this letter to the queen and then burn it' were her instructions – her erstwhile chamberlain gave Anne of Austria the information most likely to rebound upon the duke. This may have been a list of the names of the ladies with whom Buckingham had slept since he swore undying love to Anne, perhaps even including, to support its credibility, that of Henrietta herself. 'I do all this to fulfil my design' she explained to Tillières.[67]

Detail from Honthorst's Apollo (Charles I) and Diana (Henrietta Maria) where Lucy Percy leans excitedly over the queen's shoulder; Mercury is below, with Buckingham playing the role of a celestial Lord Chamberlain.

Lucy, as Henrietta's new, most intimate friend, could even have helped her to complete the list. Thanks to her not only was the Queen of England secure in her marriage, thereby eliminating Buckingham's best hope of another invitation to Paris, but she had made certain that the French queen received a timely reminder of the inconstancy of powerful men.

How Richelieu must have rejoiced when he received Lucy's reports. Louis XIII could now follow his instincts and keep Buckingham out of France. In December the duke travelled to The Hague to shore up an alliance of anti-Hapsburg states, all the more urgent because England's latest attack on the

221

Spanish port of Cadiz had just ended in humiliating failure, but still showed a willingness to drop everything and go to Paris to see the French queen. Lucy's cousin, the Earl of Holland, back in the French capital on another round of diplomacy, sent Buckingham a cryptic message about Anne of Austria's smouldering mood in cipher. The symbols he selected, a fleur de lys for the king and a heart for the queen, lacked subtlety, to say the least:

'♣ persists in his suspicions, voicing them frequently. Those closest to ♣ whisper that ♥ has infinite tenderness for... you know who for. ♥ is for you beyond all reason and would risk losing everything to satisfy her desires.'

Holland was in a complete quandary. 'Do as you will', he wrote, 'I dare not advise; to come is dangerous, not to come is unfortunate.'[68] The cardinal instructed the French ambassador at The Hague to discourage the visit, which he did with such vehemence that the duke took offence.[69] When Buckingham persisted with his plans on his return to England, Richelieu promptly repudiated the terms of the treaty agreed by his bemused ambassador, maréchal Bassompierre, and the duke, having started out for Paris, got no further than Canterbury.[70] Buckingham and Anne of Austria would never meet again.[71]

Soon Lucy wrote to an unnamed recipient, hoping he would not 'regret the favours' he had done her.[72] It seems likely this was Richelieu, for whom Lucy had become 'his humblest and faithfullest [sic] servant'. Lucy revelled in the *frisson* of her clandestine role. The cardinal's most secret agent was no longer a mere appendage of both her lover and her husband, but had an appointment and an apartment at court, the favour of the King and Queen of England, and as the Duke of Buckingham had found to his cost, an influential political role in her own right. Lucy Percy, 'beauty, wit, harlot and traitress', had finally become someone. Her career in intrigue and espionage was only just beginning.

EPILOGUE: LUCY, SKY-HIGH DEBTS AND DIAMONDS

In June 1627, when Charles I and the Duke of Buckingham inspected the fleet at Portsmouth, a hamper containing the royal plate, due to be loaded on board *The Triumph* for use at a lunch with their naval captains, instead was accidentally dropped into the Channel. It was an ill-omen for the duke's great expedition of 100 ships and 8,000 troops to support the French Huguenots at La Rochelle, launched for no other reason, most British citizens believed, than to further his vainglorious pursuit of the Queen of France. Buckingham's force went ashore on the strategically important Île de Ré outside La Rochelle but failed to capture its stronghold, Saint-Martin, their siege ladders a fatal four metres short of the top of its surrounding walls. The duke seemed to be everywhere, taking huge personal risks, but at the end of October even he had to admit defeat and sail for home, leaving 5,000 dead in the field.

In 1628 Buckingham resolved to try again but on 23 August, during the confusion caused by feverish preparations at Portsmouth, he was fatally stabbed by a disillusioned army lieutenant, John Felton. The duke's fleet still sailed for France but with much less conviction and on 28 October the unrelieved and starving garrison of La Rochelle surrendered to Richelieu.

Buckingham's demise brought Lucy Percy's husband, James Hay, Earl of Carlisle, back into favour. Charles I made him Groom of the Stool, the leading courtier privy to the mysteries of the royal bedroom; although, no doubt mercifully for Hay, the Groom no longer 'presided over the office of royal excretion'.[1] He remained tolerant of Lucy's affairs, even in 1631 when his political rival, Henry Rich, Earl of Holland, her first cousin, became her principal sexual partner.

With the king's help, Hay arranged to put his homes, lands and possessions into a trust of such complexity that it would confound his long list of creditors. When Hay died on 20 April 1636, aged about fifty-six, as Clarendon put it, he left 'not a house or an acre to be remembered by' and spectacular debts, more than £80,000.[2] His creditors, whose optimism that they would soon be

The siege at La Rochelle.

paid inevitably proved to be misplaced, attended his grand funeral at St Paul's Cathedral in London. Lucy, who was otherwise intimately engaged with the fourth Duke of Lennox at the time, did not.

The twenty-four-year-old duke, Charles I's cousin, James Stewart, was at first besotted with Lucy, who had high hopes of becoming a duchess and even more powerful at court. Events, however, conspired against her. Buckingham's daughter, Mary Villiers, known as little 'Mall', had been married, aged only

twelve, in January 1634 to the fifteen-year-old Charles, Lord Herbert, heir to the earldom of Pembroke. This arranged loveless union came to an abrupt end in January 1636 when Charles, who had set off without his wife on a grand tour of Italy, died in Florence from smallpox. Lucy, at thirty-six, could no longer compete in looks with the highly eligible fourteen-year-old widow. On 3 August 1637, given away by the king, Mary Villiers married James Stewart in the Royal Closet at Whitehall Palace. Lucy probably did not appreciate the irony of her reversal of fortune at the hands of the family she most despised.

Mary Villiers, who married James Stewart.

Charles I finally met his mother-in-law, Marie de' Medici, in October 1638 when she arrived, almost penniless, in England for what proved to be a lengthy stay. The French Queen Mother, after failing in her attempt to remove Richelieu from power in 1630, had made the tactical error of going into exile in the Spanish Netherlands, and was never allowed to return to France. In 1642, at the start of the English Civil War, Charles sent her on her travels again with a gift of £3,000. So keen was everyone but her daughter Henrietta to see her depart, this was the only grant on which he and Parliament could still agree.[3] But with her Continental creditors remorselessly closing in, the money soon evaporated. Marie de' Medici died in poverty at Cologne on 3 July, after being forced to sell her own furniture for food and fuel.

Charles and Marie de' Medici finally meet.

That perennial plotter, the duchess Marie de Chevreuse, remained a thorn in Cardinal Richelieu's side. However, after her part in yet another conspiracy was exposed, in 1637 she was forced to flee, disguised as a boy, across the frontier into Spain. Marie soon found a warm place of safety in Madrid: King Philip IV's bed. From here, she went to England, lived on credit and for two years defied the combined efforts of Richelieu, Louis XIII and her despairing husband, the duc de Chevreuse, to get her back. Charles I, entranced as ever by her beauty, refused all French requests to put Marie on a boat to France. He gallantly purchased her portrait and gave her rooms in Whitehall.

Encouraged by the duchesse de Chevreuse, Anne of Austria also became embroiled in several fresh attempts to remove Richelieu from power. Caught red-handed in treasonable correspondence with her native Spain, with whom France was at war, Anne was saved from disgrace by an astonishing, entirely unexpected pregnancy, followed by the birth in 1638 of the future Louis XIV, who was almost certainly not the son of Louis XIII.[4] When her husband died in 1643, Anne became regent against his wishes; with the help of Richelieu's successor, Cardinal Jules Mazarin, she emerged as the dominant political force during her son's minority.

Nonetheless in 1648, during the civil war known as the Fronde, the Paris Parlement refused to register her royal edict levying new taxes. Anne was obliged to pawn many jewels to meet urgent debts, in particular after her household cooks, fed up with working without pay, had gone on strike. These jewels probably included several of the diamond studs, as the necklace was cut in half; although the loose studs were later redeemed from the pawnbrokers, except perhaps the original pair stolen by Lucy Percy and given to the queen by Cardinal Richelieu, the necklace was not reassembled during her lifetime.

In 1665 Anne feared she was terminally ill with breast cancer and changed her will, with the intention of leaving all her personal jewellery to her granddaughter, Marie Louise, the daughter of her younger son, Philippe d'Orléans. Her elder son, Louis XIV, was furious at potentially losing what he saw as his entitlement and compelled his mother to revert to most of the terms of her original testament. When she died a few months later, on 20 January 1666, a detailed inventory was made of her possessions, consisting of 347 groups of articles, divided into four sections: carriages and their horses, furniture, gold and silver plate, and the personal jewellery.

Louis XIV.

As neither of her sons would trust the other, Claude Ballin, the most celebrated goldsmith in Paris, and Jean Pittan, resident goldsmith in Philippe's household, together listed and valued her jewels – at 1,300,000 livres, perhaps £6,900,000 in today's money - so that they could be divided equally between Louis and Philippe.[5] Item 298 consisted of the six studs still assembled as one half of the necklace; Item 299 the remaining six loose studs. More than forty years had elapsed since the Anne's affair with Buckingham, so it seems unlikely that anyone involved fully appreciated their real significance. All twelve diamonds were given to Philippe as part of his share.[6]

Philippe had a passion for jewels and added greatly to his collection. After his death on 9 June 1701 it was valued at 1,623,000 livres, more than £8,650,000.[7] However, the description of the items does not include anything that could be readily identified as the necklace.[8] Philippe may already have presented it, as Anne intended, to his sixteen-year-old daughter Marie Louise, on the occasion of her betrothal in 1679 to Charles II of Spain. Marie Louise's great-aunt Sophia, destined to play a significant role in British history as the mother of King George I and almost queen of England in her own right, visited the French court that year and remembered seeing a magnificent diamond necklace amongst her niece's trousseau.[9] Thereafter, it disappears without trace, swallowed up in a tragedy. Charles, the victim of chronic in-breeding, was short, lame, epileptic, senile and almost certainly impotent. Marie Louise

Philippe, brother of Louis XIV.

Marie Louise d'Orléans: ten horrendous years of marriage.

died childless, probably from acute appendicitis, after ten horrendous years of marriage.

Tréville later became Anne of Austria's secret lover after delivering her necklace intact in time for her dramatic appearance at the ball. However, it seems unlikely that she had much influence over the king when in 1634, eight years later, Louis XIII appointed him captain of his Musketeers. This coveted post normally had to be purchased for 200,000 livres, a sum far beyond Tréville's means, but Louis waived any payment. Perhaps the embarrassment back in 1626 Tréville had caused Richelieu counted in his favour.

Louis, who always regretted allowing the cardinal to recruit his own personal guard, probably expected his Musketeers under Tréville's vigorous new leadership to emerge as his army's elite force. In this he would soon have been frustrated, because the Cardinal's Guard outnumbered the King's Musketeers by three to one, were more smartly dressed, better equipped and whenever inevitably they clashed on the streets of Paris, proved themselves the superior swordsmen. It was in desperation that Tréville summoned to Paris the young blades who would become Dumas's Three Musketeers, Athos, Aramis and Porthos, all members of his extended family network, after hearing of their prowess at the illegal practice of duelling in the remote province of Béarn. In May 1640 they defeated the elite of the Cardinal's Guard in a pre-arranged clandestine multiple duel, assisted by the precocious Gascon, Charles de Batz, known as d'Artagnan, on his first day in the French capital. All four thereafter were marked men and the cardinal would prove a dangerous enemy.

Richelieu continued to receive valuable intelligence from England, where his secret agent, Lucy Percy, had become the mistress of Thomas Wentworth, Earl of Strafford, the new principal adviser to the king. With a bankrupt treasury, in

Dumas's Three Musketeers and d'Artagnan defeat the Cardinal's Guards.

November Charles I was forced to recall Parliament after an interval of eleven years; Strafford, suddenly expendable, was impeached and executed.

Lucy, possibly on Richelieu's orders, transferred her affections to Thomas Pym, a wealthy landowner and the leader of the House of Commons. In January 1642, when Charles attempted to arrest his main Parliamentary opponents for a second time, the unsuspecting Queen Henrietta disclosed the plan to Lucy, who was able to warn Pym. At the last minute he and four other Members escaped from Westminster by boat, leaving the king who had fallen into the trap to say forlornly, 'All my birds are flown'.[10] It was the first spark in the combustible chain of events that led inexorably to the English Civil War.

Although a wealthy widow, Lucy was also fending off her late husband's creditors, and as a consequence had to live within her means. She could no longer afford such grand residences as Syon Park and Essex House. Lucy was obliged to live in rented property, first at Little Salisbury House in the Strand and later in the decidedly unfashionable Drury Lane. The promise of gold from the vengeful Cardinal Richelieu induced her to set a honey trap for d'Artagnan in Paris and to arrange for his assassination by a group of English cut-throats, correctly anticipating that the Three Musketeers would come to his aid and perhaps suffer the same fate. After a fierce struggle d'Artagnan, Aramis and Porthos escaped with minor injuries but Athos, badly hurt, later died from his wounds in a nearby convent.[11]

Lucy narrowly avoided arrest and returned to England, where she conspired with the Earl of Holland on the Royalists' behalf during the Civil War. However, both had changed sides once too often. Their plans were discovered and on 9 March 1649, five weeks after beheading Charles I, the Roundheads executed Holland as a traitor. Twelve days later, on Oliver Cromwell's orders, Lucy Percy was taken back as a prisoner to the place where she had played as a girl and suffered for love as a teenager: the Tower of London.

But all this, as no doubt Dumas would have said, is another story...

FINAL CURTAIN: NOT QUITE DUMAS

Alexandre Dumas turned the real Affair of the Queen's Diamonds into one of the world's most famous romantic novels in a few frantic months in 1844, truly his annus mirabilis, when he completed 'The Count of Monte Cristo' as well as 'The Three Musketeers'. Aged forty-two, with the outline of both books in his head, Dumas set himself the target of writing and honing twenty pages every day. Such was his dedication to the task, he came to the end of Monte Cristo one afternoon but when many authors would have gone out to a restaurant to celebrate, Dumas, having written only fifteen pages since sunrise, remained seated at his large, white-wood table and wrote the opening five pages of the Musketeers. In his shabby Paris lodgings at No 22 rue de Rivoli, overlooking the claustrophobic inside courtyard, Dumas was oblivious to the outside world. His meals, brought by the landlady, remained largely untouched, as the great writer started work at seven in the morning and continued until late in the evening. Apart from two rickety chairs, his only other functioning piece of furniture was a rusty iron bed, where he snatched a few hours sleep each night but whenever an idea came to him, rose to note it down before dawn.[1]

Le Mousquetaire magazine.

Dumas was a man ahead of his time, akin to a Hollywood script writer before movies were invented, and an enthusiast for self-promotion before sophisticated marketing even existed as a concept. He understood and exploited the potential of multimedia. On the back of his phenomenal triumph came a hugely successful play that opened in 1846, entitled 'Mousquetaires de la Reine', 'Musketeers of the Queen'. Then in February 1847 Dumas launched his own theatre in Paris and named it the 'Historique'. On 12 November 1853 he founded a magazine, called, inevitably, 'Le Mousquetaire', with himself as editor and chief contributor. Dumas made a fortune but squandered it on reckless projects, none greater than a vast mansion, completed in July 1847, which his friends and enemies alike dubbed the 'Palace' of Monte Cristo.

Although Dumas died in 1870, the immortal Musketeers trilogy would become an industry in itself, spawning almost fifty films for the large and small screen, plays for stage and radio, endless new editions, toys in lead and plastic, and even a famous French operetta, 'The Musketeers at the Convent'. It opened on 16 March 1880 at the Bouffes-Parisiens Theatre in Paris. The writer, Paul Ferrier, vainly and more or less truthfully, asserted it was based on a vaudeville called 'Saint-Hilaire and Dupont'; but when the operetta had its first tour the following year to Rome, Vienna and finally St Petersburg, not everything went smoothly. Although the lyrics had been translated into Russian, the

Mousquetaires au Couvent – a scene from the production.

audience, who apparently expected unadulterated Dumas, felt short changed, and many asked for their money back. Some hasty alterations were made to the production: 'Cardinal Richelieu' was given a bigger role, sword fights were extended, the two musketeers became three, and the heroine enlisted them to recover her necklace. Unfortunately, in a scene unintentionally teetering upon comic opera, the action came to an abrupt halt because the necklace, presumably costume jewellery, could not be found. It had been stolen during the interval. Dumas, although perhaps not the real Cardinal Richelieu, would have seen the funny side of that. [2]

BIBLIOGRAPHY

and an explanation of abbreviations referring to original sources
subsequently used in the Notes.
Initial words in bold indicate how the books are described in the Notes

A.A.E. Archives des affaires étrangères, Paris

Abbot. George Abbot, Archbishop of Canterbury, *The Case of Impotency, As Debated in England, In that Remarkable TRYAL Annum 1613 between Robert, Earl of Essex and the Lady Frances Howard, who, after Eight Years Marriage, commenc'd a Suit against him for Impotency* (London: Curll, 1715)

Académie française. *Dictionnaire de l'Académie française*, 1st Edition (1694)

Additional. BL Additional Manuscript

A.G.S. Archivo General de Simancas

Akrigg. George Philip Vernon Akrigg, *Letters of King James VI and I* (Berkeley-Los Angeles: University of California Press, 1984)

Alnwick MSS. Alnwick Manuscript, Alnwick Castle, Northumberland

Anderson. Roberta Anderson, 'Diplomatic Representatives from the Hapsburg Monarchy to the Court of James VI and I', in Alexander Samson, *The Spanish Match*

Arezio. Luigi Arezio, *L'Azione diplomatica del Vaticano nella questione del matrimonio spagnuolo di Carlo Stuart principe di Galles (anno 1623)* (Palermo: Reber, 1896)

Armstrong. Sir Walter Armstrong, *Velazquez: A Study of His Life and Art* (London: Seeley, 1897)

Auchincloss. Louis Auchincloss, *Richelieu* (London: Michael Joseph, 1972)

Avenel. Georges D. Avenel [ed.], *Lettres, Instructions Diplomatiques et Papiers d'État du Cardinal de Richelieu* (Paris: 1861)

Arundel. Charles Arundel and others, *Commonwealth* (Rouen: June 1584)

Babelon. Jean-Pierre Babelon, *Henri IV* (Paris: Fayard, 1982)

Bailly. Auguste Bailly, *Richelieu* (Paris: Flammion, 1936)

Bald. Robert Cecil Bald, *John Donne: a Life* (Oxford: Clarendon Press, 1970)

Bassompierre. Marquis de Chantérac [ed.], Francois de Bassompierre, *Mémoires*, (Paris: 1870-77)

Batho C.S. Gordon R. Batho [ed.] *The Household Papers of Henry Percy, Ninth Earl of Northumberland (1564-1632)*, Camden Society (London: 1962)

Batho H.T. Gordon R. Batho, 'A difficult father-in-law: the Ninth Earl of Northumberland', *History Today* (November 1956)

Battifol. Louis Batiffol, *La Duchesse de Chevreuse*, (London: Heinemann, 1913)

Bergeron. David M. Bergeron, *King James & Letters of Homoerotic Desire* (Iowa City: University of Iowa, 1999)

Bergin 85. Joseph Bergin, *Cardinal Richelieu: Power and the Pursuit of Wealth* (New Haven: Yale University Press, 1985)

Bergin 91. Joseph Bergin, *The Rise of Richelieu* (New Haven: Yale University Press, 1991)

Betcherman. Lita-Rose Betcherman, *Court Lady and Country Wife: Two Noble Sisters in Seventeenth-Century England* (New York: Harper Collins, 2005)

Bilhöfer. Peter Bilhöfer, *Der Winterkönig. Friedrich von der Pfalz. Bayern und Europa im Zeitalter des Dreißigjährigen Krieges* (Heidelberg: 2004)

Bingham. Caroline Bingham, 'Seventeenth-Century Attitudes Towards Deviant Sex', *Journal of Interdisciplinary History*, 1, No 3 (Spring 1971)

Birch Charles. Thomas Birch [ed.], *The Court and Times of Charles the First* (London: 1848)

Birch James. Thomas Birch [ed.], *The Court and Times of James the First, illustrated by Authentic and Confidential Letters* (London: 1848)

B.L. The British Library

Blet. Pierre Blet, *Le clergé du Grand Siècle en ses assemblées (1615-1715)* (Paris : Editions du Cerf, 1995)

B.N. Bibliothèque Nationale, Paris

Boal. Ellen Teselle Boal, 'Saraband: Speed, Steps and Stress', in *Journal of the Viola da Gamba Society of America*, Vol 17 (December 1980)

Boehrer. Bruce Boehrer, 'The Privy and Its Double: Scatology and Satire in Shakespeare's Theatre', in Richard Dutton and Jean Elizabeth Howard [eds.], *A Companion to Shakespeare's Works: Poems, problem comedies, late plays* (Oxford: Blackwell, 2003)

Bolton. Solomon Bolton, *The Extinct Peerage of England* (London: 1769)

Borthwick. Borthwick Institute, University of York

Bouer. Christian Bouer, *La Duchesse de Chevreuse: L'indomptable et voluptueuse adversaire de Louis XIII* (Paris: Pygmalion, 2002)

Brenan. Gerald Brenan, *A History of the House of Percy* (London: 1902)

Brewer. John Sherren Brewer et al., *Letters and Papers, Foreign and Domestic of the Reign of Henry VIII* (London: 1870)

Brienne. Henri-Auguste de Loménie, comte de Brienne, *Mémoires* (Paris: Foucault, 1824)

Byrne. Muriel St Clare Byrne, *The Letters of Henry VIII* (Newcastle upon Tyne: 1936)

Canton. Sanchez Canton, *Carlos Stuart Principe de Gales et y el Conde de Gondamar* (Barcelona: 1948)

Carducho. Vicente Carducho, *Diálogos e la pintura: su defensa, origin, esencia, definición, modos y diferencias* (Madrid: 1970)

Carlisle. Carlisle Papers

Carlton. Charles Carlton, *Charles I, The Personal Monarch* (London: Routledge and Keegan Paul, 1983)

Carter. Charles H. Carter, 'Gondomar: Ambassador to James I' in *The Historical Journal* 7.2 (1964)

Casey. James Casey, *Early Modern Spain* (London: Routledge 1999)

Catholic Clergy. Anonymous, 'Catholic Clergy to the Pope in favour of the Spanish Match', BL

Cawthorne. Nigel Cawthorne, *The Sex Lives of the Kings and Queens of England* (London: Prion, 1994)

Chamberlain. Norman Egbert McClure [ed.], *The Letters of John Chamberlain* (Philadelphia: American Philosophical Society, 1939)

Chardon. Henri Chardon, *La troupe du Roman Comique dé voile et les comédiens de campagne au XVIIeme siecle* [Le Mans: Edmond Monnoyer, 1876 and revised edition, 1905)

Chastenet. Marquis de Puységur, Jacques-François de Chastenet, *Art de la guerre par principes et par règles* (Paris: Jombert, 1748)

Clarendon. Edward Hyde, First Earl of Clarendon, *The True Historical Narrative of the Rebellion and Civil Wars in England* (Oxford: 1702-4)

Clifford. Katherine O. Acheson [ed.], *The Diary of Anne Clifford, 1616-19* (New York: Garland, 1995)

Coke Court. Roger Coke, *The Detection of the Court and the State of England during the last four reigns* (London: Bell, 1697)

Coke Law. Sir Edward Coke, *The Third Part of the Institutes of the Laws of England, concerning High Treason and other pleas of the Crown* (London: Brooke, 1797)

Comédiens. *Nouveau documents sur les comédiens du campagne* (Paris: Picard, 1905)

Cotgrave. Randall Cotgrave, *A Dictionarie of the French and English Tongues* (London: Adam Islip, 1611)

Cottington. Sir Francis Cottington, Account Book, MS 1879, National Library of Scotland

Courtin. Antoine de Courtin, *Nouveau traité de la civilité qui se pratique en France par les Honnêtes Gens* (Paris: 1671)

C.S.P.D. Calendar of State Papers, Domestic

Dedouvres. Louis Dedouvres, *Le Père Joseph Polemiste. Ses Premiers Écrits* (Angers: Grassin, 1895)

Denbigh. Cecilia, Countess of Denbigh, *Royalist father and Roundhead son, being the memoirs of the first and second Earls of Denbigh, 1600-1675* (London: Methuen, 1911)

D'Ewes. Elisabeth Bourcier [ed.], *The Diary of Sir Simons D'Ewes, 1622-4* (Paris: Didier, 1974)

Dk. PRO, State Papers, Denmark

D.N.B. Oxford Dictionary of National Biography

Dom. MSS PRO State Papers, Domestic

Donne. William A. McClung and Rodney Simard, 'Donne's Somerset Epithalamion and the Erotics of Criticism', *Huntington Library Quarterly* 50 (1987)

Doolittle. James Doolittle, *Pattern for Nobility: the Comte de Brienne,* PMLA, Vol. 83, No. 5 (Oct., 1968)

Draper. John W Draper, 'The Queen Makes a Match and Shakespeare a Comedy', *The Yearbook of English Studies*, Vol 2 (1972)

Dudley. De l'Isle and Dudley MS

Dugdale. Richard Dugdale, *A Game at Chess being A narrative of the wicked plots carried on by Seignior Gondamore [sic] for advancing the Popish Religion and the Spanish Faction* (London: Clavell, 1679)

Dulong. Claude Dulong, *Anne d'Autriche: Mère de Louis XIV* (Paris: Hachette, 1980)

Dutton. Richard Dutton [ed.], *Thomas Middleton, 'Women Beware Women' and Other Plays* (Oxford: Oxford University Press, 1999)

Eg. Egerton MS, BL

E.L.H. English Literary History

Ellis. Sir Henry Ellis, *Original Letters, illustrative of English History* (London: Harding, Triphook and Lepard, 1825)

Erlanger Buckingham. Philippe Erlanger, *George Villiers, Duke of Buckingham* (London: Hodder and Stoughton, 1953)

Erlanger Richelieu. Philippe Erlanger, *Richelieu* (Paris: Perrin, 1969)

Estrange. Alfred Guy L'Estrange, *The Palace and the Hospital or Chronicles of Greenwich*, (London: Hurst and Blackett, 1886)

Ettinghausen. Henry Ettinghausen, 'The Greatest News Story Since the Resurrection? Andrés de Almansa y Mendoza's Coverage of Prince Charles's Spanish Trip' in Alexander Samson, *The Spanish Match*

Fagniez. Gustave Fagniez, *Le Père Joseph et Richelieu* (Paris: Hachette, 1894)

Farnham. George Francis Farnham, *Leicestershire Medieval Village Notes* (Leicester: 1929-33)

Félibien. André Félibien, *Histoire de la ville de Paris* (Paris: 1725)

Feuillerat. Albert Feuillerat [ed.], *The Complete Works of Sir Philip Sidney* (Cambridge: Cambridge University Press, 1923)

Flugel. Ingeborg and John Carl Flugel 'On the Character and Married Life of Henry VIII', in Bruce Mazlish [ed.], *Psychoanalysis and History* (Englewood Cliffs, New Jersey: Prentice-Hall, 1963)

Fonblanque. Edward Barrington de Fonblanque, *Annals of the house of Percy* (London: Clay, 1887)

Fraser Court. Antonia Fraser, *The Six Wives of Henry VIII* (London: Weidenfeld and Nicholson, 1992)

Fraser Plot. Antonia Fraser, *The Gunpowder Plot* (London: Weidenfeld and Nicholson, 1996)

Gaçeta. Alfonso de Ceballas [ed.], Gascón de Torquemada, Gerónimo, *Gaçeta y nuevas de la Corte de España desde del año 1660 en addante* (Madrid: 1991)

Gibbs. Philip Gibbs, *The Romance of George Villiers* (London: Methuen, 1908)

Girard. Guillaume Girard, *Histoire de la vie de duc d'Épernon* (Paris: 1655)

Gondi. Aimé Champollion [ed.], Jean-François-Paul de Gondi, *Mémoires de Monsieur le Cardinal de Retz* (Paris: 1859)

Goodman. Godfrey Goodman, *The Court of James I* (London: 1839)

Gordon. Philip Gordon, 'The Duke of Buckingham and van Dyck's "The Continence of Scipio" ', in *Essays on van Dyck* (Ottowa: National Gallery of Canada catalogue, 1983)

Griselle. Eugene Griselle [ed], *État de la Maison du Roi Louis XIII... et sa femme Anne d'Autriche, comprenant les années 1601-1665* (Paris: Juteau-Duvigneau, 1902)

Grouchy. Emmanuel, vicomte de Grouchy, 'Inventaire de la reine Anne d'Autriche', in *Bulletin de la Sociéte de l'Histoire de Paris* (1891, 1892)

Gurr. Andrew Gurr, *The Shakespearean Playing Companies* (Oxford: Oxford University Press, 1996)

Hackett. John Hackett, *Scrinia reserata* (London: 1693)

Hamel. Frank Hamel, *Famous French Salons* (London: Methuen, 1908)

Hammer. Paul E.J. Hammer, 'Myth-Making: Politics, Propaganda and the capture of Cadiz in 1596', *The Historical Journal* 40 (Cambridge: Cambridge University Press, 1997)

Hamy. Pierre A. Hamy, *Entrevue de Francois Ière avec Henry VIII à Boulogne-sur-Mer en 1532. Intervention de la France dans l'Affaire du Divorce. D'Après un grand nombre du Documents inédit* [from BN 10388] (Paris: Gougy, 1898)

Hardwicke. Philip York, Earl of Hardwicke, *Miscellaneous state papers from 1501-1726* (London: Strahan and Cadell, 1778)

Harl. MSS Harleian Manuscript, BL

Harrison. George B. Harrison [ed.], *Advice to his Son by Henry Percy, ninth Earl of Northumberland* (London: Ernest Benn,1930)

Havran. Martin Joseph Havran, *Caroline Courtier: the Life of Lord Cottington* (London: Macmillan, 1973)

Held. Julius S. Held, 'Rubens's Sketch of Buckingham Rediscovered', *The Burlington Magazine* No. 881 (August 1976)

Herbert. Lord Herbert, *The Life of Edward, Lord Herbert of Cherbury* (London: Warwicke, 1824)

Héroard. Eudine Soulié and Eduard De Barthélemy [eds.], *Journal de Jean Héroard sur l'enfance et la jeunesse de Louis XIII* (Paris: 1868)

Hibbard. Carol Hibbard, 'The Role of a Queen Consort: The Household and Court of Henrietta Maria, 1625-1642' in Ronald Asch & Adolf Birk [eds.] *Princes, Patronage and the Nobility 1450-1650*, (Oxford: Oxford University Press, 1991)

H.M.C. Royal Commission on Historical Manuscripts

Hoskins. Anthony Hoskins, 'Mary Boleyn's Carey children and offspring of Henry VIII' in *Genealogists' Magazine*, Vol 25 No 9 (March 1997)

Howell. James Howell, *Epistolae Hoelianae, Familiar Letters Domestic & Forren* [sic] (London: 1645)

Howells. William Dean Howells [ed], *Doña perfecta, Benito Pérez Galdós*, translated by Mary Jane Serrano (New York: Harper, 1923)

Jenkins. Elizabeth Jenkins, *Elizabeth and Leicester* (London: Phoenix Press, 2002)

Joubert. André Joubert, *Histoire de la baronnie de Craon de 1382 a 1626* (Angers: Germain Grassin, 1888)

Kennett. White Kennett (Vol III), John Hughes (Vols I & II), *A complete history of England: with the lives of all the kings and queens thereof; from the earliest account of time, to the death of His late Majesty King William III. Containing a faithful relation of all affairs of state, ecclesiastical and civil* (London: 1706)

Kettering. Sharon Kettering, 'The Patronage Power of Early Modern French Noblewomen' in *The Historical Journal*, Vol. 32, No. 4 (December 1989)

Khevenhüller. Franz Christoph Khevenhüller, *Annales Ferdinandei* (Linz: Oberstörreichisches Landesarchiv, Khevenhüller Bestand, 1623-4)

Koecher. Adolf Koecher [ed.], *Memoiren der Herzogin Sophie nachmals Kurfuerstin von Hannover* (Leipzig: Preussischen Staartsarchiven, 1879)

Lacroix. Paul Lacroix, *Henri IV et Louis XIII* (Paris: Firmin-Didot, 1886)

Lamaire. Adrian Armstrong and Jennifer Britnell [ed.], Jean Lamaire de Belges, *Épistre du roy à Hector et autres pièces de circonstance (1511-1513)* (Paris: Société des Textes Français Modernes, 2000)

La Porte. 'Mémoires de Pierre de La Porte, premier valet de chambre de Louis XIV, contenant plusieurs particula-rites des regnes de Louis XIII et de Louis XIV', in A. Petitot and Monmerque [eds.], *Collection des mémoires relatifs a l'histoire de France*, Ser. II, Vol. LIX (Paris: Foucault, 1827)

Lee. Maurice Lee Junior, *Great Britain's Solomon: James VI and I in his Three Kingdoms* (Urbana: University of Illinois Press, 1990)

Lemberg. Margret Lemberg, *Eine Königin ohne Reich: Das Leben der Winterkönigin Elisabeth Stuart und ihre Briefe nach Hessen* (Marburg: Elwert Verlag, 1996)

Levens. Peter Levens, *The Path-Way to Health* (London: 1654)

Levi. Anthony Levi, *Cardinal Richelieu and the Making of France* (London: Constable Robinson, 2000)

Lindley. David Lindley, *The Trials Of Frances Howard: Fact And Fiction At The Court Of King James* (London: Routledge 1993)

Lockyer. Roger Lockyer, *Buckingham: The Life and Political Career of George Villiers, First Duke of Buckingham, 1592-1628* (London: Longman, 1981)

London. Geraldine Edith Mitton and John Cunningham Geikie, 'Hammersmith, Fulham and Putney', in *The Fascination of London* (London: Black, 1903)

Louis XIII marriage. Anonymous, 'Détail singulier de ce qui se passa le jour de la consummation du marriage de Louis XIII' [1616], reprinted in *Revue retrospective ou bibliothèque historique* (Paris: 1834)

MacCulloch. Diarmaid MacCulloch, *History of the Reformation* (New York: Viking, 2003)

Macdonald. Roger Macdonald, *The Man in the Iron Mask: The True Story of the Most Famous Prisoner in History and the Four Musketeers* (London: Constable Robinson, 2005; revised and enlarged edition, Constable, 2008)

Marston. Richard W. Marston, *'Old Nottinghamshire Marriage Romances'* (High Barnet: 1926)

Marvick. Elizabeth Wirth Marvick, *Louis XIII: The Making of a King*, (New Haven: Yale University Press, 1986)

Mattingly. Garrett Mattingly, *Renaissance Diplomacy* (London: Jonathan Cape, 1955)

Maximes. François, duc de La Rochefoucauld, *Réflexions ou sentences et maximes morales* (Paris: 1665)

McGowan. Margaret McGowan, 'Ballet for the Bourgeois', in *The Journal of the Society for Dance Research*, Vol 19, No 2 (winter 2000)

Mémoires. Joseph François Michaud and Jean Joseph François Poujoulat, *Nouvelle collection des Mémoires relatifs de l'histoire de France* (Paris: 1866)

Mendoza. Miguel Cabas Agrela [ed.], *Bernardino de Mendoza, un escritor soldado al servicio de la monarqua catalica (1540-1604)* (Diputacian de Guadalajara: 2001)

Millanges. Simon Millanges, *La Royalle Reception de leurs Maiestez tres-chrestiennes en la ville de Bordeaus, ou le Siècle d'or ramené par les alliances de Frances et d'Espagne, recueilli par le commandement du Roy* (Bordeaux: 1615)

Michael. Ian D.L. Michael, *King James VI and I and the Count of Gondomar: two London bibliophiles, 1613-18 and 1620-22* (Newark, Delaware: Juan de la Questa, 2002)

Monsieur. *Inventaire après décès de Monsieur*, 17 June 1701, AN 300 AP I

Monson. *Notes and Queries,* 18 May 1907, 10S VII, 'Viscount Monson'

Moote. Alanson Lloyd Moote, *Louis XIII, the Just* (Berkeley: University of California Press, 1989)

Mounts. Charles E. Mounts, 'Spenser and the Countess of Leicester', *ELH*, Vol 19 No 3 (September 1952)

N.A. National Archive

Neale. John Ernest Neale, *Queen Elizabeth* (London: Jonathan Cape, 1934)

Nicoll. Allardyce Nicoll, *Stuart Masques and the Renaissance Stage* (New York: Harcourt Brace, 1938)

Nicholls. Mark Nicholls, *Investigating Gunpowder Plot* (Manchester: Manchester University Press, 1991)

Nichols. John Nichols, *The Progresses, Processions and Magnificent Festivities of King James the First* (London: 1828)

Nicot. Jean Nicot, *Le Thrésor de la langue francoyse* (1606)

N.L.S. National Library of Scotland

Ogg. David Ogg, *Cardinal de Retz* (London: Methuen, 1912)

Oglander. Francis Bamford [ed.], *A Royalist's Notebook: The Commonplace Book of Sir John Oglander, Knight, of Nunwell* (London: Constable, 1936)

Oman. Carola Oman, *The Winter Queen: Elizabeth of Bohemia* (London: Hodder and Stoughton, 1938)

Osborne Edinburgh. Francis Osborne, 'Traditional Memoirs', in *Secret History of the Court of King James the First* (Edinburgh: 1811)

Osborne original. Francis Osborne, 'Traditional Memorials on the Reign of King James' (first published 1658) in *The Works of Francis Osborn* [sic] (London: 1673)

Pagan. Blaise François de Pagan, *Les fortifications de Monsieur le Comte de Pagan avec ses théoremes sur la fortification* (Paris: 1624)

Palais Royal. Victor Champier and Roger Sandoz, 'Du cardinal de Richelieu à la revolution' in *Le Palais Royal d'après des documents inédits* (1629-1900) (Paris: 1900)

Pavie. Eusébe Pavie, *La Guerre entre Louis XIII et Marie de' Medici 1619-1620* (Angers: 1899)

Peyton. Sir Edward Peyton, 'The Divine Catastrophe of the Kingly Family of the House of Stuarts', in Sir Walter Scott [ed.], *Secret History of the Court of James the First* (Edinburgh: 1811)

P.M.L.A. Publications of the Modern Language Association of America

Pontchartrain. P. Phéypeaux de Pontchartrain, 'Mémoires concernant les affaires de France sous la régence de Marie de Médicis', in Joseph François Michaud & Jean Joseph François Poujouat [eds.] *Nouvelle Collection des Mémoires*, 2nd series. Vol V (Paris: 1837)

Pour mon fils. Philippe Alexandre and Beatrix de l'Aulnoit, *Pour mon fils, pour mon roi: La reine Anne, mère de Louis XIV* (Paris: Robert Laffont, 2009)

P.R.O. Public Record Office: The National Archive, Kew, Richmond, Surrey

Puttenham. Richard Puttenham, *The Art of English Poesie* (London: Richard Hall, 1589)

Raumer. Friedrich Ludwig Georg von Raumer, *Briefe aus Paris zur Erlauterung der Geschichte des sechzehnten und siezehnten Jahrhunderts* [Letter from Paris, being a commentary on 16th and 17th century history] (Leipzig: 1831)

Raymond. George Davies [Ed.], *Autobiography of Thomas Raymond* (London: Royal Historical Society, 1917)

R.B. Real Biblioteca, Madrid

R.B.M. Journal of Rare Books and Manuscripts

Redworth Letters. Glyn Redworth, 'Of Pimps and Princes: Three Unpublished Letters from James I and the Princess of Wales Relating to the Spanish Match' in *The Historical Journal*, Vol 37 No 2 (June 1994)

Redworth Y.U.P. Glyn Redworth, *The Prince and the Infanta: The Cultural Politics of the Spanish Match* (New Haven: Yale University Press, 2003)

Regan. Geoffrey Regan, *Royal Blunders* (London: André Deutsch, 2002)

Relf. Frances Helen Relf, 'Notes on the debates in the House of Lords', *Royal Historical Society* (1929)

Renaissance. Ann Rosalind Jones and Peter Stallybrass, *Renaissance Clothing and the Materials of Memory* (Cambridge: Cambridge University Press, 2000)

Richelieu. *Mémoires du Cardinal Richelieu* (Paris: Laurens, 1912-27)

Robb. Graham Robb, *The Discovery of France* (London: Picador, 2007)

Rochefoucauld. 'Mémoires de la Rochefoucauld', in Joseph François Michaud and Jean Joseph François Poujoulat, *Nouvelle Collection des Mémoires pour Service a l'Histoire de France* (Paris: 1850)

Roederer. Antoine-Marie Roederer, *La Famille Roederer 1676-1790* (Paris: Firmin-Didot, 1849)

Roth. Yves Roth, 'Tanneguy II leveneur de carrouges, comte de Tillières (1585-1652)' in *Bulletin de la Societé Historique et Archéologique de l'Orne*, Vol 124, No 4 (2005)

Ruigh. Robert E. Ruigh, *The Parliament of 1624* (Cambridge, Massachusetts: Harvard University Press, 1971).

Rushworth. John Rushworth, *Historical Collections of Private Passages of State, 1618-29* (London: 1721)

Sackville. Kent Archive Office, Maidstone, Kent, Sackville MS

Saintsbury. George Saintsbury, *Minor Poets of the Caroline Period* (Oxford, 1921)

Samson. Alexander Samson, *The Spanish Match: Prince Charles's Journey to Madrid, 1623* (Aldershot: Ashgate, 2006)

Schoppe. Kaspar Schoppe, *Ecclesiasticus auctoritati Jacobi regis oppositus* (1611)

Schreiber. Roy E. Schreiber, 'The First Carlisle: Sir James Hay, First Earl of Carlisle as Courtier, Diplomat and Entrepreneur', *Transactions of the American Philosophical Society*, New Series, Vol. 74, No. 7 (1984)

Sévigné. Marie de Rabutin-Chantal, *Lettres de Madame de Sévigné* (Paris: Monmerqué, 1862)

Sidney. Centre for Kentish Studies, Maidstone, Sidney Papers

Sinclair. James Sinclair [ed.], Sholto and Reuben Percy, *More Percy Anecdotes Old and New* (London: 1826)

Sloane. Sloane MSS, British Library

Smuts. Malcolm Smuts, 'Religion, European Politics and Henrietta Maria's Circle, 1625-41' in Erin Griffey [ed.], *Henrietta Maria: Piety, Politics and Patronage* (Aldershot: Ashgate, 2008)

Southworth. John Southworth, *Fools and Jesters at the English Court* (Stroud: Sutton, 2003)

S.P. State Papers

Spurr. Harry Spurr, *The Life and Writings of Alexandre Dumas* (London: Dent 1902, revised edition 1929)

Stanley. Arthur Penhryn Stanley, *Historical Memorials of Westminster Abbey* (London: 1882)

Starkey. David Starkey, *Henry: Virtuous Prince* (London: Harper Perennial, 2009)

Stewart. Alan Stewart, *The Cradle King: A Life of James VI & I* (London: Chatto and Windus, 2003)

Stone. Lawrence Stone, *The Family, Sex and Marriage in England 1500-1800* (London: Pelican, revised edition, 1979)

Strafford. The Earl of Strafford, *Letters* (London: 1739)

Strong. Roy Strong, *Henry, Prince of Wales, and England's Lost Renaissance* (New York: Thames and Hudson, 1986)

Suckling. Thomas Clayton [ed.], *Suckling, Works* (Oxford: Clarendon, 1971)

Tallemant. Antoine Adam [ed.], Gédéon Tallemant, sieur des Réaux, *Historiettes* (Paris: Gallimard, 1967)

Tanner. Bodleian MS Tanner

Tawney. Richard Henry Tawney, *Business and Politics under James I* (Cambridge: Cambridge University Press, 1958)

Thomas. Phillip Drennon Thomas, 'The Tower of London's Royal Menagerie', *History Today*, Vol. 46 (August 1996)

Tillières. Maurice Hippeau [ed.], *Mémoires Inédit du comte Leveneur de Tillières, ambassadeur en Angleterre, sur la cour de Charles Ier et son marriage avec Henriette de France* (Paris : Poulet-Malassis, 1862)

T.L.S. Times Literary Supplement

Tratados. Samuel Rawson Gardiner [ed], Francisco de Jesús, *El Hecho de los tradados del matrimondo pretendido por el Principe de Gales conc la serenenissima Infanta de España* (London: Camden Society, 1869)

Trumbull. Berkshire Record Office, Reading, Downshire Papers, Trumbull-Downshire MS

Turner. Edward Sackville Turner, *The Court of St. James's* (New York: St Martin's Press, 1959)

Univers. Marie Touannin and Jules Van Gaver, *L'Univers* (Paris: 1840)

Vallière. Louis César de La Baume Le Blanc, duc de La Vallière, *Ballets, opéra et autres ouvrages lyriques, par ordre chronologique, depuis leur origine* (Paris: C.-Jean-Baptiste Bauche, 1760)

Varlow A.D. Sally Varlow, *The Lady Penelope: The lost tale of love and politics in the reign of Elizabeth I*, (André Deutsch, London, 2007 and second edition 2009)

Varlow H.R. Sally Varlow, 'Sir Francis Knollys's Latin dictionary: new evidence for Katherine Carey', *Historical Research*, vol.80, no. 209 (August 2007)

Verney. Sir Ralph Verney, *Notes on the Long Parliament*, [ed. John Bruce] (London: Camden Society, 1845)

Vérité. Anonymous, *La Vérité prononcant ses Oracles* (Paris: 1652)

Villiers. Frederick William Fairholt [ed.], *Poems and Songs relating to George Villiers* (London: Percy Society, 1850)

Waldman. Milton Waldman, *Elizabeth and Leicester* (New York: Houghton Mifflin, 1945)

Waller. Edmond Waller, *Poems* (London: 1645)

Walton. Izaak Walton [ed.] 'The Life of Sir Henry Wotton' in *Reliquiae Wottonianae* (London: 1651)

Weir. Alison Weir, *Henry VIII: King and Court* (London: Jonathan Cape, 2001)

Weldon James. Anthony Weldon, 'Court and Character of King James' in Sir Walter Scott [ed.], *The Secret History of the Court of James the First* (Edinburgh: 1811)

Weldon Scot. Anthony Weldon, *A Perfect Description of the People and Country of Scotland* (London: 1618)

White. Christopher White, *Peter Paul Rubens: Man and Artist* (New Haven: Yale University Press, 1987)

Williams E. Ethel Carleton Williams, *Anne of Denmark* (London: Longman, 1970)

Williams N. Noel Williams, *A Fair Conspirator: Marie de Rohan, duchesse de Chevreuse* (London: Methuen, 1913)

Williamson. Hugh Ross Williamson, 'The Poisoning of King James I' in *Enigmas of History* (London: Michael Joseph, 1957)

Willson. David Harris Willson, *King James VI & I* (London: Jonathan Cape, 1956)

Wilson. Arthur Wilson, *The History of Great Britain, being the Life and Reign of King James I* (London: 1653)

Wotton. Sir Henry, *Reliquiae Wottonae* (London: 1654)

Wood. Walter Wood, *The East Neuk of Fife: its histories and antiquities* (Edinburgh: Oliver and Boyd, 1862)

Wright. Louis B Wright, 'A Game at Chess', TLS, I6 February 1928

Wroth. Lady Mary Wroth, *The Countesse of Mountgomeries Urania* (London: Marriott and Grismand, 1621)

Wynn. Richard Wynn's account, in Thomas Hearne, *Historia vitae et regni Ricardi secundi*, appendix iv, 297-341 (Oxford: 1729).

Young. Michael Young, *King James & the History of Homosexuality* (New York: New York University Press, 2000)

NOTES

CURTAIN RAISER: *A Game at Chess*

[1.] Strictly, of course, no longer 'Shakespeare's Globe', since the bard had already retired from London before his theatre was set alight on 29 June 1613 by a cannon ball fired during a production of *Henry VIII*. The Globe was rebuilt the following year with a new roof of tiles to replace the flammable straw. The Globe was patronised by the social elite as well as by working men and riff-raff; it competed for local custom with taverns that were little more than brothels, or offered bear-baiting and cock-fighting.

[2.] Performances took place between 2 p.m. and 5 p.m. because the Globe had no lighting. The King's Men were the successors to 'Her Majesty's Servants', Shakespeare's troop, which had enjoyed royal patronage.

[3.] PRO SP, Spain, 94/31 fol. 132.

[4.] Gondomar suffered from an anal fistula, a severe abscess of the bowels; a special chair accompanied him around London, with a whole cut in the centre of its seat. See Gurr, 142.

[5.] Wright,112, concludes that Middleton would hardly have written a play that he could foresee would displease James I 'without some assurance of reward'; he had 'authority from some source high in power, most likely Buckingham'. It still cost him a spell in the Fleet.

[6.] Saintsbury, Vol III, 6.

PROLOGUE
(between pages 1 and 10)

[1.] Macdonald (2008 edition) 293-4.

[2.] Roederer, 11.

[3.] Long afterwards, in 1853, he was allowed to publish a truncated version of his father's papers.

1: ANOTHER BOLEYN GIRL
(between pages 11 and 38)

[1.] Starkey, 337-8. Dukes of Buckingham were created twice, the first line in 1444, the second line (beginning with George Villiers) in 1623.

[2.] Thomas Stafford's son Henry at first was stripped of his title altogether. It was restored but only as Baron Stafford. See Bolton, 40.

[3.] In 1534 Henry VIII was accused to his face of "meddling" with Elizabeth Boleyn. Weir, 126, states that 'an early liaison... with Lady Boleyn cannot be ruled out'.

[4.] Flugel, 146.

[5.] Interviewed in February 2009. Dr Starkey remains to be convinced that Henry VIII is the father of Mary Boleyn's son. For the most likely date of Catherine's birth, coinciding with a grant of land to William Carey, see Estrange, Vol. I, p. 192.

[6.] Hoskins, 345–52, concludes that Henry VIII sired both of Mary's children.

[7.] Brewer, Vol. VIII, 567, records the following remark made in 20 April 1535 by John Hale, vicar of Isleworth, to the Royal Council: *"Morever, Mr. Skydmore dyd show to me yongge Master Carey, saying that he was our suffren Lord the Kynge's son by our suffren Lady the Qwyen's syster, whom the Qwyen's grace might not suffer to be yn the Cowrte."* Henry Carey was aged nine at the time. Two weeks later Hale was executed for ostensibly unrelated reasons.

[8.] The tower was built by Duke Humphrey of Gloucester on Greenwich Hill in about 1433 and demolished to enable the construction of the Royal Observatory in 1675.

[9.] Puttenham, Chapter XXIII, unnumbered but para.13. The book was published anonymously because Richard Puttenham was in prison at the time. It is often wrongly attributed to his brother, George Puttenham, but he never left England and the book's contents show that the author (as did Richard) visited other princely courts in France, Italy and Spain. An adjacent reference to Catherine of Aragon and that the king 'found himselfe grieued that the Emperour should take her part and worke vnder hand with the Pope to hinder the divorce' confirms that the anecdote refers to Henry VIII.

[10.] Sir Andrew Flamock, 'a merry conceyted man and apt to skoffe', clearly liked to live dangerously. His derogatory rejoinder to Henry's verse was 'Within this hour, She pissed full sour, And let a fart'. Henry's momentary anger evidently passed because Flamock was granted lands belonging to Kenilworth Abbey after the dissolution of the monasteries. The trip down river (or sometimes up river, from Greenwich Palace) was not an isolated event. On a previous occasion recorded by Puttenham, upon entering the boundary of Greenwich Park, Henry, no doubt full of eager anticipation at seeing Mary Boleyn, blew his hunting horn and Flamock, probably not by accident, promptly farted with equal volume.

[11.] Fraser, 136.

[12.] The author of *The Other Boleyn Girl* was interviewed for a Historic Royal Palaces Video, 'Henry VIII: Love Sex and Marriage' (2009).

[13.] Anne Boleyn took to her bed at Hever with the sweating sickness on the very same day but recovered.

[14.] Byrne, 71.

[15.] Hamy, 62-8. Anne Boleyn opened the dancing with Francis I. The other ladies with Mary were Lady Derby, Lady Fitzwalter and Lady Wallop. The hypothesis that Mary Boleyn remained a member of the inner circle of the Tudor Court for much longer than previously supposed is persuasively developed by Hilary Mantel during her brilliant characterisation of Thomas Cromwell in *Wolf Hall* (Harper Collins, 2009). Mary remained on the market for another husband, even, in one of Mantel's more fanciful moments, considering Cromwell himself. Of the Howards and the Boleyns, she has Mary say: 'I want to marry a man who frightens them.' (page 139).

[16.] William's grandfather, Humphrey Stafford, backed the wrong horse at Bosworth in 1485 and was executed as a traitor at Tyburn, his lands forfeit; Henry VIII restored some of them to his family in 1515.

17. NA, King's Bench 8/9, May 1536 records the charge of incest with her brother George Boleyn made against Anne. Written in Latin, it alleges that Anne 'tempted her brother with her tongue in the said George's mouth and the said George's tongue in hers' and that the pair then had sexual intercourse 'contrary to all human laws'.

18. Like many of the dates for Mary Boleyn, there is little agreement. Some sources give the date of her death as 19 July 1543, others 30 July.

19. Stanley, 183, 193.

20. The Imperial ambassador Ernest Chapuys, in reporting Anne Boleyn's execution to Vienna, was at a loss to explain what Henry saw in her successor as queen, Jane Seymour, whom he thought a rather plain girl with beady eyes and a double chin. Chapuys speculated that her appeal lay in her 'enigme' or 'secret' parts, meaning he had heard that she possessed a prehensile vagina.

21. Varlow HR, 315-323. This research is of particular significance as it established for the first time the correct date of Lettice's birth – three years earlier than historians previously had believed it to be.

22. Hoskins states that Lettice's documents were lodged with those of Henry III, Henry VI, Mary II, William III, Prince George of Denmark, Queen Anne and Queen Caroline.

23. Neale, 242; Waldman, 159.

24. Mounts, 194.

25. Neale, 242; Feuillerat, Vol III, 396, refers to an even earlier secret and hasty marriage between the couple that did not satisfy the bride's relatives.

26. Lettice would live even longer than Elizabeth, to the considerable age of ninety-one, dying on Christmas Day 1634.

27. Arundel. This polemic tract, unpaginated in its original form, was assembled in 1584 by English Catholics in exile in Paris. It accused Leicester of adultery and murder.

28. Varlow AD, 263-7.

29. Ibid, 28.

30. Mendoza, 113. For the best account of Lettice's relationship with Elizabeth I, see Jenkins, 279, 314 et seq.

31. Draper, 64. Draper states that the couple parted by mutual consent in July 1587.

32. Ibid.

33. Harrison, 79.

34. Draper, 64.

35. The anonymous comment is dated 1607, indicating that Dorothy's marriage remained contentious at that point. Draper [cited above, footnote, 63] takes the view that preparations for a marriage and reception on this scale would have taken at least six months. Her first husband was known to be alive in January 1595. See Batho, Third Series, 92, xlviii and xlix. Sinclair, Vol II, 116 states that Perrott lived into the reign of James I.

36. According to Lucy's brother-in-law, the Earl of Leicester, she was born about Michaelmas 1599 (Dudley, 6.623).

37. The great hall and long gallery were transformed by Robert Adam who introduced a gilt and marble decor from 1761. Syon House was formerly a royal residence. In January 1547 Henry VIII's coffin was left overnight in the chapel en route to his burial at Windsor. His bloated corpse

forced open the coffin as it expanded and deposited a hideous collection of bodily fluids on the floor, whereupon they were lapped up by dogs.

[38.] Batho, 744.

[39.] London, 75. The house, once known as 'The Palace' because of its royal visitors, no longer exists but Lacy also gave his name to a nearby, surviving street.

[40.] Batho, 744.

[41.] Nicholls, 102, 224.

[42.] Percy was accepted into Petersham College, Cambridge on 4 July 1579.

[43.] Nicholls, 109 n. 47.

[44.] Varlow AD, 225.

[45.] James invited him to 'lay in his chamber' for several nights so that they might discuss the matter further, but in all probability had a sexual motive; in any event, Percy declined.

[46.] Goodman, Vol 1, 102. Fraser Plot, 204-5, draws attention to Goodman's failure to identify his source.

[47.] The Earl of Northumberland said at his trial in June 1606 that he had always thought Percy loyal but since his arrest he had discovered that Percy had expressed these hopes 'behinde his backe'.

[48.] SP 14/216/225.

[49.] Secret correspondence between Lord Henry Howard and James VI, 1602.

[50.] Tanner 75, folio 203. These contain copies of parts of Fawkes' interrogation under torture on 11 and 30 November 1605; the originals are missing.

[51.] Betcherman, 66.

2: BEDFELLOWS
(between pages 39 and 62)

[1.] Oglander, 193.

[2.] CSP Scotland VI, 149.

[3.] Willson, 85.

[4.] Sir Dudley Carleton wrote in 1613, *The queen shooting a deer mistook her mark and killed Jewel, the King's most special and favourite hound; at which he stormed exceedingly awhile.*' See Williams E, 164-5.

[5.] CSP Scotland IX, 701-6.

[6.] Lee, 241.

[7.] Osborne, 89.

[8.] Oglander, 196-7.

[9.] Weldon Scot., 75. When his tract appeared in print, there was uproar in Scotland, and James was forced to remove him from office.

[10.] Weldon James Vol 2, 75: 'I wish this Kingdom have never any worse...for he lived in peace, dyed in peace; and left all his Kingdomes in a peaceable condition'.

[11.] Ibid.

[12.] Wood, 393.

[13.] CSP Venetian, 1603-07, No 206, 143.

14. Harl. MS 1581, fo. 336, BL.

15. Schreiber, 10. A masque supplied a mixture of dance, mime, song and verse, combined as a scenic spectacle.

16. Osborne, Vol I, 275.

17. Chamberlain, Vol I, 495.

18. BL Additional 4129 fol. 18 and Lindley, 109-12.

19. See Donne, 95.

20. Bergeron, 76.

21. Akrigg, 336-7.

22. James I, however, did not take this for granted. At Carr's trial, two men stood ready to throw a heavy cloak over him to muffle his words and remove him from the Lords, if he made any reference to the king's private affairs.

23. CSP Venetian, 1613-15, Nos 870-1, 481-2.

24. Urania , Vol I ii 2-3.

25. HMC, xx (1969), part 6, p 84; see also HMC xxii (1971) 160-2.

26. In July 1616 Dorothy's mother, the Countess of Northumberland, unaware of her elopement, was still concerned that another suitable match would be found for Robert. See Chamberlain Vol 1, 498 and Alnwick, 101, fol 78.

27. Strong, 86-7.

28. Fonblanque, ii 342-3.

29. Chamberlain, Vol I, 570.

30. Brenan, Vol II, 191.

31. Clifford, 30.

32. Nicoll, 216.

33. Chamberlain to Carleton, 8 March 1617, CSPD, 'James 1 - Vol 90: March 1617', C James I, 1611-18 (1858), 439-456.

34. Chamberlain, Vol 2, 77.

35. Ibid, Vol 2, 84-5.

36. Clarendon, 1702-4.

37. Renaissance, 20.

38. Kennett, Vol II, 703.

39. Chamberlain, Vol 2, 24.

40. Ibid, Vol 2, 94.

41. The Spanish king also sent James I an elephant, which would only drink wine – a gallon a day. Animals were kept at the Tower from c.1204 until 1835. See Thomas, 29-35.

42. Ellis, 2nd series, Vol III, 247. The royal physician in question was Theodore de Mayerne, whose parallel roles at the English and French courts are described in the next chapter.

43. Oman, 84.

44. Willson, 192, 286, 388.

45. DNB, entry on Hay by Roy E Schreiber: 'Domestic career'.

46. Chamberlain, Vol II, 181.

47. Ibid, 195.

48. On 23 May 1618 Count Jaroslav Martinitz and Count Wilhelm Slavata were thrown out of

a window from a height of 27 ells, an Imperial measure equivalent to 100 feet, so they had a lucky escape; this is generally regarded by historians as the event that precipitated what became known as the Thirty Years War.

49. Lemberg, 26.

50. Cynics suggested at the time that his conversion to a faith that countenanced wedlock had been prompted by his dogged pursuit of Anne More, the great-niece of Sir Thomas Moore. Anne was the daughter of a wealthy landowner and knight of the realm, who try as he might was unable to prevent them marrying in secret. It proved to be a sensuous match that produced twelve children in sixteen years. David Renaker, Professor of English at San Francisco State University, believes on the evidence of Donne's poetry, 'We may have underestimated the sexual inventiveness of the aristocracy of seventeenth-century England'. See The Atheist Seventeenth Century website, 'On the History of Renaissance Literature', *Oral Sex: A Theme in Donne and Some Cavalier Poets* (1991).

51. Chamberlain, Vol II, 237.

3: RISING STAR
(between pages 63 and 86)

1. Univers, 312n.

2. Farnham, Vol II, 61.

3. Borthwick, Star Chamber proceedings, 1607, Attorney General hearing probate caveats of 11 November 1606. He declined to set aside Sir William Reyner's will in favour of his sister's children, a will that made no mention of Mary Villiers. See also Marston, 12 September 1925, High Barnet Library. The principal witness against Lady Villers was a servant, John Siston, first employed by the late Lady Aubrey and clearly not enamoured of Mary's rapid climb up the social ladder. Siston was sent to London to pawn the plate in December 1605.

4. Additional, 11,402. 147v.

5. Blois was then part of the diocese of Chartres, which Valençay, who would become a loyal supporter of Cardinal Richelieu, took over on Christmas Eve 1620. See Blet, 82.

6. Sloane, 2089 fol. 27v.

7. Avenell, Vol 1, 13-55.

8. Bergin, 103.

9. M.C., LXXII, 277.

10. The rue du Battoir became the rue de Quatrefages in the 19th century, renamed after the famous botanist Jean Louis Armand de Quatrefages de Bréau.

11. Anne Aston instead married a Colchester gentleman, Sir Thomas Perient, and disappears into obscurity.

12. For example, Ingram lent the Earl of Nottingham £1,840 against the security of a diamond ring worth considerably less. See Renaissance, 27.

13. Akrigg, 201.

14. Walton, 209.

15. Lockyer, 35. Lockyer gives a formidable list of sources for this episode, of which the most reliable is probably HMC Supp., 66-7.

16. James had all the details suppressed, telling Cecil that no reproach of the queen 'can ever be separated from the dishonour of me and all my posterity'. The king's letter is reproduced in Akrigg, 286-7.

17. Stewart, 184.

18. Williams E., 30.

19. Turner, 123.

20. HMC Hastings IV, 16.

21. Young, 135.

22. Young, 49 and 172 (73n.); CSP (Hardwicke) Vol I, 454.

23. Stone, 266.

24. Lockyer describes him as the 'son of an Elizabethan seadog' (page 35). However, this was not his father but his grandfather, who ran away to sea from Balliol College, Oxford.

25. Chamberlain Vol II, 144.

26. Buckingham was joint commander of the fleet from October 1618 and appointed Lord High Admiral in his own right on 28 January 1619.

27. Young (page 56) states that *Corona Regia* was published in 1615.

28. According to Walton, 65, one of Schoppe's contemporaries.

29. Bald, 349-50. Elizabeth, who did not speak a word of Czech, was already unpopular with the Prague population.

30. Wotton, 343.

31. Lemberg, 21. The original sentence in German has a much greater sense of foreboding and finality: *'Ach, nun geht die Pfalz in Böhmen'.*

32. Tillières to Puysieux, 12 November 1619.

33. Waller, 96, lines 19-26. Many subsequent editions expurgated these lines.

34. CSP Venetian, 1619-21, No 86, p 49.

35. Carleton to Chamberlain, 1 January 1620, The Hague: PRO SP 84/94, fos 5th – 6th.

36. Carlisle, 2595 fol 164.

37. Wilson, 149.

38. Donna Hollandia owned the Manor from 1603 to 1632 before selling up and returning to Brussels. In 1626 Charles I introduced an Act against 'bawdy houses' and many were suppressed. Riotous behaviour at the Manor as it went down market led to an unsuccessful attempt in December 1631 by the Sheriff of London to arrest Dame Hollandia and her prostitutes. The drawbridge had a secret lever that enabled a central section to be opened without warning, plunging the Sheriff's men into the stinking moat. See Simpson, 68-9.

39. Goodman Vol II, 189-91.

40. Gordon, 53-5. Publius Cornelius Scipio's magnanimity took place in 209 BC after the capture of modern-day Cartagena from the Carthaginians (see Livy, Ab urbe condita, XXVI, 50).

41. Lockyer, 60.

42. Schoppe, 196. Wotton's famous saying in its original Latin is *Legatus est vir bonus peregre missus ad mentiendum rei publicae causa.*

43. Gondomar's cruel comparison was prompted by Frederick's creation at Heidelberg in 1614 for his wife Elizabeth of a baroque garden in Italian Renaissance style. See Bilhöfer, S. 24. 24.

44. A German song, written at Michaelmas 1620, coined the epithet that stuck with Frederick for

the rest of his life. It began:
Oh! Poor winter king, what have you done?
How could you steal the emperor's crown
By pursuing your rebellion.

4: AMBASSADORS
(between pages 87 and 106)

[1.] See Hammer, 621-642.

[2.] Anderson, 212, 216.

[3.] Afterwards Gondomar's uncle tried unsuccessfully to claim the credit. See Michael, 421-5.

[4.] DIE, iii, 85.

[5.] Willson, 365.

[6.] See Carter, 189-208. In an effort to mollify Gondomar, James I had shown the Spanish ambassador the orders given to Raleigh before he sailed. Gondomar was able to press vigorously for Raleigh's execution, which took place on 29 October 1618.

[7.] See Dutton. Gondomar's anal discomfort was cruelly exposed, as in 4.2.7: 'There's a foul flaw in the bottom of my drum'.

[8.] Carter, 195-98. Buckingham was added to the list of Spanish pensioners early in 1618.

[9.] Mattingly, 260-1.

[10.] Carter, 197, n.18. Gondomar was practically never in funds himself and almost certainly borrowed the money: he was probably the London moneylenders' best customer.

[11.] Dugdale, reproduced in Harl. Miscellany, Vol III, 313-26.

[12.] Mattingly, 262.

[13.] Arter, 205.

[14.] Raymond, 25.

[15.] Catholic Clergy, undated, folio 294.

[16.] Dom.MSS 14. 86.95. The incidents took place in March and June 1616 respectively.

[17.] A Scottish observer used Buckingham's prowess as a dancer to illustrate his rise, saying of this masque that he 'jumpt higher than any Englishman did in so short a time'.

[18.] MacCulloch, 500.

[19.] Willson, 374-6.

[20.] Robert Anderson, 218-9. Gondomar arrived in August 1613 and left on extended leave on 16 July 1618. He returned on 7 March 1620 and had an audience with the king at Whitehall on 12 March. He returned to Spain to progress the Match in July 1622.

[21.] Redworth Letters, 155 n. 22.

[22.] Canton, 146, dates the letters to the summer of 1620 but they may extend over a longer period ending in October 1622.

[23.] Redworth Letters, 405 n.17. Here Redworth quotes from this earlier letter with its postscript from the prince, citing MS II-2108, fol. 74c.

[24.] Ibid.

[25.] CSP Venetian Vol 18 (1912), 502-13.693. Mme Saint-Luc later fell out badly with Marie' de Medici.

[26.] Raumer, Vol II, 259-78. Von Raumer was Professor of Political Science and History at

Berlin University from 1819 to 1847. Some, but by no means all, of Raumer's source material appears in the compilation of Tillières's memoirs subsequently published in 1852 (listed under Tillières in the bibliography). The authenticity of the manuscript has been questioned because the handwriting is clearly the work of more than one person. However, it is known that the ambassador delegated much of his written work to his confidential secretary in England, Du Moulin.

[27.] Raumer, Vol II, 269.

[28.] Gibbs, 91-97.

[29.] Willson, 245.

[30.] Relf, 10 March 1621, 14.

[31.] Lockyer, 94.

[32.] Sackville ON. 2461.

[33.] Raumer Vol II, 269 and see Lockyer, 120.

[34.] Raumer Vol II, 261. Raumer quotes directly from Tillière's dispatch in the original French, presumably deciding that the story was too distasteful to translate for the benefit of his German readership. The English translation of Raumer's history published in 1835 omits this episode, which occurred in 1620, altogether. Tillières does not supply the Christian name of Buckingham's niece in his dispatch but her identity can be established. One of Buckingham's half brothers, Sir William Villiers, had two daughters by Rebecca Roper but whilst the exact date of birth of female children was rarely recorded, neither Catherine nor Ann could have been aged 'nine or ten' in 1620. Elizabeth Villiers, the daughter of Buckingham's other half brother, Sir Edward Villiers, by Barbara St John, was born in 1610 and meets the necessary criteria. Elizabeth went on to marry Robert Douglas, the future Earl of Morton, in April 1627. She died on or about 15 December 1654.

[35.] Young, 61.

[36.] Raumer, Vol II, 261.

[37.] The French poet Théophile de Viau, noted for his scandalous verses, in 1623 addressed an obscene poem to Buckingham, 'Par ce doux appétit des vices', which left nothing to the imagination. Viau listed a number of homosexual pairings and included the couplet:
'And it is well known that the King of England
Fucks the Duke of Buckingham.'

[38.] Coke Law, 57-8.

[39.] Bingham, 447-68. The trial took place in 1631.

[40.] Peyton Vol II, 346-353.

[41.] CSP Scotland, IX, 701.

[42.] The term derives from cheating at the card game of faro. Tiny strips were cut off certain cards, so that a dealer in the know could tell where they lay in the deck. When the cards were cut convex or concave, it was called 'both ends against the middle'.

[43.] CSP Venetian 1623-1625, no. 459, pp 360-1.

[44.] Sydney, Vol I, 126.

[45.] Chamberlain, Vol 2, 333.

[46.] Although invented by Sir John Harington in 1596. He installed one at Richmond Palace for his godmother, Queen Elizabeth I, but allegedly she refused to use it because she thought the flushing mechanism made too much noise.

47. Chamberlain, Vol 2, 381.

48. See Woodford to Trumbull letter of 31 July 1621, Trumbull, 49: no 28.

49. Chamberlain, Vol 2, 390.

50. Hay to Calvert, 28 August 1621, Moissac; PRO, SP 78/69, fos 176a-177b.

51. John Woodford to Nethersole, 13 September 1620; PRO., SP 81/18, fol. 74a.

52. CSP Venetian 1621-23, no. 338, pp. 244-5; Chamberlain, Vol 2, 424.

5: THE HOUSE OF THE SEVEN CHIMNEYS

(between pages 107 and 136)

1. Tillières to Puisieux, 18 May 1622 London; PRO, 31/3/56, fol 36b.

2. Tillières to Puisieux, 1 September 1622 London; PRO, 31/3/56, fol 103b.

3. Gondomar to Ferdinand, 26 November 1621, AGS, Estado Libro, fol 363v.

4. Howell, 129.

5. RB, MS 2-2108, no. 69.

6. Lockyer, 162.

7. RB, MS 2-2108, no. 69.

8. Harl. MS 1583, fos 349-350.

9. See Sir Horace Vere's entry in DNB, 1885-90. Vere, a professional soldier, led a volunteer force to the Palatinate and divided his troops among the three most important strongholds. He occupied Mannheim himself, stationed Sir Gerard Herbert in Heidelberg Castle, and ordered Sir John Burroughs to defend Frankenthal.

10. Relf, 1624, iii, 221-2. Buckingham gave his account of the visit to Spain in the Lords soon after his return.

11. Bergeron, 5.

12. Havran, 70.

13. Sackville, ON. 7748.

14. Brett did not return to England until March 1624. In July of that year, when James I was hunting in Waltham Forest, Brett ignored Buckingham's strictures to keep away from the king, rode up to him, and seized the bridle of his horse. He was sent to London's Fleet prison for six weeks and forbidden thereafter to come within ten miles of the court. See Williamson, 139.

15. Trumbull, 18.88. William Monson, who would be made an Irish Peer, had an eventful career. He refused to pay Ship Money, Charles I's illegal tax, and was appointed a judge at the king's trial in January 1649; but withdrew after the opening sessions and refused to sign the death warrant. Nonetheless at the Restoration in 1660, Monson was accused along with the other Regicides, stripped of his property and titles, and drawn on a cart from the City of London to Tyburn and back with a halter around his neck, before starting life imprisonment. He died in Fleet prison in 1673. See Monson, 381.

16. Cottington to James, 8 April 1623, NLS, Advocates ms 33.1.10, Vol Xxvii, no 20, fols 53-54.

17. Gibbs,140.

18. Trumbull, 7.179.

19. Wotton, 84.

[20.] Robb, 140. In 1789 it would take a week for the news of the fall of the Bastille to reach Beziers, 520 miles on post roads from Paris, at an average speed of less than four m.p.h.

[21.] The post-horses system was established in 1464, at first in a limited form, by Louis XI of France. See Jean Lamaire de Belges, *Épistre du roy à Hector et autres pièces de circonstance (1511-1513)*, 44.

[22.] Nonetheless it seems that Prince Charles and Buckingham were recognised before the end of their day's sightseeing in Paris. Gibbs, 144, concludes that 'sharp eyes were upon them, piercing their disguise'.

[23.] Lockyer, 139.

[24.] Vallière, 75.

[25.] Ettinghausen, 79 n.14.

[26.] According to Gibbs, 145, Lord Herbert sent a messenger after Buckingham and Prince Charles, warning them of the pursuit, and urging them to make all the haste they could out of France.

[27.] Carlisle to Conway and Calvert, 24 February 1623, Boulogne; PRO, SP 78/71, fos 43a.

[28.] Herbert, 135.

[29.] Venetian ambassador to France, Giovanni Pesaro, letter to the Doge, 12 March 1623, CSP Venetian, XVII, 586.

[30.] Levi, private papers, consisting of unpublished extracts from La Rochefoucauld's memoirs. See also note 20 in chapter eight.

[31.] Robb, 160.

[32.] Wotton, 87.

[33.] Ibid.

[34.] Ibid.

[35.] Robb, 57. Jean Racine was writing in 1661.

[36.] Robb, 21.

[37.] Anthony Levi, private papers. Richelieu did not yet reside permanently in Paris but was present for a meeting of the Council.

[38.] Bergin, 264-5.

[39.] See, despite significant inaccuracies in the account of this anecdote, Anderson, 214 and Redworth YUP, 80. Carlos Columna represented Spain in London from April 1622 to October 1624.

[40.] Howell, 132.

[41.] Tratados, 203.

[42.] Gibbs, 151, says the pretence that the Prince of Wales had not accompanied Buckingham was maintained while Buckingham and Digby were smuggled into the royal palace to be received by the King of Spain.

[43.] Tratados, 325-6.

[44.] Harl. 6897.153. Edward VI made Sir John Dudley, a commoner, Earl of Warwick then, on 11 October 1551, Duke of Northumberland. His father, Edmund Dudley, had been executed for high treason in August 1510. John Dudley would suffer the same fate in August 1553.

[45.] Bergeron, 127-8 and 160-.1. The letter was sent on 1 April 1623.

[46.] Cottington, unnumbered.

47. Casey, 82.

48. PRO, SP 14/140, fo.84. The Crown Jewels were first kept in the Tower in 1303 and various items in the collection had a chequered history: pawned by Edward III and sold by Oliver Cromwell. The British ambassador in Madrid, Digby, had the dangerous task of bringing back the diamonds from Spain when the Match fell apart.

49. Nichols, Vol iv, 823, quoting from a letter from Buckingham to the king, 17 March 1623.

50. Carducho, 436-7.

51. Ellis, Vol iii, 137.

52. Gibbs, 171-2.

53. Southworth, 141-2.

54. Gaçeta, 156.

55. Tratados, 252 . His undated letter (believed to have been transcribed, and perhaps prompted, by Hay early in May 1623) was extremely critical of Buckingham, whereas the duke had engineered a much more innocuous letter from the fool to James dated 28 April by means of putting Archie's supposed thoughts on paper himself.

56. Schreiber, 50.

57. Ellis, First series, Vol III, 113-14.

58. Birch James, Vol ii, 399.

59. CSP Venetian 1623-5, nos 36 and 42, pages 25 and 28.

60. Digby's gloomy assessment was borne out in diplomatic circles. Alvise Valaresso, the Venetian ambassador in London, said of the prince's arrival in Madrid, 'No action more remote from all imagination or belief ever took place, or less founded in likelihood to say nothing of reason, utterly unknown to everyone and approved by nobody'. 10 March 1623, CSP Venetian, 583.

61. Bergeron, 186-8, Charles and Buckingham to James, 9 March 1623.

62. Bergeron, 158-60, 25 March 1623. Henri IV formally renounced Protestantism for good on 25 July 1593. Whether he actually said *Paris vaut bien une messe'*, 'Paris is worth a mass', seems unlikely: the earliest reliable references come from Catholic nobles, who intended to cast doubts on their sovereign's sincerity.

63. Arezio, 78.

64. Redworth, 107.

65. Tratados, 230.

66. Howell, 288.

67. Additional 18,201 fol 13-16v.

68. Tratados, 48.

69. Ibid, 231-2.

70. Lockyer, 158.

71. Wynn, 316.

72. Tanner 306, fol. 258.

73. Willson, 437.

74. Hackett, 136.

75. Tratados, 246.

76. Calvert to Conway, 26 July 1623, PRO, SP 14/149, no. 53.

77. Cottington, exhausted by his travels, fell gravely ill and converted to Catholicism; but just as quickly retracted when he unexpectedly recovered.

78. Armstrong, 54.

79. CSP Venetian Vol 19 (1913), 1625-6, 597 et seq. ('finalmente della Contessa d'Olivares gli fu sopra l'appuntamento di goderla posta in letto la più infettata femmina di Spagna').

80. Clarendon [quoted in Gibbs, 174].

81. His daughter would die in 1626 giving birth to a stillborn boy.

82. Howells [ed], Introduction, III.

83. Lockyer, 162.

84. Gibbs, 172, 190.

85. Tratados, 254.

86. Khevenhüller, x, 96.

87. Rushworth, Vol I, 123.

88. Bristol's *Defence*, 50.

89. Bergeron, 168-9, 21 July 1623.

90. HMC, Eighth Report, Appendix Part 1 Section 1, 215-6.

91. Tratados, 242.

92. Howell, 150.

93. D'Ewes, 163.

94. RB, MS 2590 fol. 4.

95. Gibbs, 191.

96. Tawney, 235.

97. Lockyer, 175.

98. Williamson, 135.

99. Nojosa to James I, Tanner no 82, fos 207-208.

100. Samson, 221.

101. Tillières to Pusieux, 7 November 1623, PRO Sig. C3v 31/3/57 fol 260r.

6: ESCAPE FROM BLOIS

(between pages 137 and 160)

1. Babelon, 877.

2. Marvick, 121.

3. Héroard: Vol I, 34-6, also records that such was the emphasis on Louis's genitals, instead of offering his hand to courtiers to kiss, he would put forward his penis.

4. Regan, 76.

5. Louis XIII Marriage, 105.

6. Starkey, 331-6: Catherine told her father, King Ferdinand II of Aragon, that she had a miscarriage in May 1510 when it had actually occurred on 31 January that year, so she was capable of lying if it suited her purpose.

7. Tallemant (see note 12) had access to Dr Héroard's journal but dismissed it as 'several volumes in which you will find nothing except what time he [Louis XIII] awakened, breakfasted, spat, pissed, crapped, etc.'

8. Hamel, 6-7.

9. Levi, 266, n.16.

10. Macdonald (2008 edition), 3.

11. Ibid, 3-4.

12. Tallemant, Vol 1, 333-5.

13. Ibid.

14. Louis XIII marriage, First series, 250-52.

15. Héroard, Vol 2, 186.

16. Herbert, 160. In 1619 Herbert presented his credentials to Louis XIII in Paris as British ambassador and this was his first impression of the king.

17. Moote, 85.

18. Louis announced to his escort as he joined Anne on the bed that he was 'going to piss into her body'.

19. Moote, 142.

20. Auchincloss, 21.

21. The Estates-General would not meet again until 1789, on the eve of the French Revolution.

22. In 1617 he would sell his post for 70,000 livres in cash and goods. See Bergin, 85, 72.

23. Bergin, 91, 161.

24. Pontchartrain, 2nd series. Vol V (1837), 511-2.

25. Erlanger, Richelieu, Vol 1, 56.

26. *Oracles*, 16.

27. François de Bassompierre, *Mémoires*, ed. Marquis de Chantérac (Paris: 4 Vols published 1870-77), Vol III, 81.

28. Batiffol, 3. This is thought to be a reference to the mother of Louise-Roger de La Marbelière, who in 1638, aged seventeen, gave birth to an illegitimate son by Gaston d'Orléans, Jean Louis, the future comte de Charny.

29. Batiffol, 17.

30. Bailly, 167.

31. *Pour mon fils*, 41.

32. Tallemant, Vol 1, 334. This incident is difficult to date precisely because of differences of opinion over Louis's level of influence in matters of state but it was probably during the summer of 1618. Lacroix, 149, states that his majority was formally recognised on 2 October 1614.

33. BN, *fonds français* 10210.

34. *Pour mon fils*, 55.

35. Macdonald (2005), 23.

36. Ibid.

37. BN, fonds francais 10210.6.

38. *Pour mon fils*, 57. The entry appears on 18 March 1619.

39. Levi, 63.

40. Edmondes to Windwood, 12 June 1617, PRO SP 78/67 fos. 130-1.

41. Pavie, 41n.

42. Girard, 201.

43. Battifol, 43.

44. Ibid, 23.

45. Ibid, 32.

46. Herbert, 58.

47. Sévigné Vol II, 694. Madame de Sévigné advised her daughter to leave nothing to chance if she wanted to avoid a further pregnancy. 'I beg you, my love, do not trust to two beds; it is a subject of temptation. Have someone sleep in your room.'

48. Bouer, 30.

49. Macdonald (2005), 25; the first black slaves were sold to the French nobility by slave traders on a freelance basis, but official trading posts were established in French Guiana, Saint Kitts and Senegal in 1624.

50. *Pour mon fils*, 72.

51. Levi, private papers, 2005.

52. Later known as the Salle Lacaze, after the art collection given to the nation by Louis La Caze and displayed at the Louvre.

53. Levi, 64.

54. Battifol, 36.

55. *Historiettes*, Vol 1, notes, 905-7. In conversation with Marie de' Medici, Richelieu is supposed to have described the feelings her playing of the lute aroused in him, 'Madame, si ma robe était de plomb, vous entendriez sonner le tocsin !'('Madam, if my robe was made of lead, you would hear my heart ringing like a tocsin!') However, Richelieu had a way with words, and 'sonner le tocsin' was also a metaphor for 'stirring up adverse public opinion', so he might have been deliberately ambiguous.

56. Auchincloss, 116.

57. Erlanger, Vol 2, 90-1.

58. Boal, 38-9. Memorialists suggest that the dance was performed by Richelieu in 1635.

59. Brienne, Vol 1, p. 274. 'On rioit a gorge deployée; et qui pouvait s'en empecher, puisque apres cinquante ans j'en ris encore moi- meme?' ('Everyone roared with laughter; and who could help it, since fifty years afterwards I am still laughing myself?') In his biography of Richelieu, Erlanger adds this footnote on page 153: 'However far-fetched it may seem, this story may well be true. We know that in 1630, just before the Day of Dupes [10 November: the dupes being those who wrongly thought Richelieu was finished], Richelieu, wishing to reinstate himself in Marie de' Medici's good books, played the guitar to her in a boat.'

7: DANGEROUS LIAISONS
(between pages 161 and 190)

1. Lockyer, 152.

2. Bergeron, 138-9. The original letter is in Tanner, 72 fol 14.

3. Lockyer, 169.

4. Carlton, 108.

5. Villiers, 9.

6. Wotton, 219.

[7.] Dom.MSS. 14. 159.76.

[8.] Holland to Buckingham, 26 February 1624, Harleian 1581, fol. 39-40.

[9.] Osborne original, 511 and see also 534-5.

[10.] Clarendon, Vol 1, 138.

[11.] *Pour mon fils*, 86.

[12.] Battifol, 56, attributing the remark to La Rochefoucauld.

[13.] Ibid.

[14.] Carlisle, 2595, folio 14.

[15.] SP 14/183/50, for example, on 13 February 1625.

[16.] This changed when Buckingham's wife Kate gave birth to a boy, Charles, on 17 November 1625 but he died very young and the title eventually went to his second son, George, born on 30 January 1628.

[17.] McClure, Chamberlain, Vol 2, 607, 23 March 1625. The child was born in late September 1624. Howard was excommunicated by the ecclesiastical court.

[18.] Holland to Charles, 9 March 1624, Harl. 1581, fol 24a-b.

[19.] Carlisle and Holland to Conway, May 1624; PRO, SP 78/72, fos. 241-242, PRO.

[20.] C.S.P.Venetian, 1623-25, no. 437, p.344.

[21.] Villeauxclercs to Tillières, various dispatches 11-15 June 1624 (N.S.), fos. 211-215.

[22.] Hay to James I, 14 June 1624; PRO, SP 78/72, fos. 351-353.

[23.] Hay and Holland to Conway, 7 August 1624; PRO, SP 78/73, fos. 5-6.

[24.] Charles I to Hay, PRO, SP 78/73/139.

[25.] Lockyer, 243.

[26.] Battifol, 59.

[27.] CSP Venetian, Vol 19, 1625-1626 (1913), 9-24.

[28.] Levi, 83.

[29.] Harleian MSS 1580.25.

[30.] Lockyer, 239.

[31.] Ibid.

[32.] Battifol, 12-13.

[33.] *Pour mon fils*, 88.

[34.] The sister of Charles, the younger brother of Louis-François, duc de Villars, was one of Anne's ladies. Charles was Anne's gentleman of honour from 1661 until her death in January 1666.

[35.] Courtin, 103. This book on etiquette first appeared in January 1671 and by October had been translated into English and printed in London, indicative of its popularity.

[36.] Tillières, 61.

[37.] La Porte, 295.

[38.] White, 190.

[39.] Held, 547.

[40.] None of the other surviving copies, to be found in the Prado, the Rijskmuseum and the Duke of Marlborough's collection, includes the bust of the duke. The queen is shown wearing a wedding ring in the Rijskmuseum picture.

[41.] Anne of Austria may have deliberately disguised the picture given to her by the duke as portraying her sister-in-law, Elisabeth of France, who became queen consort of Spain in 1621.

It was not conclusively identified until Nicolas Bailly produced a comprehensive catalogue of leading French art in 1709. In 1685 the marquis de Louvois bought the picture on behalf of Louis XIV and hung it at Versailles, perhaps unaware of its significance. It is now on display in the Louvre. See also Erlanger, 166-7.

[42.] Originally at York House but when Buckingham went to sea with the fleet, the queen's portrait was displayed with similar Madonna-like reverence in the Lord High Admiral's cabin, where it was seen by a French envoy, the baron de Saint-Seurin.

[43.] La Porte, 7.

[44.] Erlanger Richelieu, Vol II, 91.

[45.] Buckingham to Effiat, 11 February 1625; Kings MS. 135, fos. 449-50, BL. The Île de Ré was seized by the Huguenots in January 1625 and recaptured by the Duke of Guise for Louis XIII in the following September.

[46.] Mercure de France, Vol II, 366.

[47.] *Pour mon fils*, 83.

[48.] Brienne, *Éclaircissements Historiques*, Note A, 331 and see Betcherman, 85.

[49.] Battifol, 64.

[50.] Gondi, Vol 3, 198.

[51.] Ogg, 20.

[52.] Levi, 308, n.15.

[53.] Battifol, 63.

[54.] Levi, private papers.

[55.] Gondi, Vol 3, 238. Marie de Chevreuse's third daughter, Charlotte-Marie de Lorraine, was also numbered among Retz's mistresses.

[56.] Levi, 64, 84.

[57.] Tillières, 62.

[58.] Doolittle, 1314.

[59.] Brienne, Vol 27, 40.

[60.] Henrietta-Maria would return to Paris as a political refugee and fund-raiser for her husband, Charles I, during the English Civil War.

[61.] Doolittle, 1317.

[62.] Battifol, 68.

[63.] Brienne, 41.

[64.] Battifol, 63.

[65.] Rochefoucauld, Vol 5, 382.

[66.] Williams N, 37.

[67.] Honoré d'Albert, first Duke of Chaulnes, was a Marshall of France; see La Porte, 297-99.

[68.] Lockyer, 240.

[69.] *Pour mon fils*, 97. Madame de Motteville's mother was one of Anne's maids of honour at the time of the Amiens episode.

[70.] Griselle, para. 3514; Marie de Pagan was not paid a wage but received expenses, which had to be decided by the king.

[71.] Griselle, para. 3345.

[72.] Blaise-François de Pagan had already written, aged 20, what was regarded as the definitive work on fortifications (see Pagan, bibliography) and later taught the great engineer, Sébastien Le Prestre de Vauban, his trade. Pagan was blinded in an accident in 1642 and Marie de Pagan, after 21 years service with Anne of Austria, retired from court to care for him.

73. Erlanger Buckingham, 166.

74. Battifol, 73.

75. Williams N, 40.

76. CSP Venetian, Vol 19: 1625-1626 (1913), 95-111.

77. Ibid, 1-8.

78. Lockyer, 242.

79. Kettering, 824.

80. Brienne, *Éclaircissements Historiques*, Note A, 331.

81. Carlton, 67.

82. Katherine Gorges to Hugh Smyth, 7 December 1625, Bristol Public Record Office, Ashton Court, Muniments, 47. Katherine Gorge was distantly related to Susan Villiers and occasionally accompanied her to court.

83. Mead to Stutteville, 2 July 1625, Court I, 40.

84. Carlton, 68.

85. Macdonald, 331.

86. BN Dupuy 403, 37v.

87. Battifol, 79.

88. Chamberlain to Carleton, 25 June 1625, Birch Court, Vol 1, 35. To allay 'stinking breath' Chamberlain apparently believed in a combination of 'aniseed, mint and cloves soaked in wine'. For the full account of many unattractive remedies, including the application of chicken dung, thought effective in the seventeenth century, see Levens [an Oxford M.A], 22 *et seq*. The book was sold rather surreptitiously from the White Lion pub near the Old Bailey in London.

89. Battifol, 81.

8: 'THE KILLING BEAUTY'

(between pages 191 and 222)

1. William Congreve, *The Mourning Bride* (1697), Act III, Scene II.

2. Williams, 40; Lockyer, 241.

3. CSP, 1634-35, 229.

4. Schreiber, 97.

5. Eg 2597, fol. 13, BL.

6. Schreiber, 97.

7. Smuts, 37.

8. Battifol, 87.

9. Coke Court, Vol I, 68.

10. All that survives of York House is the stone water gate built in 1626 where the Thames once lapped at the edge of its grounds, a triumphal arch that created a spectacular access to the gardens and the property. See Harl. MSS, 7000.

11. Lockyer, 409.

12. Williams N, 41.

13. Félibien, Vol II, 86.

14. For example, notice of one month and four days was given for the same event in 1927. See McGowan, 125, n. 18.

15. The Mercure François, initiated in 1605, was purchased in 1611 by two brothers, Jean and Etienne Richer, who altered its design and increased its circulation.

16. Levi, private papers, quoting an unpublished extract from La Rochefoucauld (see footnote 20) stating that Joseph and Richelieu jointly came up with the plan to expose Anne of Austria's relationship with Buckingham by forcing her to confess what she had done with the diamond necklace. See also Fagniez, Vol 1, 68 and Dedouvres, 68-71. Abbé Dedouvres identified a number of unsigned letters and documents as witten or dictated by Joseph.

17. At the siege of La Rochelle, the duc de La Rochefoucauld brought a force of 1,500 men to fight for Louis XIII, telling Cardinal Richelieu that every man was related to him in some way.

18. Maximes.

19. *Pour mon fils*, 100.

20. Levi, private papers, unpublished extracts from the memoirs of Francois VI, duc de la Rochefoucauld. Levi examined the original manuscripts of La Rochefoucauld's memoirs and discovered that some of their contents had been excised before publication. According to Levi, de Wicquefort, an agent of Cardinal Mazarin, Richelieu's successor, inspected the first draft of the memoirs in 1661 and prevented a printer in Rouen from publishing it. La Rochefoucauld then defiantly sent the manuscript abroad. De Wicquefort, acting on the instructions of the French foreign minister, Hughes de Lionne, was sent to track it down. He followed its trail from Cologne to Brussels and finally to Amsterdam where the prospective Dutch printer, Elzevier, reluctantly agreed to remove several passages identified by de Wicquefort. What apparently prompted the censorship was not the Affair of the Queen's Diamonds itself, as La Rochefoucauld was still permitted a passing reference to it, but his identification of Tréville as Anne of Austria's lover at the critical time of the conception of the future Louis XIV.

21. Gibbs, 233.

22. PRO 31/3/64, fol 114.

23. Betcherman, 81.

24. The house of Sir Abraham Williams, who was agent for the exiled Queen of Bohemia.

25. Chamberlain, Vol II, 627.

26. Brienne, 334.

27. 6 March 1626: CSP Venetian, Vol. 19, 1625-26 (1913), 322-336.

28. George Heriot died on 12 February 1624 and was buried at St-Martin-in-the-Fields, Westminster, London.

29. The full account of what took place at the bal du roi appears in Brienne, *Éclaircissements*, 339-345.

30. Chastenet, 42.

31. Levi, 97.

32. B.N. Archives des affaires étrangères, Vol XXXIX (1626), fol. 315-8, and another unnumbered bound volume referring to the same year, have several examples of this in Cheré's handwriting.

Dulong, 121 suggests that 'La Chesnelle' was chosen for the queen because Louis XIII's code word was 'Le Chesne', a majestic species of oak (see Nicot: chesne) but Anne's code was used first and it is much more likely that Louis's code word was prompted by Anne's code, rather than the other way around.

[33.] Cotgrave includes 'chesnelle' or 'chesnette' as a 'little chain'. Among the contemporary inventories, a pendant consists of 'une chesnelle d'or de deux rubiz'. (Joubert, 8).

[34.] Académie francaise.

[35.] Williams, 48. The remark is attributed to the Princess de Condé, Charlotte de Montmorency.

[36.] Battifol, 95.

[37.] Levi, 98.

[38.] Battifol, 101.

[39.] Williams N, 57.

[40.] BN, Archives des affairs étrangères, Vol 39, fol. 18.

[41.] Battifol, 113.

[42.] Battifol, 93. Louis said of Anne on his deathbed: 'In my present state I am bound to forgive her, but I am not obliged to believe her!'

[43.] Williams N, 79.

[44.] Richelieu, Vol 6, 215.

[45.] Schreiber, 99.

[46.] Williams N, 96; Richelieu, Vol 6 178-9.

[47.] BN, Archives des affaires étrangères, *Angleterre*, Vol. 41, fol. 16. Bautru was in need of Richelieu's protection to avoid a beating or worse because it had been discovered that he was the author of a play, *Ozonandre*, which had ridiculed the duc de Montbazon.

[48.] Lockyer, 276.

[49.] Suckling, Vol I, 31.

[50.] Ibid, Vol I, 31-2.

[51.] Rushworth, Vol I, 357.

[52.] Tillières, 109.

[53.] Charles I to Carleton, 12 July 1626, Bib. Regia, 219-21.

[54.] Carlton, 89.

[55.] Charles I to Buckingham, 7 August 1626, Harl. MSS 6988, 11.

[56.] Hibbard, 405.

[57.] Catherine de Tillières to her husband, 9 August 1626. See Roth, 1-25.

[58.] Denbigh, 49.

[59.] Tillières, 135.

[60.] Betcherman, 89. Dispatch dated 24 July 1626.

[61.] Schreiber, 97.

[62.] Battifol, 75.

[63.] Cawthorne, 56 and see Betcherman, 93.

[64.] PRO 31/3/64 fol 114, Mende.

[65.] Tillières, 35, quoting Bassompierre; and on the diamond bracelet, a report in April 1627 by the acting chargé d'affaires in London, sieur Du Moulin. B.N., archives des affaires étrangères, fonds de la correspondance politique, Angleterre, Vol XLII, fol. 45v.

66. PRO, SP 16/101/43.

67. Tillières, 253-4 and La Rochefoucauld, Levi private papers, concerning the destroyed central sheet shown to Anne of Austria. The surviving part of the letter is undated but refers to Bassompierre as French ambassador. Bassompierre's brief tenure in London began on 7 October and ended on 2 December 1626.

68. Gibbs, 232.

69. PRO, Dk 6.218.

70. Lockyer, 352. This was Bassompierre's third consecutive diplomatic failure, following hard upon fiascos in Spain and Switzerland.

71. Betcherman, 93.

72. Ibid. Early in 1627.

EPILOGUE: LUCY, SKY-HIGH DEBTS AND DIAMONDS
(between pages 223 and 230)

1. Bruce Boehrer 78. Elizabeth I balked at the idea of a man attending to her bowel movements and under Charles I 'stool' became 'stole', referring to the long robe of the monarch.

2. Strafford, 479.

3. CSPD, 1641-3, 73-5.

4. Macdonald(2008), 11-26.

5. Ibid, 330, Note on 'The value of [17thC] money'.

6. Grouchy, 1891, 175-186 and 1892, 7-27.

7. Monsieur, 17 June 1701, AN 300 AP I, 746.

8. Palais Royal, 191-2.

9. Koecher, Vol. 4, 116. After the exclusion of the Catholic Stuarts, Sophia became heir to the English throne and in 1714 failed by only a five weeks to outlive Queen Anne.

10. Verney, 138-9.

11. Macdonald (2008), 81-5.

FINAL CURTAIN
(between pages 231 and 233)

1. Dumas's son, Alexandre Dumas fils, aged twenty at the time, the only person allowed to interrupt the great writer, recorded these aspects of Dumas's eccentric life in various introductions to nineteenth-century editions of 'The Three Musketeers'. See also Spurr, 64-7.

2. Chardon, limited edition 1905, special preface by the author.

INDEX

George Villiers, Duke of Buckingham, 1592-1628.

ABOUT ROGER MACDONALD

Oxford historian (M.A. Hertford College) Roger Macdonald is a member of the University's advisory board on development for the Humanities. His media career began in Fleet Street on the *Daily Mail* and *The Times* before he moved to the BBC as a producer and editor for more than twenty years.

The Press Association won its largest ever contract for the provision of electronic news during his period as PA's marketing and development director. His previous history book, about the real Man in the Iron Mask, was the central theme of a documentary in *'The Legend Detectives'* series made for the Discovery Channel.

The author on location in France with the Legend Detectives (left to right), Tessa Dunlop, Massimo Polidoro and Ronald Top.

Praise for *The Man in the Iron Mask: the true story of the most famous prisoner in history and the Four Musketeers:*

"One of the greatly romanticised periods of history is brought to glittering life in this extraordinary and absorbing book."
The Good Book Guide

"A fine read, with lashings of sex, intrigue and derring-do."
Oxford Times

"Wonderful research – and it reads like a who-dunnit!"
Professor Nicholas Cronk, Director Voltaire Foundation